D0875545

Staging Motherhood

Staging Motherhood

British Women Playwrights, 1956 to the Present

Jozefina Komporaly

First published 2006 by
PALGRAVE MACMILLAN
Houndmills, Basingstoke, Hampshire RG21 6XS and
175 Fifth Avenue, New York, N.Y. 10010
Companies and representatives throughout the world

PALGRAVE MACMILLAN is the global academic imprint of the Palgrave Macmillan division of St. Martin's Press, LLC and of Palgrave Macmillan Ltd. Macmillan® is a registered trademark in the United States, United Kingdom and other countries. Palgrave is a registered trademark in the European Union and other countries.

ISBN-13: 978–1–4039–9909–2   hardback
ISBN-10: 1–4039–9909–0   hardback

This book is printed on paper suitable for recycling and made from fully managed and sustained forest sources.

A catalogue record for this book is available from the British Library.

Library of Congress Cataloging-in-Publication Data

Komporaly, Jozefina, 1969-
   Staging motherhood: British women playwrights, 1956 to the present / Jozefina Komporaly.

      p.cm.
   Includes bibliographical references and index.
   ISBN 1–4039–9909–0
   1. English drama–Women authors–History and criticism.
2. Motherhood in literature. 3. English drama–20th century–History and criticism.
4. Women and literature–Great Britain–History–20th century.
5. Feminism and literature–Great Britain–History–20th century. I. Title.

PR739.M68K66 2006
822'.9109928--dc22   2006044832

10   9   8   7   6   5   4   3   2   1
15   14   13   12   11   10   09   08   07   06

Printed and bound in Great Britain by
Antony Rowe Ltd, Chippenham and Eastbourne

Contents

List of Illustrations

- **(Chapter 1)**
  Figure 1 Edith Evans, Peggy Ashcroft and M Walker in *The Chalk Garden*, by Enid Bagnold, Haymarket Theatre, London, 1956 (credit: Angus McBean photograph © Harvard University, Courtesy of the Harvard Theatre Collection, The Houghton Library).

  Figure 2 Ensemble in *Rites* by Maureen Duffy, Royal National Theatre, 1969 (photo: John Timbers, reproduced by photographer's permission).

- **(Chapter 2)**
  Figure 3 Sheila Allen and Iain Mitchell in *Queen Christina* by Pam Gems, RSC Other Place, 1977 (credit: Joe Cocks Studio Collection © Shakespeare Birthplace Trust).

- **(Chapter 6)**
  Figure 4 Image from *Yerma's Eggs* by Anna Furse, Athletes of the Heart at the Riverside Studios, 2003 (photo: Hugo Glendinning, reproduced by photographer's permission).

Acknowledgements

This study brings together my preoccupations in the area of British women's writing for performance and the stage representation of motherhood. I wish to convey my thanks to all the playwrights and practitioners who inspired my interest in the subject and responded to my queries, in particular Trish Cooke, Anna Furse, Jackie Kay, Charlotte Keatley, Kaite O'Reilly, Jenny Sealey, Michelene Wandor, Timberlake Wertenbaker and Sarah Woods. I am grateful to the staff at the V&A Theatre Museum, the Shakespeare Birthplace Trust and the Harvard Theatre Collection in helping me locate images by Joe Cocks and Angus McBean, as well as to the photographers Patrick Baldwin, Hugo Glendinning and John Timbers. My thanks also go to the publishers and copyright holders who have kindly granted me permission to reproduce extracts from the various plays I discuss (Bloodaxe Books, Faber and Faber Ltd, Methuen Publishing Ltd, Nick Hern Books, Oberon Books, as well as Anna Furse, Dominick Jones and Michelene Wandor), and to Tess Buckland at De Montfort University, Leicester in facilitating a grant to cover copyright-related expenses. Particular thanks are due to those who commented on my manuscript at various stages of its planning, writing and editing process: Mary Brewer, Colin Chambers, Nicoleta Cinpoeş, Geraldine Cousin, Maggie B Gale, Gabriele Griffin, Tony Howard, Rossitza Ivanova, Márta Minier, Carol Rutter, Lib Taylor, Laura Vroomen, and to Paula Kennedy at Palgrave, who has been a patient and supporting editor. This study, however, would not have been realized without the long-standing encouragement of Sue Wiseman, who believed in my ability to finalize this project whenever I faltered. Last but not least, I am grateful to my husband, whose concerns that we shall never go on holiday again led to his thorough scrutiny of my manuscript and resulted in me observing the final deadline.

Chapter 1

1. Enid Bagnold, *The Chalk Garden* (London: Samuel French, 1956) – © Enid Bagnold. Reprinted by permission of Dominick Jones.
2. Shelagh Delaney, *A Taste of Honey* (London: Methuen, 1988) – © Shelagh Delaney. Reprinted by permission of Methuen Publishing Ltd.

3. Ann Jellicoe, *The Sport of My Mad Mother* (London: Faber, 1985) – © Ann Jellicoe. Reprinted by permission of Faber and Faber Ltd.
4. Jane Arden, *Vagina Rex and the Gas Oven* (London: Calder and Boyars, 1971) – © Jane Arden.
5. Maureen Duffy, 'Rites', in *Plays by Women*, vol. 2., ed. by M. Wandor (London: Methuen, 1983) – © Maureen Duffy. Reprinted by permission of Methuen Publishing Ltd.

Chapter 2

1. Pam Gems, 'Queen Christina', in *Plays by Women*, vol. 5., ed. by M. Remnant (London: Methuen, 1986) – © Pam Gems. Reprinted by permission of Methuen Publishing Ltd.
2. An early version of the section on Pam Gems was first published in article form as 'Is Queen Christina a Woman? Gender, Performance and Feminist Experimentation in Pam Gem's *Queen Christina'*, *European Journal of Women's Studies*, vol. 11 (2004), pp. 143–58.
3. Caryl Churchill, *Owners*, in Churchill, *Plays: One* (London: Methuen, 1985) – © Caryl Churchill. Reprinted by permission of Methuen Publishing Ltd.
4. Caryl Churchill, *Top Girls* (London: Methuen, 1991) – © Caryl Churchill. Reprinted by permission of Methuen Publishing Ltd.

Chapter 3

1. Louise Page, *Salonika* and *Real Estate* in Page, *Plays: One* (London: Methuen, 1990) – © Louise Page. Reprinted by permission of Methuen Publishing Ltd.
2. Shelagh Stephenson, *The Memory of Water* (London: Methuen, 1997) – © Shelagh Stephenson. Reprinted by permission of Methuen Publishing Ltd.
3. Winsome Pinnock, 'Leave Taking' in *First Run: New Plays by New Writers*, ed. by K. Harwood (London: Nick Hern Books, 1989) – © Winsome Pinnock. Reprinted by permission of Nick Hern Books.
4. Charlotte Keatley, *My Mother Said I Never Should* (London: Methuen, 1997) – © Charlotte Keatley, 1997. Reprinted by permission of Methuen Publishing Ltd.
5. Diane Samuels, *Kindertransport* (London: Nick Hern Books, 1996) – © Diane Samuels, 1996. Reprinted by permission of Nick Hern Books.

6. Phyllis Nagy, *Butterfly Kiss*, in Nagy, *Plays: One* (London: Methuen, 1998) – © Phyllis Nagy, 1998. Reprinted by permission of Methuen Publishing Ltd.

Chapter 4

1. Women's Theatre Group, 'My Mother Says I Never Should', in *Strike while the Iron is Hot: Three Plays on Sexual Politics*, ed. by M. Wandor (London: The Journeyman Press, 1980) – © Michelene Wandor, 1980. Reprinted by permission of Michelene Wandor.
2. Grace Dayley, 'Rose's Story', in *Plays by Women*, vol. 4. ed. by M. Wandor (London: Methuen, 1985) – © Grace Dayley, 1985. Reprinted by permission of Methuen Publishing Ltd.
3. Sharman MacDonald, *When I Was a Girl, I Used to Scream and Shout...*, in MacDonald, *Plays: One* (London: Faber and Faber Ltd', 1995) – © Sharman MacDonald, 1995. Reprinted by permission of Faber and Faber Ltd.
4. Trish Cooke, 'Back Street Mammy', in *First Run*, volume 2., ed. by K. Harwood (London: Nick Hern Books, 1990) – © Trish Cooke, 1990. Reprinted by permission of Nick Hern Books.

Chapter 5

1. Gay Sweatshop and Michelene Wandor, 'Care and Control', in *Strike while the Iron is Hot: Three Plays on Sexual Politics*, ed. by M. Wandor (London: The Journeyman Press, 1980) – © Michelene Wandor, 1980. Reprinted by permission of Michelene Wandor.
2. Michelene Wandor, 'AID Thy Neighbour', in *Plays* (London: Journeyman Playbooks, 1984) – © Michelene Wandor, 1984. Reprinted by permission of Michelene Wandor.
3. Sarah Daniels, 'Neaptide' and 'Byrthrite', in Daniels, *Plays: One* (London: Methuen, 1986) – © Sarah Daniels, 1986. Reprinted by permission of Methuen Publishing Ltd.
4. Jackie Kay, *The Adoption Papers* (Newcastle upon Tyne: Bloodaxe Books, 1991) – © Jackie Kay, 1991. Reprinted by permission of Bloodaxe Books.
5. Claire Luckham, 'The Choice', in *Plays by Women*, vol. 10., ed. by A. Castledine (London: Methuen, 1994) – © Claire Luckham, 1994. Reprinted by permission of Methuen Publishing Ltd.

6. Timberlake Wertenbaker, *The Break of Day* (London: Faber, 1995) – © Timberlake Wertenbaker, 1995. Reprinted by permission of Faber and Faber Ltd.
7. Earlier versions of the sections on Claire Luckham and Timberlake Wertenbaker were published in article form as 'De-sexing the Maternal: Reproductive Technologies and Medical Authority in Comtemporary British Women's Drama', in *Gramma*, vol. 10 (2002), pp. 133–42; and as 'Maternal Longing as Addiction: Feminism Revisited in Timberlake Wertenbaker's *The Break of Day*', *Journal of Gender Studies*, vol. 12, no. 2 (2004), pp. 129–38.

Chapter 6

8. Kaite O'Reilly, *Peeling* (London: Faber, 2002) – © Kaite O'Reilly, 2002. Reprinted by permission of Kaite O'Reilly and Faber and Faber Ltd.
9. Sarah Woods, *Cake* (London: Oberon Books, 2003) – © Sarah Woods, 2003. Reproduced by kind permission of Oberon Books.
10. Anna Furse, *Yerma's Eggs* (unpublished) – © Anna Furse, 2003. Reprinted by permission of Anna Furse and Nina Klaff; extracts from Lorca's 'Yerma', translated by P. Luke, in Lorca, *Plays: One* (London: Methuen, 1987). Reprinted by permission of Methuen Publishing Ltd.

The author and publishers have made every attempt to contact copyright holders, but if any have inadvertently been overlooked the publishers will be pleased to make the necessary arrangements at the first opportunity.

Introduction

The topic of motherhood has been extensively debated by post-war and contemporary women playwrights in Britain, often in a process that also addresses the relationship between theatre and feminism in a British context. As I seek to analyse the ways in which transformations in women's personal and public lives have impacted women's theatre, I scrutinize the strategies employed by women in their writing and performing practices. I also examine the extent to which feminist ideas have been formulated or appropriated by women playwrights and practitioners, and interrogate correspondences between theoretical, social, political, economic, medical as well as dramatic and performance contexts. The time span surveyed constitutes a period of unprecedented prosperity for women's voices in the public sphere, and I duly acknowledge the impact of second-wave feminism; however, I equally examine the years leading up to the Women's Liberation Movement and its aftermath. In this way, I reference the climate of five decades – from the mid-fifties to the present – and I investigate constantly changing conditions, in particular as far as the aesthetic and economic circumstances of women's theatre are concerned.

I argue that the fifties playwrights anticipated – even if obliquely at times – most of the topical concerns of the late sixties and seventies. Similarly, many playwrights writing after the heyday of second-wave feminism continued to revisit the seventies. Thus, the playwrights created opportunities for confronting both the achievements and shortcomings of feminist interventions, often speculating on the necessity of a next phase in women's orchestrated self-assertion. Rather than privileging one single feminist stance, I link together dramatists writing from a variety of ideological positions, emphasizing the importance of co-existence and multiplicity. Throughout this study I map out some of the major directions in feminist thinking, aiming to help contextualize both women's stage work and feminist theory in relation to the defining historical, political and cultural phenomena at a given moment, and I reference relevant intersections with psychoanalytical and post-colonial theory. My predominant methodology in this study is dramatic criticism, as I engage with the textual nature of work produced by women playwrights. I also utilize performance documentation and criticism, especially in the chronologically more recent sections, aiming to stress the gradual move from text-based work to non-playwriting performance practices. It is particularly significant that even published authors, such as Phyllis Nagy, contend that their ultimate goal is to write for performance.[1]

For my analysis I have chosen playwrights active in Britain even if they are of Irish or American origin, and aimed at reflecting regional and racial, as well as stylistic and ideological, difference.[2] I have selected the playwrights and practitioners on account of their preoccupation with motherhood and parenthood and, throughout, I examine the extent to which their gender identification was significant to their creative processes. My editorial decisions have been governed by the desire to reflect frequently encountered thematic approaches, and to allow for a chronological and contextual situation of the work discussed. Because several plays follow a variety of thematic strands, there are occasional overlaps between sections; for instance, women's wage work or mother–daughter relationships appear in a multitude of plays and are signposted throughout the study, even if the plays in question are discussed in the context of another theme. Thus, the study addresses the following; motherhood as a biologically unavoidable yet empowering experience (Chapter 1); the tensions between motherhood and female career, where the urge to have and care for children clashes with competing desires (Chapter 2); relationships between mothers and daughters across generations (Chapter 3); maternal desire as a route for agency on behalf of the teenage subject (Chapter 4); the impossibility of parenting, for reasons including personal choice and medical condition (Chapter 5); and recent preoccupations with rewriting the maternal body (Chapter 6).

Apart from being thematic units, the chapters are also organized to reflect work produced throughout the successive decades (for instance, the fifties or the early twenty-first century). This study follows a trajectory from the proto-feminism and aesthetic diversity of the fifties (via the work of Enid Bagnold, Shelagh Delaney, Doris Lessing and Ann Jellicoe) and sixties (Jane Arden, Maureen Duffy) to the co-existence of liberal, radical and socialist–feminist tendencies in the seventies and early eighties, contemporaneous with Thatcher's election (as reflected by Pam Gems and Caryl Churchill).[3] The climate of the late seventies and eighties is scrutinized through the juxtaposition of plays by Michelene Wandor, Louise Page and Charlotte Keatley, all affiliated to socialist feminism yet to different aesthetic principles; for instance, Keatley argues for theatre as an art form not a platform, as opposed to Wandor, who puts across her explicit political views. A certain didacticism is also practised by the Women's Theatre Group – later replicated by young emerging authors such as Grace Dayley, whose unadulterated style, however, is more of a consequence of inexperience than political agenda. Sarah Daniels gives voice to radical feminism in eighties drama, reflecting up-to-date concerns in feminist theory, while Sharman MacDonald and Shelagh Stephenson write from seemingly opaque political positions, representing white middle-class perspectives, and are concerned primarily with the individual rather than the community. Winsome Pinnock, on the other hand, aware of her emblematic position as a successful black woman playwright, voices issues rooted in the experience of immigrants from the Caribbean and discusses cultural hybridity. Similarly, Diane Samuels references her Jewish heritage by revisiting the Holocaust and examining ethnic origin as a potentially problematic 'other'. The end of the eighties and the nineties are connected to the emergence of ideological distantiation and the fragmentation of political platforms, and are discussed via the plays of Trish Cooke, Claire Luckham and Timberlake Wertenbaker. The nineties also launch the careers of younger playwrights, such as Phyllis Nagy or Sarah Kane, who distance themselves from agendas traditionally associated with women writers and claim the right to address any topic of their choice. The early years of the third millennium are represented via work by Kaite O'Reilly, Sarah Woods and Anna Furse, and call attention to emerging practices in terms of dramatic form as well as content. As these examples show, there is a significant shift from text-based to devised and collaborative work, often involving new technologies, and in O'Reilly's case a women-centred focus is also juxtaposed to the disability agenda, in an attempt to intertwine two major human rights causes.

A number of the playwrights discussed have had initial problems with theatre managements, as their plays were not considered to fit conventions then in operation regarding dramatic form or content. Paradoxically, it was this contestation of norms that made me decide to start my investigations in 1956, a year associated with male authors and destabilized in importance in recent years. Utilizing Enid Bagnold's case,

I wanted, on the one hand, to establish a link with the significant inter-war tradition of women's playwriting, while, on the other, I wished to signal the fact that even established women writers encountered difficulties when tackling new subject matter. Thus, Bagnold's *The Chalk Garden* (1956) premièred in the United States and not in England, and only in the wake of its overseas acclaim did it première in Britain. In a similar vein, Delaney's *A Taste of Honey* (1958) was patronizingly labelled a naïve text at first; Jellicoe's *The Sport of My Mad Mother* (1958) became marginalized for its anarchic structure, while Gems's *Queen Christina* (1977) was initially turned down due to its apparent lack of appeal to audiences. Another significant opposition was manifested regarding women's non-linear treatment of time, involving constant journeys between past and present and, often, erasures of hierarchies between the characters. Keatley's 1987 *My Mother Said I Never Should* is perhaps the best known example in this sense, a play initially labelled inadequate for the stage that later became one of the most successful plays by a British woman author. With regard to the experimental treatment of time, however, the impact on forthcoming playwrights of Churchill's *Top Girls* (1982) is perhaps second to none. By juxtaposing arbitrary moments in history, Churchill not only succeeded in merging past and present, but she also devised a subsequently very influential technique of overlapping dialogue to create an impression of simultaneity and fragmentation.

Though very different in style and ambition, both *Top Girls* and *My Mother Said I Never Should* bear connections to Julia Kristeva's theory on 'women's time'.[4] The lack of chronological unity and the encounter of characters from different historical moments link the two plays with regard to the subversion of linear – and hence, 'patriarchal' – time and advocate a sense of rhythmic, female-identified cyclicality, characteristic, according to Kristeva, to the second phase of (radical) feminism. For Kristeva, female subjectivity is connected to 'cyclical time' (repetition) and 'monumental time' (eternity) as far as the perspective of motherhood and reproduction is concerned (as opposed to the time of history which is deployed as a progression). Kristeva explored the various perceptions of time in relation to the different stages in the feminist movement. While the first generation of feminists claimed equal rights with men (including the right to be located in linear time), the second wave stressed sexual difference and demanded women's situation outside history and patriarchy. Rejecting both earlier options, the third generation of feminists emerging in the late seventies – with whom Kristeva identified herself – made an attempt at reconciling maternal and linear time.

This perspective not only destabilized the mutual exclusion between the two earlier perceptions but also problematized the very notion of identity in order to privilege individual differences within (rather than between) sex/gender categories. Besides *Top Girls* and *My Mother Said I Never Should*, Sharman MacDonald's *When I Was a Girl, I Used to Scream and Shout ...* (1984), Trish Cooke's *Back Street Mammy* (1989), Phyllis Nagy's *Butterfly Kiss* (1994), Diane Samuels's *Kindertransport* (1996) and Shelagh Stephenson's *The Memory of Water* (1997) frequently divert time from linear into cyclical patterns. Connecting the present of stage time to both the past and the future, these plays also present heterogeneous rather than homogeneous views of women, allowing for the co-existence of parallel practices.

In other instances, theory only confirmed the innovative contributions of earlier plays, as in the case of Jellicoe's *The Sport of My Mad Mother*. As a proto-chronic exercise of *écriture féminine*, this play prophetically illustrates Hélène Cixous's subsequent concept of writing in the maternal white ink as a replication of the rhythm of the female body. Jellicoe's play equally performs the function of 'linguistic flesh' as theorized by Chantal Chawaf. Both aim at the 'disintellectualization' of writing and an articulation of a sensual corporeality in order to make a political statement. Jellicoe's Greta also implicitly invokes the tarantella dance performed by the hysterical woman in her ritualistic process of contestation, though Catherine Clément's thesis finds further correspondences in Gems's eponymous character in *Queen Christina*, as well as in Gret and Angie in Churchill's *Top Girls*.[5] According to Clément, through the somatization of formerly repressed emotions the dancing hysterical subject rebels against the perpetrator of her oppression, and claims her right to agency.

Although I discuss the various plays in thematic units, doubled by a sense of chronology – to stress the interdependence between social, political context and theatrical discourse – I also read them as intertextual with each other. For example, I highlight the ways in which Michelene Wandor reworked the English drawing room comedy in *AID Thy Neighbour* (1978) and reconsidered the tradition of Enid Bagnold. Trish Cooke's protagonist in *Back Street Mammy* reconnects to Delaney's Jo in *A Taste of Honey* both as a female adolescent and as a daughter reenacting her mother, particularly in terms of teenage pregnancy. The two plays also share a Northern working-class location, but, while Cooke featured a traditional family of Caribbean descent, Delaney's white protagonists disrupted the conventional family structure of the fifties.

Delaney and Cooke, as well as the Women's Theatre Group, MacDonald and Dayley, focus on adolescents, while most other playwrights centre on mature professional women. These figures constitute some of the strongest characters in contemporary British theatre and enact the full range of attitudes towards motherhood. But while the protagonists of the seventies and eighties lead their lives in the public sphere (Gems's *Queen Christina,* Churchill's Marlene and Marion in, respectively, *Top Girls* and *Owners,* 1972), women of the nineties are often presented as looking back on careers. These characters are regularly preoccupied with their desire for a child, which they have kept postponing in order to achieve professional success first (Luckham's *The Choice,* 1992; Wertenbaker's *The Break of Day,* 1995). Work emerging in the early years of the twenty-first century, on the other hand, reintroduces cases of practising motherhood (Woods's *Cake,* 2003) and connects parenthood to other debates, such as disability and human rights concerns (O'Reilly's *Peeling,* 2002) and the appropriation of reproductive technologies (Furse's *Yerma's Eggs,* 2003).

Despite this variety of work produced under constantly altering circumstances, women dramatists and practitioners need continued attention and support in order to carry on. Following the disbanding of many feminist groups, the nineties backlash has extended to women playwrights too. The number of companies producing plays by women has continued to be low ever since, despite the fact that more women are currently writing for the stage than ever before, and that the work of women playwrights – in terms of experimentation with form and fresh topics – is being extensively discussed. The most frequently staged English-language woman playwright continues to be Agatha Christie, although plays by Churchill, Wertenbaker and Kane in particular have enjoyed notable success and have been integrated into school and academic syllabi, thus gaining a sort of canonical status.[6] A related cause of women playwrights' limited visibility has been identified in the fact that most influential theatre critics are men (middle-aged and white) who often exercise negative judgement with regard to experimental work. Writers as diverse in approach as Keatley, Pinnock and Wertenbaker have commented not only on the likelihood of critics coming to performances with preconceived ideas, but also on the inadequacy of the methods employed in theatre criticism. Beyond critical response, as some of the playwrights have pointed out in interviews conducted for this study, becoming accepted more widely is a matter of time and of more women coming forward. Despite a decrease in the visibility of women's work, women have not given up working in the theatre. Even if they have continued to be under-represented, an increasing number of women practitioners have occupied influential positions in recent years, as directors, agents and artistic directors, albeit not at the most prestigious and influential institutions.

In such conditions, the importance of theatres in sustaining new work is particularly decisive. Referencing material under discussion in the forthcoming chapters, for instance, *The Break of Day* was co-produced by Leicester Haymarket and Out of Joint, while Woods's *Cake* was staged at the Birmingham Rep. The latter also established a relationship with the Asian women-led company, Tamasha, whose production of Ruth Carter's *A Yearning* they staged in 1995. The Traverse in Edinburgh regularly stages new work by women playwrights (see plays by Liz Lochhead and Rona Munro, alongside the equally risk-taking agenda of producing foreign plays). In London, the Royal Court has epitomized the nurture of new writing under the artistic directorships of Max Stafford-Clark, Stephen Daldry and Ian Rickson, and several playwrights discussed have held either appointments as resident playwrights or had work staged there (Churchill, Page, Wertenbaker, Daniels, Kane). Equally crucial is the role of the Soho Theatre. Led by Abigail Morris, the theatre pioneered the short, no-interval drama, and its productions include Samuels's *Kindertransport* as well as Laura Wade's *Colder Than Here* (2005). Among major venues supporting experimental work by women, particularly important are the Riverside Studios and the Battersea Arts Centre, to date having hosted productions by Furse and Woods, among others. Apart from funding, critical attention and suitable venues, women's playwriting is equally dependent on constant audience feedback. It also needs the consideration of theatre scholars and academics, with a view to ensuring that this type of practice gets documented and brought to the attention of younger audiences. This study hopes to contribute to this agenda, together with signalling the validity of contact and support within the feminist theatre community.

1
Rethinking Motherhood: Instances of Proto-Feminism

Characteristic of the thematic and stylistic diversity of women's theatrical production in mid-fifties Britain, was the fact that playwrights continued to utilize the conventions of commercial theatre yet moved on to previously unexplored subjects, while a new generation of authors emerged who radically changed style and introduced working-class experience into mainstream drama. Through cases studies such as Enid Bagnold's *The Chalk Garden* (1956), Shelagh Delaney's *A Taste of Honey* (1958), Doris Lessing's *Play With a Tiger* (1958) and Ann Jellicoe's *The Sport of My Mad Mother* (1958), this chapter shows that women playwrights predominantly focused on the domestic or female-only environments to revisit received notions of social and psychological issues. In fact, playwrights embarked on a fresh examination of women's roles, examinations that often led to a subversion of mainstream ideology. The authors considered here investigated different perceptions of the fifties family as a structure of social organization, and often scrutinized conflicts between generations, focusing on the figure of the mother. They depicted extended families incorporating several generations and classes, units led by single mothers, as well as alternative arrangements disconnected from marriage and direct bloodlines. The playwrights also presented parenthood in a variety of manifestations. Contented motherhood was almost entirely absent, as a range of plays centred on women negotiating motherhood with an independent life, and on women's resistance to give birth or to nurture, attention often being channelled to surrogacy. In terms of form, the playwrights emphasized opposing tendencies too, ranging from the inter-war tradition of bourgeois theatre to the world of predominantly realist drama and experimentalism.

Compared to the economic austerity of the forties and early fifties, the final years of the fifties emerged as a period of unprecedented prosperity, as a result of the reforms introduced by the Labour Government that came into power after World War Two. The establishment of the National Health Service, the introduction of free secondary education, the building of new housing facilities – all within the creation of the Welfare State – contributed to a context in which gradual changes in the social structure could take place. Since Labour was defeated in 1951, however, the fifties have been associated with a certain sense of political unity generated through three successive Conservative administrations. The fifties, however, failed to conform to a homogeneous pattern. The end of Labour's first post-war government ironically coincided with the 1951 Festival of Britain, intended as a celebration of the party's achievements and of reconciliation. Two subsequent moments also stood for contradictory tendencies. The year of the Coronation, 1953, symbolized consensus and stability, while 1956 introduced fracture and dissent via events on a variety of terrains, including the Soviet invasion of Hungary and the Suez crisis in politics, the instant popularity of rock n' roll in popular culture, and, in theatre, the emergence of Samuel Beckett and the premiere of John Osborne's *Look Back in Anger*. The decade also accelerated the disintegration of the Empire, in parallel with an increase in immigration into Britain from the former colonies. Finally, it was the fifties that witnessed the infiltration of sexuality into public discourse: 'Sexual potency in men and sexual responsiveness in women began to be seen as explicitly desirable qualities', while divorce or sexual reform became widely debated matters.[1]

The end of the war facilitated men's re-entry into peacetime employment, whereas for women it generated a return to the home to take up their traditional roles as wives and mothers. This 'backlash against feminism' reached its peak in the early fifties, and was widely aired in the media.[2] Domestic activities were presented as attractive occupations, housework being shown as a particular kind of job, just as important as paid employment. However, not all women opted for this pattern, and statistics proved that – despite ideological opposition – women's presence in the labour force consolidated following the war. Alva Myrdal and Viola Klein's 1956 study *Women's Two Roles: Home and Work* aimed at legitimizing the compatibility between family responsibilities and employment. The authors made it clear that women's work was needed by the labour market, and stressed that – from an economic perspective – children were a burden rather than an asset, especially for the poor. Since families had considerably reduced in size, the study also explored the psychological frustration of women who had no preoccupation other than their families. Writing at a time of a renaissance in family values, in which the focus of research in psychology was primarily on the welfare of the child, Myrdal and Klein's opening up of alternatives for women was both subversive and innovative.[3] As they urged women to harmonize employment with motherhood, Myrdal and Klein concluded: 'We are convinced [...] that work and family are not in principle two irreconcilable alternatives.'[4]

While, in a British context, Myrdal and Klein presented dual roles as feasible options – and Hannah Gavron signalled the inner conflicts of housebound women and mothers in *The Captive Wife* (1966) – Betty Friedan pointed out a total lack in American women's life-style choices. According to Friedan's analysis (*The Feminine Mystique*, 1963), the US-based married woman had reached an identity crisis, realizing her dissatisfaction with her social position and unable to cope with her public image. As a result of the 'sexual sell' that had taken place via her marriage, she had sentenced herself to a comfortable yet inescapable 'concentration camp'. According to Friedan, however, the problem for women was not simply sexual, but 'of identity': 'The feminine mystique says that the highest value and the only commitment for women is the fulfilment of their own femininity. [...] However, special and different, it is in no way inferior to the nature of man, it may even in certain respects be superior.'[5] In Friedan's view, woman's mistaken choice had been 'living by her sex alone, trading in her individuality for security', and she stated that a woman without an ambition – beyond biological functions – was 'committing a kind of suicide'.[6]

Friedan's text, often cited as a key document of liberal feminism, prioritized the issue of identity as opposed to biology for women, yet it was nevertheless emblematic for a feminism unconcerned with the possibilities of radical change in society. Later stances – inspired by the emergence of the Women's Liberation Movement – were characterized by a far more interventionist tone. The British context in which some of these radical views emerged coincided with legislative acts introduced by the Labour Government of Harold Wilson, regulating aspects of family life and women's health. Among the acts most relevant for the purposes of this discussion were the following: The Family Provision Act (1966), The Matrimonial Homes Act (1967), The NHS Family Planning Act (1967), the long overdue Abortion Act (1967) and Sexual Offences Act (1967), The Maintenance Orders Act (1968), The Family Law Reform Act (1969), The Divorce Reform Act (1969), The Children and Young Persons Act (1969), The Equal Pay Act (1970). Although this legislation paved the way for gradual transformations, it did not manage to achieve an overnight amelioration in the social condition of women or to enthuse the population at large. On the contrary, the immediate outcome of these attempts was a shift of support from Labour to Conservative, recalling the 1951 elections when Labour's efforts to establish the Welfare State ushered in more than a decade of Conservative rule.

Returning to the world of theatre, the early fifties featured women playwrights perpetuating practices reminiscent of the inter-war period. Via playwrights like Enid Bagnold, however, a gradual shift emerged, by carrying on the conventions of West End theatre, yet in content sketching subsequent preoccupations of new theatre with regard to sexual politics and class dynamics. In her 1956 play, *The Chalk Garden*, for instance, Bagnold featured an alternative family that included three members of a female lineage as well as characters of both sexes belonging to different classes, and subverted male authority through female creativity and intellect. Equally, she explored female bonding across generations and social status, stressing the rivalries and difficulties in communication between women, a theme taken up by several playwrights discussed in the subsequent chapters, including Caryl Churchill in the seventies, Charlotte Keatley in the eighties, Timberlake Wertenbaker in the nineties and Kaite O'Reilly in the early noughties. Unlike Bagnold, Shelagh Delaney rejected drawing room drama to produce a play rooted in the immediate experience of working-class characters and audiences. *A Taste of Honey* (1958) also features an alternative family in opposition to a mother–daughter relationship; but while the alternative partnership works as a paradigm of mutual support, the actual blood link between mother and daughter appears more problematic. Delaney also asked for the time revolutionary questions regarding women's association with childbirth and nurture, and she can be seen as intuitively forecasting issues developed by the Women's Liberation Movement and feminism.

Doris Lessing's *Play With a Tiger* (1958) does not problematize the practice of motherhood; instead it looks at the circumstances in which women consider having and raising children. Lessing examined the destinies of women and men confronted with decisions regarding parenthood and she offered alternatives, via the characters' opposing views. Contrasting conventional and avant-garde characters and exploring the boundaries of social norms, however, is but an aspect of the play. Lessing was equally concerned with the inner lives of her protagonists, their irrational fascination with one another and with issues of power in human relationships. Ann Jellicoe in *The Sport of My Mad Mother* (1958) also examined power and authority, juxtaposed with the mysterious and threatening facets of female fertility. Written in an experimental style, the play attempts to explore natural impulses and emotions associated to the feminine. The protagonist's fertility constitutes the major ground for audience support and secures her ultimate claim to authority. Greta's maternity, however, is a symbolic rather than literal asset; it stands for the possibilities inherent in the marginal female subject to move centre-stage, while it equally marks a route towards female essentialism.

The Chalk Garden

Although contemporary with the work of John Osborne, Enid Bagnold's *The Chalk Garden* deliberately ignores the progressive historical, political and cultural climate of its time. By the early fifties Bagnold was an established novelist and playwright for the commercial theatre; however, despite her previous success, Bagnold encountered difficulties similar to other women playwrights when she first approached theatre managements. *The Chalk Garden* premièred in the United States as a result of the American theatre being 'more receptive to fresh work than the English'.[7] Bagnold and her manager, Irene Selznik, worked for over a year on the script until they succeeded in putting on the play. Eventually, it opened on 26 October 1955 at the Barrymore Theater in New York, directed by George Cukor, with Gladys Cooper as Mrs St Maugham and Siobhan McKenna as Miss Madrigal. Starting from immediate positive reactions, the play achieved long-term acclaim on Broadway and Bagnold received the American Academy of Arts and Letters Silver Medal for distinguished achievement in drama. Reworked for the British première in 1956, the play ran for 658 performances and received equally appreciative reviews, which climaxed in Kenneth Tynan's comment: 'the finest artificial comedy to have flowed from an English (as opposed to an Irish) pen since the death of Congreve' by Enid Bagnold (Figure 1).[8]

Despite continuing the commercial success of productions acclaimed in the West End during the inter-war period and the early fifties – works that did not attempt to transgress the boundaries of the genre in which they were written – Bagnold's plays also share common ground with the emerging proto-feminist writers of the late fifties. Lib Taylor has classified Bagnold's work as feminist/reflectionist, owing to her representation of women's experience alongside her attempts at disrupting social and gender stereotypes and 'dislodging entrenched beliefs'.[9] Bagnold often features upper middle-class households, like in *The Chalk Garden*, where she engages with class relations via the employee versus the employer relationship; but she also addresses differing class structures more directly, as in the stage adaptation of *National Velvet* or in *Lottie*

Figure 1   Edith Evans, Peggy Ashcroft and M Walker in *The Chalk Garden*, by Enid Bagnold, Haymarket Theatre, London, 1956 (credit: 'Angus McBean photograph © Harvard University, Courtesy of the Harvard Theatre Collection, The Houghton Library').

Dundass and *Poor Judas*. The power relations in these scenarios are not automatically negotiated along the class divide and social conventions are often disregarded. Although in *The Chalk Garden* Bagnold situates her working-class characters as domestic servants – replicating the conventions of drawing room drama – she makes them challenge and ultimately dominate their social superiors. *The Chalk Garden* is set in Mrs St Maugham's country home, involving a cluster of female and male protagonists. Bagnold sets an unconventionally structured family at the centre of her play, which consists of Mrs St Maugham, her granddaughter Laurel and Laurel's governess, Miss Madrigal. Laurel's mother, Olivia – who is initially presented as uncaring, and who separated from her daughter in order to remarry – only appears towards the end. The maternal function, therefore, is distributed between a number of other characters: Mrs St Maugham, a manservant called Maitland, but above all Miss Madrigal, the emblematic surrogate mother.

In *The Chalk Garden* everybody's actions, Madrigal's excepted, are symbolically supervised by an unseen man, the disabled butler Pinkbell. He is the authority figure unconditionally accepted by Mrs St Maugham, but finally challenged by the newcomer Madrigal. Pinkbell's authoritarian regime appears strikingly obsolete and inefficient to Madrigal. Her gradual introduction of new working methods are steps towards Pinkbell's elimination, and his death in the final section of the play marks her victory. At the end she and Mrs St Maugham are seen attending to the garden together – trying to make it fertile. From this stage onwards, 'maternal order is the natural order' in the chalk garden.[10]

However, the title refers not merely to Mrs St Maugham's actual garden but also to Laurel, ignored by her biological mother, neglected by her grandmother and desperately longing for attention. Bagnold suggests that without enthusiastic caring intervention, neither the garden nor the girl can develop normally:

> MRS ST MAUGHAM: [...] The child's a flower. She grows in liberty!
> MADRIGAL: Weeds grow as easily.[11]

In this way, Bagnold calls attention to the destructive potential of inadequate care and points the finger at Mrs St Maugham as the embodiment of the irresponsible grandmother, and indeed mother, on the account of her earlier failed attempts at nurturing Olivia: 'I had conceived Mrs St Maugham as making a muddle of everything, her garden and her grand-daughter.'[12] Crucially, Bagnold does not dwell significantly on Mrs St Maugham's inability to exercise her maternal function – or indeed to carry out any practical or emotional role adequately – but shifts the responsibility for this inadequate care from the 'bad mother' (Mrs St Maugham and Olivia) to the patriarchal regime of Pinkbell. Only after Madrigal challenges his authority and manages to introduce her own methods can the garden and Laurel suddenly flourish. Madrigal proves that besides technical expertise one must rely on affection and creativity in order to succeed as a carer. Yet Madrigal herself, as a middle-aged unattached woman with no children, does not conform to any stereotype of the ideal nurturer.

In Madrigal Bagnold creates a character with a strong will, able to confront opposition. She also imagines someone with a vast and uncommon personal experience, considerably removed from the average middle-class woman's. Madrigal has encountered both exposure in the public sphere (through her trial for murder) and total isolation and claustrophobia (in prison), before experiencing a certain sense of refuge in Mrs St Maugham's home. Refusing to sentimentalize her, Bagnold makes a case for the possibility of experimenting with gender roles and stereotypes. She indicates that one needs neither to be a biological mother to nurture, nor a stay-at-home housewife to be able to meet the needs of a child.

At the end of the play, nevertheless, Laurel is reclaimed by her birth mother. Laying the blame for her inadequate performance as a mother on her own lack of a satisfactory relationship with Mrs St Maugham, Olivia emerges as a woman matured by her experiences: 'Things come late to me. Love came late to me. Laurel was born in a strange virginity. To have a child doesn't always make a mother.'[13] As she pleads her suitability for the role of the perfect carer, she confronts her mother's desperate attempt to keep Laurel, labelling it a compensatory exercise for their own failed mother–daughter bond:

MRS ST MAUGHAM: [...] Laurel came to me of her own free will – and I have turned my old age into a nursery for her.
OLIVIA: And God has given you a second chance to mother. [14]

In spite of Laurel's reservations, this championing of direct biological bonds is supported by Madrigal, despite the fact that in this way she undermines her own legitimacy as a surrogate mother. As a result, however, her connection with Mrs St Maugham intensifies. Lacking an object of attention, the two women develop a relationship of a new kind: Madrigal teaches Mrs St Maugham gardening (and by extension, nurturing skills), while Mrs St Maugham accepts to renegotiate their class division.

As for the male characters' caring capacities, Bagnold offers less versatile options despite mapping out two contradictory trends. She makes an attempt via Maitland to present genuine concern, yet she overshadows this by the women's intricate bonds. Her presentation of Pinkbell shows men simply exercising control and authority, without any genuine desire or potential for interpersonal and inter-gender communication. Thus, she predominantly maintains the division of labour between the sexes as far as the practice of nurture is concerned. She ascribes it to the female realm, with significant alterations to the actual stereotype of the carer.

Following the American success, the British production opened in Birmingham on 21 March 1956 before transferring to the Theatre Royal, Haymarket. Directed by Sir John Gielgud, Madrigal was played by Peggy

Ashcroft and Mrs St Maugham by Dame Edith Evans, whose performance connoted, according to Tynan, 'a crested wave of Edwardian eccen-
tricity vainly dashing itself on the rocks of contemporary life'.[15]
Through this performance, Tynan claimed, West End theatre had justi-
fied its otherwise anachronistic existence. He equally stressed, however,
that this production of *The Chalk Garden* 'mark[ed] the end of an era;
Miss Stott's [Laurel's] farewell to Dame Edith Evans, as irrevocable as
Nora's departure in *A Doll's House*, represent[ed] the future taking leave
of the past'.[16] After almost another two decades, *The Chalk Garden* was
revived at the Haymarket, and again in 1992. The play received positive
reviews on both occasions for its fine craftsmanship and innovative-
ness. Setting the play in the broader context of theatre history, Charles
Spencer contended:

> *The Chalk Garden* is an exotic bloom from the 1950s which miracu-
> lously retains its freshness more than 35 years after its première. [...]
> [After] John Osborne's *Look Back in Anger* [...] elegant, well-made
> drawing-room plays were supposedly consigned to the dustbin of
> theatrical history. Yet it is Osborne's drama which now seems stri-
> dent, sentimental and old-fashioned.[17]

A Taste of Honey

Shelagh Delaney's debut play, *A Taste of Honey,* was instantly recognized
as a promising work by a potentially major talent. It was staged by Joan
Littlewood's Theatre Workshop in1958, and has subsequently been
identified as a pre-feminist classic.[18] For example, Trevor R. Griffiths and
Margaret Llewellyn-Jones singled out the year of its first production as
the start for their investigation of post-war British drama, on the
grounds that Delaney's play initiated a 'new way forward for women's
theatre'.[19] In Raymond Williams's view it was *A Taste of Honey* rather
than *Look Back in Anger* that became representative for the new British
theatre, owing to its synthesis of 'general restlessness, disorganisation
and frustration'.[20] A similar claim has been made by Dominic Shellard,
who contended that despite the fact that *A Taste of Honey* 'reached the
stage later' than *Look Back in Anger,* it 'has an equal, if not greater, claim
to be a break point of the British theatre'.[21] Susan Bennett has argued
that Delaney pushed the boundaries of social realism considerably further than Osborne, despite being 'as far as the (theatre) histories go, in
the shadow of Jimmy Porter's legendary presence'.[22]

In a 1959 review, T.C. Worsley classified *A Taste of Honey* as a play '"about" a tart, a black boy giving a white girl a baby, a queer. The whole contemporary lot, in short.'[23] Though ironic and dismissive, this synopsis highlighted most of Delaney's themes, while also suggesting the innovative nature of her approach and her preoccupation with issues of her own time. A comment from Littlewood also reiterated Delaney's focus on ordinary daily life, together with commending the celebration of a register so far absent from British theatre: 'at least you can hear the real English language in the theatre, and people on the stage move like human beings.'[24] Predominantly centred on Jo, the play offers an insight into the disintegrating family life of a mother and daughter in the Salford slums. Though forced by poverty to share the same bed, Helen and Jo inhabit different worlds. The lack of actual communication between Helen and Jo, rooted partly in their different expectations from life but mainly in the generation gap between them, is addressed by Helen: 'You bring them up and they turn round and talk to you like that. I would never have dared to talk to my mother like that when I was her age. She'd have knocked me into the middle of next week.'[25] Despite the fact that she does not consider Jo an adult yet, Helen's plans for the future concentrate on herself. Regretting having given birth to Jo as a result of a brief relationship, Helen seems to be only concerned with finding an opportunity to leave her daughter behind.

Not only does Helen completely lack domestic abilities, but she is also frank and ironic about the fact that she never aspired to be a good mother:

> JO: You should prepare my meals like a proper mother.
> HELEN: Have I ever laid claim to being a proper mother?[26]

Despite this, however, the relationship between Helen and Jo is arguably the strongest interpersonal connection in the play. While usually contradicting each other, Helen and Jo cannot avoid relating to one another and, in most cases, Jo re-enacts Helen's past. Jo is not always aware that her actions parallel Helen's; in fact, she insists on her 'uniqueness'. Nevertheless, the Helen–Jo encounters can be read as double-acts in a music-hall routine – music-hall was one of the major influences on Delaney's style – and Jo consistently picks up on Helen's cues throughout the play. Jo's replication of Helen is especially ironic in the light of her desire for difference, and thus, despite the play's realist setting, none of the protagonists' claims are to be taken literally.

The play is set in a domestic environment – though neither woman performs any housework – and especially the kitchen becomes the background for the tentative bond between mother and daughter. For instance, after having just moved into their new flat, Jo is making coffee for Helen who has caught a cold. This gesture symbolizes a reversal of relationships between mother and daughter as Jo acquires a vaguely nurturing role. The genuine embodiment of caring, however, is Geof, whose appearance in the play coincides with Jo's financial independence and move away to a flat of her own. In fact, Geof becomes the surrogate parent *par excellence*, who assumes the responsibility of attending to Jo during her pregnancy and prepares for the arrival of her baby. 'It comes natural to you [...] you'd make somebody a wonderful wife', Jo observes, emphasizing that it is such an alternative arrangement that can potentially lead to happiness; in a 'family' that 'breaks all the rules and in which the central role, that of the mother, is detached from the biological mother and becomes a subject of negotiation'.[27]

Written prior to second-wave feminism and in a style antithetical to theorizing, Delaney's play nevertheless anticipates psychoanalytically motivated arguments on negotiated parenting. According to Dorothy Dinnerstein's *The Mermaid and the Minotaur* (1976), men's fear of women is determined by women's domination of childcare and the only solution to this problem is dual parenting, an idea explored further by Dinnerstein in *The Rocking of the Cradle and the Ruling of the World* (1987). Delaney recommends such an arrangement via the relationship between Jo and Geof, the success of which she roots in the elimination of sexual components. For Jo, Helen's sexual availability for others has always connoted lack of maternal affection: 'I used to try and hold my mother's hands, but she always used to pull them away from me. [...] She had so much love for everyone else, but not for me.'[28] In fact, as a result of Helen's inadequate parenting, Jo is prepared for neither emotional involvement nor the sheer physical pleasure of sex, yet her curiosity makes her open to temptation. Jo is desperate for affection but is unable to offer or receive it, mainly due to the lack of emotional support she received as a child. Thus, for instance, when Geof gets her a doll on which to practice baby-care, she immediately bursts out in anger and smashes it: 'I'll bash its brains out. I'll kill it. I don't want this baby, Geof. I don't want to be a mother. I don't want to be a woman.'[29]

In this sense, Delaney also anticipates Nancy Chodorow's claims in *The Reproduction of Mothering* (1978). Chodorow distinguished between the nurturing of children of different sexes, from the perspective of the mother. In her view, mothers perceive daughters as extensions of their

selves, considering them in a symbolic sense as continuous with themselves, whereas sons are seen and urged to see themselves as different
entities. Mothered by women, girls perceive themselves as less separate
from the mother than boys: 'In relation to their mother [girls] experience themselves as overly attached, unindividuated and without
boundaries.'[30] Girls' education into acknowledging female care basical-
ly excludes their introduction to other options: 'As a result of having
been parented by a woman, women are more likely than men to seek to
be mothers, that is, to relocate themselves in a primary mother-child
relationship, to get gratification from the mothering relationship, and
to have psychological and relational capacities for mothering.'[31] Thus,
according to Chodorow, the lack of maternal attention leads to a lack of
desire to mother when the girl reaches adulthood. Although Jo is not
entirely an adult yet (she had to be portrayed over 16 and hence legal-
ly entitled to marry and become a mother, to avoid censorship), her
manifesto claim – 'I hate babies' – is a rebellion against motherhood and
against biological and social destiny.[32] She is positive that she does not
want to follow in her mother's footsteps, yet she is unable to find another feasible option. The realization that female destiny is thrust upon her
triggers her deepest fears, conveyed most convincingly when she talks
about breastfeeding: 'I'm not having a little animal nibbling away at
me, it's cannibalistic. Like being eaten alive.'[33]

In the final scene, however, having eliminated their men and aspirations, mother and daughter find themselves united again. By bringing
the Helen–Jo relationship to the fore once more, Delaney revisits the
start of the play: mother and daughter confined to a claustrophobic
domestic space. This reunion has been interpreted in multiple ways to
fit both conservative and subversive arguments, ranging from an
emphasis on Delaney's reinforcement of women's biological destinies as
mothers to the acknowledgement of her critique of sexual politics. On
the one hand, the two women appear to unite in order to assume and
affirm the biological role as female and mother, despite previous
attempts at challenging its supremacy. Bringing together the two
women to undertake the responsibility of motherhood stands thus for
the failure of either Helen's or Jo's dreams of breaking through social
conventions and indicates a cycle whereby Jo replicates the life of her
mother. Nevertheless, in Michelene Wandor's words, the play crucially
identified the problem that 'motherhood [was] thrust upon some
women', and, via Geof's departure, that 'some men [were] denied the
chance to nurture'.[34] On the other hand, Jo remains abandoned
onstage, as Helen leaves for a drink after hearing about the baby's black

father. Thus, one can identify yet another break in the mother–daughter relationship between Helen and Jo, suggesting – apart from racism – Helen's ultimate inability to assume her maternal role.

A Taste of Honey is frequently mentioned as a proto-feminist text. Sue-Ellen Case argues, for instance, that the play's lyrical suspension corresponds to Delaney's own isolation as a young woman writing before the emergence of an adequate context, that of second-wave feminism.[35] The play has been categorized by Lib Taylor as a 'feminine/reflectionist' piece,[36] owing to its emphasis on women characters and on the female condition. This label, however, describes texts that engage with the experience of women yet fail to challenge the dominant ideology. Helen and Jo avoid conforming to the role of traditional homemakers and identify motherhood as a burden, not as a source of joy or fulfilment. Jo willingly accepts the domestic support of Geof, removing care from the terrain of women. Both Jo and Helen make significant attempts at subverting expectations concerning motherhood and femininity, even if they are eventually forced to confront the perpetuation of motherhood as a woman's realm.

In spite of high expectations, Delaney did not produce further successes for the stage. Her second play, *The Lion in Love* (1960), achieved only a moderate run and Delaney moved on to film-script writing. From the perspective of forthcoming women playwrights, however, the emergence of Jo as a young female protagonist had the significance of a breakthrough. Confident in her gender and class role, Jo appears as a subject throughout and almost never as an object of male desire. Her future as a single mother does not appear to destabilize her position, and although Helen advises Jo to avoid her mistakes, her reservations are less about teenage pregnancy than associated with Geof's suspected homosexuality and the baby's colour. The mere presence of Geof, in fact, acts as a taboo-breaking device: for his vaguely contoured yet obvious homosexuality, and for his inclination towards caring. While problematizing pregnancy and parenthood, Delaney draws up an ambivalent image: on the one hand implying the constraining nature of motherhood as a repetitive cycle, but on the other hand suggesting a celebration of birth and nurture in connection with human bonding and the affirmation of women as independent sexual beings.

Play With a Tiger

In a vein similar to Delaney's obsession with being contemporary, Lessing's play is set in 1958 – the year when it was written. Unlike

Delaney, however, Lessing concentrated on removing associations with realism from her play. She acknowledged the fact that in terms of subject matter and setting (rootless and classless people living in bed-sits) her play followed the emerging pattern of kitchen-sink drama, yet she aimed – via language and style – to move the play into an experimental realm. The London-based play centres on two outsiders, an Australian woman and an American man, both people who have renounced conventional morality and live according to their own rules. The most innovative section of the play is Act Two, where these characters, alone on the stage, role play with their pasts and futures, projecting an expressionist aura. Through this meta-theatrical game between Anna and Dave, as well as the removal of physical boundaries between the various elements of the set, Lessing achieved a move from naturalism; however, the detailed stage directions and the plausibility of human types and situations she employed constantly hark back to an aesthetic she tried to avoid.

The play, directed by Ted Kotcheff, was first produced at the Comedy Theatre, London, on 22 March 1962 by Oscar Lewenstein, with Siobhan McKenna as Anna Freeman. It ran for about two months, receiving mixed reviews; however, a version with a different cast was broadcast on BBC2 on 18 December 1967. Lessing considers *Play With a Tiger,* together with *Each His Own Wilderness* (which premièred at the Royal Court in 1958), her best plays. Both works reflect Lessing's razor-sharp observation of social and political concerns, and examine the emergence of a post-war classless society: the challenges of negotiating the personal with the public in *Play With a Tiger,* and the feasibility of the socialist ideal in *Each His Own Wilderness.* In 1972 Lessing added a postscript specifying that *Play With a Tiger* should not be interpreted as a woman's play, as it does not privilege a female point of view despite featuring female protagonists and addressing gender issues. I argue, however, that through Anna, and Myra in *Each His Own Wilderness,* Lessing investigates pathways of human consciousness that have paved the way for her analysis of female artistic creativity, later identified as *avant la lettre* feminism, in *The Golden Notebook* (set in 1957, first published in 1962). Moreover, the play presents a similar cluster of characters as *The Golden Notebook.* Anna Freeman resembles Anna Wulf in being a single mother in search of an integrated professional and emotional life, and Dave Miller recalls a character appearing towards the end of *The Golden Notebook* with whom Anna Wulf falls in love. There is also a parallel between the play's Mary and the novel's Molly, both mothers having raised children on their own while struggling with the various other

facets of their lives. Both play and novel feature protagonists confronted with fragmentation, negotiating professional anxieties alongside the
complexities of their sexuality and the tensions of friendship and family.
Unlike *The Golden Notebook*, however, *Play With a Tiger* does not
concentrate in detail on political commitments, and does not offer a
parallel to the sophisticated structure of the novel that allows for the
simultaneous examination of the protagonist's fragmented selves.

The three-act play takes place in Anna's home. She remains on stage
throughout and interacts directly with all the protagonists, though
most of her attention is dedicated to Dave. Lessing emphasizes in her
preface the importance of the fact that the play is not about young people, – everyone but Janet is over 30, – and the idea of humour coming
from getting older.[37] Life experience, therefore, is crucial and the characters emphasize the importance of choice. Thus, Anna chooses to
remain single in order to maintain her personal and economic independence, despite a brief engagement to Tom. Dave chooses to continue being rootless on principle and to move from one sexual conquest to
another without the responsibility of settling down, Harry opts to
remain married despite numerous affairs, and Mary, though less of a
defiant character than Anna, refuses to marry just for the sake of getting
married. In opposition to this cluster of independent-minded people,
Lessing presents Tom who becomes the employee of someone he detests
for reasons of economic convenience, and Janet who perpetuates the
fifties idea that marriage and a family constitute the ultimate career for
a woman. She intends to 'trap' Dave into marrying her despite knowing
of other women in his life.

One such woman Dave constantly returns to is Anna, who is also in
love with him. She is, however, like Delaney's protagonists, able to separate sex from love and her sexuality from her motherhood. Like
Jellicoe's Greta and Delaney's Helen and Jo, Anna is a free agent of her
own will and desire, and her motherhood is not located explicitly in the
framework of female biology or tradition as suggested in Bagnold's and
Delaney's plays (though the Anna–Mary bond can arguably be viewed
as an alternative family arrangement and their age difference can also
allude to a mother–daughter relationship of a kind). Anna's motherhood is a result of personal choice, which instead of diminishing the
protagonist's power gives her stability and a sense of security in her
interactions with men. As far as Dave is concerned, women's maternity
in particular and female sexuality in general are a major source of anxiety, and in Wandor's words: 'Marriage and family, according to Dave,
are no longer adequate compensations for the alienation of America.'[38]

This disillusionment – echoing Osborne's contemporaneous character, Jimmy Porter – is transferred into the fear of female sexuality; however, unlike in Osborne, where Jimmy delivers a major speech on the subject, in Lessing the issue is articulated by a woman: Anna on Dave's behalf. Thus, Anna not only formulates her own views but also acts as the most lucid observer and commentator of other stances.

Unlike Delaney and Bagnold's protagonists as well as the subsequent views advocated by the Women's Liberation Movement, Anna's motherhood is not immediately associated with female solidarity. In fact, Anna refuses to own up to having anything in common with Janet when finding out about the latter's pregnancy and desperation to marry. Covertly, however, this triggers Anna to revisit her own life back in Australia. Marriage and motherhood were supposed to be synonymous for her too, and she needed to insist on choice. This major political decision for the post-war period (the episode invoked would have taken place in the late forties) is rooted in disenchantment with the lives of the previous generation that privileged motherhood and domesticity above all, and Anna refuses to replicate her mother's life. In a later scene, as part of Anna and Dave's exploration of their inner worlds, they revisit together this episode. Anna projects herself as her mother, while Dave speaks Anna's father's thoughts. Both parents are made to reveal their frustration at having remained in an unhappy marriage for the sake of their children, and regret having missed out on a different life-style: geographical freedom for the father and a career for the mother – precisely the achievements Dave and Anna were able to obtain by staying single.

Anna knows, however, that Dave's idea of marriage is closer to Janet's understanding than hers, as a trap meant to put an end to men's independence. She is also aware of the impact of Dave's presence on her as the epitome of freedom. In this sense, she is able to juxtapose love to the liberation associated with the company of a fellow free spirit. Since Anna not only dissociates between love and sex, but also between being a respectable member of society and being an intellectual, she is in a position to address lucidly the clash of positions displayed by men and women. However, when it comes to unborn babies becoming casualties in this sex war, both realize the limitations of their liberal-cum-libertine positions. Lessing, like Delaney, was writing at a time when abortions were illegal and extremely dangerous in Britain. Contraception, available in the late fifties in a secretive way, is not mentioned at all in the play, as if reinforcing the fact that such phenomena were not really supposed to be talked about at the time. Thus, when Janet makes another attempt to locate Dave, he leaves without hesitation, triggering Anna to contemplate a new status quo not only in her relationship with Dave but also as far as her own politics is concerned. The play ends, thus, with a moment of hesitation, emblematic of the uncertainty character-izing women's social and political situation at the time. It also ends though with Mary's return, and consequently, with Lessing's acknowl-edgement of a potential for women's solidarity and ability to cope with social and emotional hardship.

The Sport of My Mad Mother

Delaney's treatment of space and time were less naïve than critics orig-inally supposed. Covering a linear time span slightly over the nine-month gestation period, *A Taste of Honey* establishes a set of correspon-dences between Jo's and Helen's lives: incomplete education, unstable sexual relationships and teenage pregnancy – thus also referencing a timeframe situated outside immediate chronology. Jo, like Helen, learns to cope with her pregnancy, while her frustration finds its only expres-sion through outbursts of rage and violence. The latter are central features of Ann Jellicoe's *The Sport of My Mad Mother* (1958) too; a play set in a quasi-mythic, primitive environment. This play privileges the somatization of emotions, intending to establish an immediate – intel-lectually unmediated – mode of communication between the characters onstage and the audience.

In contrast to Bagnold's – and to an extent to Delaney and Lessing's – work, it can be argued that Jellicoe's revolutionized theatrical form. Jellicoe was interested in recording feelings rather than their descrip-tion, attempting to 'releas[e] emotions' both in characters and audi-ences, as well as to 'assault the tyranny of intellectual discourse'.[39] Owing to its celebratory approach to motherhood, its evocation of a mythical female figure and its subversion of conventional gender role patterns, *The Sport of My Mad Mother* constitutes a successful anticipa-tion of feminist theatre. Feminist dramatic criticism has identified in Jellicoe's play an *avant la lettre* application of 'writing the body': main-ly due to the play's non-linear structure, the use of language to render emotions rather than facts, and the utilization of music and rhythm to dictate pace. Investigated by a number of French feminist scholars, the concept of 'writing the body' has dominated the radical feminist theo-ry scene of the seventies. Chantal Chawaf argued in 1976 for the articulation of the body as an ultimate goal of writing. Utilizing terms such as 'linguistic flesh' or 'corporeality of language' she emphasized the need to 'disintellectualize writing' and to explore its 'sensual' potential.[40] In the same year, Hélène Cixous posited *écriture féminine* not only as a form of writing inspired by the body but also connected to the maternal; hence reiterating correspondences between Jellicoe's theatre – her protagonist's self-expression via giving birth and communicating in a non-articulate manner – and French feminist thought: 'By writing her self, the woman will return to the body which has been more than confiscated from her. [...] It's with her body that she vitally supports "the logic" of her speech. Her flesh speaks true [...]. There is always within her at least a little of that good mother's milk. She writes in white ink.'[41]

Although Jellicoe herself refused to theoretically interpret feminism, suggesting that definitions were for academics, she stated that 'rationalisation, objectivity [...] are not states of mind which will help an audience to surrender', as the appeal in the theatre must be 'to the senses, emotions and instincts'.[42] Unlike her subsequent community plays – where she considered herself 'a craftsperson' who enjoyed 'delivering the goods as skilfully' as possible – *The Sport of My Mad Mother* was written 'intuitively, sensing along', 'with eyes closed'.[43] The play is an abstract piece, creating the impression of a set of notes, temporarily jotted down, which later would have to be developed into a more comprehensible text. In fact, John Russell Taylor claimed at the time that the script must have been intended as an *aide-mémoire* to the director in the 'transference of her initial conception from the stage of her own mind to a real, physical stage'.[44] As Jellicoe herself argued, the play was not written 'intellectually according to a pre-arranged plan. It was shaped bit by bit until the bits felt right in relation to each other and to the whole. It is an anti-intellect play, not only because it is about irrational forces and urges, but because one hopes it will reach the audience directly through rhythm, noise and music and their reaction to basic stimuli'.[45] Jellicoe also made it very clear from the very beginning that her play was a new kind of play which demanded a new approach; in Tynan's contemporary words, Jellicoe's 'use of music and dance' indicated that she knew 'the direction in which theatre' was moving: 'In jazz parlance her play is "far out", but it is far out in the future, not in the past'.[46]

Jellicoe's intention was to offer an insight into the lives of incoherent people, who felt insecure and afraid, without even realizing it or being aware of the reasons, and who compensated for their frustrations by directing their violence against someone else, often in an equally problematic condition. However, instead of explaining the details of the plot, Jellicoe aimed at showing events to the audience directly. In a way this recalls the aesthetics of the Artaudian 'Theatre of Cruelty'; Jellicoe expressed her suspicion of theatre which aimed to work predominantly through verbalization. As Artaud claimed in his groundbreaking manifesto with regard to the language of theatre:

> It runs through our sensibility. It aims to exalt, to benumb, to bewitch, to arrest our sensibility. It liberates a new lyricism of gestures which because it is distilled and spatially amplified, ends by surpassing the lyricism of words. Finally it breaks away from language's intellectual subjugation by conveying a sense of a new, deeper intellectualism hidden under these gestures and signs and raised to the dignity of special exorcisms.[47]

Like Artaud, Jellicoe also made an attempt at removing theatre from its elitism, hoping to make it available to everyone. She focused on audience participation and on conveying the workings of a sort of primitive unconscious. In fact, she argued, as soon as 'we deliberately extract ourselves from participation in what is happening and ask what any particular line or section means, we are lost and the play is lost to us'.[48] Despite some acclaim, however, the risks and limits of this technique were equally emphasized and hostile critics argued that the dichotomy between theatricality and the anarchic vision was too great. Critics have also signalled the (partial) inaccessibility of Artaud's – and indeed Jellicoe's – work to the general public. Thus, the play had only a short run at the Royal Court where it was first performed, on 25 February 1958, directed by George Devine and Jellicoe herself. It was, in Philip Locke's terms, a 'flop *d'estime*',[49] a painful experience for Jellicoe despite her winning third prize for the *Observer* playwriting competition and the play's immediate publication.

The Sport of My Mad Mother takes the form of a ritual, involving a few street-gang members from the tabloid headlines. Yet Jellicoe used this format to address remarkably similar issues to those raised by Bagnold, Lessing and Delaney, such as motherhood and the crisis in contemporary perceptions of masculinity. Repetition is a key technique in the play, the various characters echoing each other and functioning as a chorus. Their dialogue has, in fact, an 'incantatory effect';[50] the sounds they produce being mostly of an inarticulate nature while their interactions and frequent mood-swings are underlined by an onstage musician. Steve, the musician who does not leave the set during the performance, acts as a link between the audience and the characters' ritualistic world. Wandor saw him as 'the personification of the unconscious onstage', which – due to his auxiliary role to the action – becomes part of the theatrical illusion and a reassuring real presence.[51]

The play is based on a myth that simultaneously deals with the issue of motherhood and insecurity. It is concerned with 'fear and rage at being rejected from the womb or tribe', reworking an ancient tale according to which 'a man, rejected by his mother, castrates himself with a stone knife'.[52] Discussing the various forms the representation of the mother took in post-war British drama, Wandor concluded that it was only Jellicoe who addressed the myth of man's rejection by his mother. Most leading male playwrights – such as Wesker, Arden or Pinter – stressed the necessary emotional distance between their heroes and the maternal figure, while Osborne's Jimmy Porter advocated the total destruction of maternal power in order to be able to discover his identity as a man. Jellicoe's play does not, in fact, even feature what one might call an actual mother. The 'mad mother' of the title refers to the character of Greta, the spiritual leader of the gang, who is generally interpreted as an embodiment of Kali, the Indian goddess of creation and destruction: 'All creation is the sport of my mad mother, Kali.'[53] Another layer of correspondence links Kali's rejection of her son to Greta's turning away from Cone, the male character most attached to her, before she gives birth. In response, Kali's son castrates himself, according to the ancient Hindu myth, while Cone commits suicide.

Motherhood does not appear till a relatively advanced stage in the play, but Greta, the young woman who is eventually revealed as pregnant, is a dominant figure in the group long before any reference to birth. Jellicoe's stage directions require that 'the focus of attention' should go with her whenever she moves away from the rest of the group. It is Patty, the character who encapsulates the conventional stereotype of femininity (pretty and passive, wearing make-up and always curling her hair) who first refers extensively to Greta. Patty makes a long speech about the absent Greta that culminates in a desire for identification with her: 'I wish I was Greta. [...] anyone'll do anything for her.'[54] Later, despite Greta's attempt at remaining incognito, she is spotted and challenged by Dean. Almost instantaneously the play turns into a sequence of ritualistic violence during which Greta is seen as both beating and saving someone from being beaten, being always in control and acknowledged as an authority figure. In Keyssar's reading it is crucial that Greta remains a remote and isolated character, since her pregnancy 'only names but does not emotively convey the attractive fruitful side of her character'.[55] Moreover, when she appears as pregnant in front of the gang, the respect she has been inspiring is doubled by a fear of her maternal power.

This fear is particularly enhanced by the Dean–Greta conflict that underpins the negotiation of gender roles as well as positions of power throughout the play. Both Dean and Greta are outsiders to the community (Dean is American, Greta speaks with an Australian accent) and hence their confrontation can be read as a battle for territory. Their opposition re-enacts the dichotomies between masculine and feminine, civilized and primitive, rational and instinctive, mind and body, culture and nature. Greta also connects herself to the figure of Lilith, Adam's first wife who killed her babies and then gave birth to new ones:

> DEAN: And each Friday you dip it [her hair] in blood - in human blood.
> GRETA: In baby's blood.[56]

Dean's discourse on the need for morality and kindness, however, is suddenly brought to an end by the start of Greta's birth-pains. In vain does he repeat: 'You're not fit to have a child. [...] You gross thing. Man/woman, cruel. Unstable. Frigid.'[57] Greta still gives birth at the end of the play.

Thus, the 'bloody organic confusion'[58] of birth prevails and leads to the castration-cum-death of male characters. Greta not only succeeds in maintaining her power but also intensifies it, and makes a symbolic claim for the continuation of life by expressing her desire to give birth to hundreds and hundreds of children: 'Rails, rules, laws, guides, promises, terms [...] into the pot with the whole bloody lot. Birth. Birth. That's the thing. Oh, I shall have hundreds of children, millions of hundreds, and hundreds of millions.'[59] Apart from being a statement on Greta's maternal power, this monologue is also an indication of her active sexuality. As in Helen's case in *A Taste of Honey*, motherhood is not meant to be an alternative to sexuality for Greta; all her contacts with the males contain a sexual dimension. Nevertheless, the men feel threatened by Greta's ability to mother, a feature that recalls the perception of the maternal as sinister by a range of male characters in contemporaneous male-authored plays.

What is more relevant from the perspective of a feminist analysis, however, is that unlike Osborne's Alison and much more like Delaney's Helen and Jo or Lessing's Anna, Greta presents her own view of herself and the world. In this process she locates herself as her own agent, achieves a position of authority in a male-dominated sub-culture while equally asserting her right to become a mother as well as a sexual being. Motherhood for Jellicoe is removed from its connotations of female biology, tradition and duty, as present in the subtext of both Bagnold's and Delaney's plays. It appears as an exercise of free choice, while being a form of symbolic assumption of power and strength. It is not located within the context of a mother–daughter relationship or female sisterhood, not even a plausible family arrangement, but in a primitive environment, prior to the formation of social units. Jellicoe, however, also presents Greta's motherhood as potentially destructive, despite its connotation to the prolific – a theme that she returned to in *The Rising Generation* (1960).[60] Here, the protagonist, Mother, seeks control over the world, attempting to eradicate men entirely. Despite Mother's eventual failure (the world is destroyed but there are both male and female survivors who leave the Earth to establish a new life) and Jellicoe's juxtaposition of maternal and patriarchal qualities, the play emphasizes the potential for empowerment inherent in maternity and signals yet another breakthrough concerning dramatic structure.

More than a decade after the staging of *The Sport of My Mad Mother*, Jellicoe briefly returned to the Royal Court as its literary manger. This event is particularly relevant in the context of this study, as Jellicoe was one of the first women literary managers in a key institution of contemporary British theatre. Since its inception, the Royal Court has constituted a unique forum for the staging of new plays and the encouragement of first-time authors, although it often displayed a male bias. Jellicoe herself has made a sustained effort to produce work by women playwrights. As she said herself, she 'found' at least three major women writers – Mary O'Malley, Felicity Brown and Lee Langley, and tried to stage Pam Gem's *Queen Christina*. Looking back on her time as a female senior management worker in a male-dominated environment and as the first woman playwright whose work was produced by the English Stage Company at the Royal Court, she contended that she did not feel isolated, as she was 'awfully blind': 'I felt I'd done something remarkable, being a woman who'd got through [...] at the same time I didn't appreciate what tremendous disadvantages I was working under [...] the men didn't take a woman seriously.'[61] Working in what she termed a 'feminine way' – not privileging 'rational' argument over intuition – was a major impediment for her, however, as was the fact that she had not constructed a career plan. Her male colleagues' patronizing attitude made her resign from the job and settle down in Dorset in 1979. She has become a writer of community plays, through which she claims to have found her true vocation: 'I'm trying to make theatre valued and respected – which it certainly is not at the moment – to make people understand the excitement of a work of art. I think the beginning is asking them to do something. Not just saying, "It's wonderful, come along and watch it", but saying, "help make it"'.[62]

Conclusion

Although they wrote before the emergence of second-wave feminism, the playwrights considered in this chapter – Bagnold, Lessing, Delaney and Jellicoe – displayed elements that establish a direct connection with preoccupations of the Women's Liberation Movement. All feature independent women protagonists in charge of their lives; however, for none is womanhood fully dissociated from maternity, be it in a literal or symbolic dimension. Lessing locates her protagonist as an emancipated single mother who has a seemingly good relationship with her absent son, although the play's focus is on her ability to lead an intellectually and emotionally challenging life rather than the daily practice of parenthood. Delaney presents Helen and Jo attempting to separate the experience of being a woman from giving birth and nurture, yet when they become pregnant they learn to accept motherhood and see it as a direct outcome of their female destiny. Bagnold calls attention to one woman who is unable to deal with her maternal responsibilities and exercises a destructive influence on her daughter and granddaughter (Mrs St Maugham), and another who has temporarily lost contact with her child (Olivia) only to discover a subsequent longing to re-establish the bond with her estranged daughter. Jellicoe removes motherhood entirely from a family environment, inscribing it exclusively to Greta, a woman functioning as an independent agent of her own will. Jellicoe also associates motherhood – and giving birth – with authority and power over others.

In both Jellicoe's and Bagnold's view, gaining authority for a woman acts as a challenge to dominant patriarchal regimes. Before Madrigal's victory a symbolic sense of paternity prevailed in 'the chalk garden': in its totalitarian version via Pinkbell and in a caring form via Maitland. Delaney, on the other hand, treats male desire for parenting with considerably more sympathy and support, connecting it to emotional engagement and genuine interest in surrogacy. Geof longs to exercise care and domesticity, unrivalled by any of the other (female or male) characters. Bagnold presents Madrigal as a paragon of surrogate parenting too, yet she eventually renounces this role, privileging instead the mother–daughter bond between Olivia and Laurel. Thus, both *The*

Chalk Garden and *A Taste of Honey* end with the re-union of biological mothers and daughters, following the subversion of successful surrogate bonds. While in *The Chalk Garden* Bagnold indicates that there are chances for developing a successful relationship between mother and daughter; in *A Taste of Honey* Delaney warns against the lack of promise concerning improvement. Although they anticipated the gradual disintegration of the nuclear family and the rise of alternative structures, Bagnold and Delaney could not entirely remove themselves from the norms of their time. It is crucial to stress, nevertheless, that they initiated a transition from the inter-war conservatism of women's theatre by tackling topical issues of sexual politics and, in Delaney's case, by incorporating elements of social realism and music-hall.

Lessing's and especially Jellicoe's work, on the other hand, constitute explicit instances of innovation. Though Lessing sets her play in a naturalistic framework, she markedly stresses her intention of undermining the conventions of naturalism and switches from a plausible environment to the inner worlds of her protagonists. She explores varieties of individual freedom via Anna and Dave, juxtaposing men's lack of accepting responsibility for fatherhood to women's resistance to matrimony as a route towards genuine independence. Jellicoe's emphasis is on female empowerment – and the utilization of non-verbal devices to convey emotions rather than ideas – which anticipates feminist writing in its most radical form. It can be read as a direct forerunner to subsequently emerging dramatic 'writings of the body', including Jane Arden's *Vagina Rex and the Gas Oven* (1969), Maureen Duffy's *Rites* (1969) or Claire Luckham's *Trafford Tanzi* (1978).[63] Collating various instances of women's experience, Arden, Duffy and Luckham emphatically located woman as the subject of their plays (replicating not only Jellicoe, but also Bagnold, Lessing and Delaney).

In opposition to many playwrights discussed in his volume, Duffy was commissioned by the National Theatre to write a short play for a so-called Ladies' Night, intended to compensate for the lack of contemporary roles for women. *Rites* was directed by Jane Plowright, and was presented at the Jeanetta Cochrane Theatre, at the time the National's Studio, in February 1969 with a cast including Geraldine McEwan and Jane Lapotaire. The play, labelled as a black farce by Duffy, is a reworking of Euripides's *The Bacchae*, but in contrast to the home terrain of many plays it is set in a female lavatory and examines the confrontation of female versus male territories. Aiming to retell Agave's story rather than that of Pentheus, Duffy investigates the boundaries of female social space, climaxing in a suspected male intrusion followed by an instantaneous female solidarity to punish this transgression.[64] As it happens, the intrusive figure was a lesbian, and hence the women's violence ends up oriented against otherness on a sexual terrain. Another intrusion, also sanctioned, is that of a boy doll brought along by its mother. Through this auxiliary figure Duffy posits the issue of motherhood as a marginal phenomenon, although she equally explores this topic in its symbolic dimension, via Ada and Meg's caring service deployed for the benefit of the women visiting the lavatory (Figure 2).

In Arden's *Vagina Rex and the Gas Oven* motherhood is only one among women's many roles, performed away from a domestic environment. First produced in 1969 at Jim Haynes's London Arts Laboratory, Arden's was one of the first plays in alignment with – rather than prefiguring – the demands of the Women's Liberation Movement, and caused uproar with its thesis on women's political and personal oppression, and with its explosive dénouement transforming female victimhood into radicalism. Bringing together a surrealist strand with Artaudian 'theatre of cruelty' and elements of music and ritual rooted in sixties counter-culture, Arden locates women in opposition to male-identified discourse ('we must destroy the language', women 'have no language') and urges the necessity of an adequate discursive system to

Figure 2   Ensemble in *Rites* by Maureen Duffy, Royal National Theatre, 1969 (photo: John Timbers, reproduced by photographer's permission).

reflect women's experience: 'the words of women have yet to be written.'[65] As it examines aspects of the female and the feminine the play presents and subverts types and stereotypes, including the woman as mother and whore. Reminiscent of Jellicoe's Greta, birth emerges as an archetypal, empowering and uniquely female experience – 'The uterus is the great divider'[66] – not merely presenting a potential threat to the male-dominated world but able to encompass women's visionary energies: 'The rage is still impacted within us – I am frightened of the oncoming explosion.'[67] Like Jellicoe, therefore, Duffy and Arden called for women to find an adequate language and space of their own, and as the forthcoming chapters demonstrate, paved the way for an alternative women's history in British theatre.

2
Irreversible Choice: Female Professional Success

Following the initial undivided response to the emergence of second-wave feminism, feminists in the seventies were gradually faced with dilemmas, in particular regarding the possibility of making 'a separate culture' or demanding 'access to the mainstream'.[1] Most supporters of the movement joined the debate and thus, a binary opposition was set up: women promoting either a radical feminist stance – in isolation from the male world, or advocating the achievement of equality with men on the public and class terrain – in agreement with the respective principles of liberal and socialist feminism. Later in the decade the concept of the 'third way' also emerged, according to which the distinct nature of being a woman could be acknowledged in conjunction with an engagement with mainstream currents and institutions. In fact, women's location with regard to a male-dominated culture has concurrently developed into a central question for feminism, which has not been entirely settled to this day. In the seventies this dilemma was positioned at the very core of women's intervention – from politics to sociology, theory to fiction, the visual arts to popular culture.

Helène Cixous, for instance, contested the binary opposition between woman and man, feminine and masculine, positing a third way that celebrated the space in between polar opposites.[2] In theatre, as this chapter explores, Caryl Churchill interrogated traditional gender stereotypes in relation to property and parenthood in *Owners* (1972), and Pam Gems examined the case of a woman first socialized as a man and then required to suddenly identify as a woman and give birth in *Queen Christina* (1977). A decade later Churchill returned to the idea of a professionally successful female protagonist in *Top Girls* (1982); this time, however, she rooted her achievements in intra-gender exploitation and the renunciation of traditional feminine values, such as motherhood.

In fiction, Angela Carter featured a woman born out of a man's body in her allegorical novel *Passion of New Eve* (1977), whereas in film, Laura Mulvey's *Riddles of the Sphinx* (1975) scrutinized the idea of symbolic fusion between the two sexes and genders, while focusing on the social and emotional aspects of parenting. In visual arts, Wendy Taylor's *Brick Knot* (1978) showed the artist caught inside the knot, and metaphorically focused on the complexities of finding a satisfactory remedy to women's social and psychological dilemmas. Though being caught inside the knot might have warned against (female) biological supremacy, it also signalled an awareness of the initially unacknowledged flaws in feminist intervention. Fuelled by the realization of the 'immensity of what had been undertaken',[3] considerable caution as well as ideological divergence took over in feminist work, in place of the previous unity and expectation of immediate solutions.

This context of theoretical complexity and lack of certainty was matched in the political arena by frequent changes in government: a Conservative government was elected in 1970, Labour returned to power in 1974 and in 1979 the Conservatives were elected again. Despite this lack of continuity, the seventies boasted major regulations in social work, the health service and local government: the Equal Pay Act (1970), the Family Income Supplement Act (1971), the Divorce Reform Act (1971), the Race Relations Act (1972) and the Sex Discrimination Act (1975) aimed at creating a framework for a fairer negotiation of power relations between employees and employers. However, the period continued to witness increases in unemployment and trade union protests, intensification in race riots, as well as a more severe control on immigration. To cope with a situation of extremely low economic growth that ultimately triggered recession, the British government adopted a number of deflationary policies, which resulted in the subversion of the economic progress women as a social class had made so far.

The seventies represented a decade of transformations from the perspective of women's voice in the public sphere. Following the first major conference of British feminists at Ruskin College in Oxford in 1970, Women's Liberation demonstrations – for abortion rights and equal opportunities and payment – occurred on a regular basis. Apart from direct campaigning or support for trade unions, women's activism also became channelled towards a women-oriented press (Virago, The Women's Press, *Spare Rib*), and the medium of theatre, leading to the formation of women-centred theatre groups, such as the Women's Theatre Group, Monstrous Regiment, Spare Tyre or Siren. The British political scene, meanwhile, featured an exhausted Labour Government, losing popularity by the day. The decay culminated in the 1978–79 'Winter of Discontent', when low-paid public-sector employees rebelled against their wages. It was in this context of popular disappointment with the inefficiency of the State that the Conservative leader Margaret Thatcher emerged, with a totally different view of society, highlighting the merits of individualism and self-help. Winning the election in 1979, Thatcher set out to bring together 'the instincts of individual greed and collective self-righteousness into a coherent model of the world, in which the rhetoric of freedom [could] co-exist with the reassertion of virtue'.[4]

This focus on individualism had the effect of subduing the general public's expectations of the State as benefactor, expectations labelled unjustified and exaggerated by right-wing liberal analysts and politicians. However, what the Right was offering in return, according to Stuart Hall, was but a populism of a different kind: 'an authoritarian populism of the right', drawing upon nationalistic and anti-collective sentiments.[5] Instead of addressing the welfare of the nation, the new government recommended achieving success on an individual basis. Thatcher claimed that she came to office to change Britain from 'a dependent to a self-reliant, from a give-it-to-me to do-it-yourself society; to a get-up-and-go instead of a sit-back-and-wait-for-it Britain'.[6] While in the early stages of her political career Thatcher insisted on women's presence in the labour market, by the time she became prime minister she advocated that the family unit needed to remain 'secure and respected' and that 'bringing up the family [was] the most important thing of all'.[7] She pointed out that there was nothing to correct further in women's condition, as the battle for women's rights had been won. In fact, the Conservative government reduced the value of maternity and child benefits, already among the lowest in Western Europe, while Thatcher, as education secretary in 1971, earned the nickname 'Milk-snatcher' for cutting government funding for children's school milk.

Alongside increasing economic difficulties, women's unemployment rose between 1979 and 1986. The only increase occurred in part-time work, largely in the lower-paid service industries. It was these conditions of polarization between middle-class professionals and less-qualified part-time workers that confirmed the emergence of 'two nations' within modern Britain, of a society divided between the 'haves' and the 'have-nots'. In the wake of the Employment Act, employers could more easily refuse maternity leave to their women employees, thus restricting women's choices concerning not only the timing but also the assumption of childbirth. This lack of encouragement for parenthood, however, did not lead to a professional promotion of women. Thatcher did not indicate any interest in women's networks ('I hate those strident tones we hear from some women's Libbers'), yet she would not have been able to win several elections without the support of women voters.[8] Encapsulating duality between appearances and essence, the figure of the woman prime minister was clearly female but not exactly feminine, apparently traditional yet at the same time artificial. In the words of the Labour politician Barbara Castle, Thatcher sported a 'combination men fear most: a brain as good as theirs plus a mastery of the arts of femininity'.[9] According to Beatrix Campbell though, Thatcher 'has not feminised politics, but has offered feminine endorsement to patriarchal power and principles'.[10]

This unique combination of traits attributed to masculine and feminine values became emblematic for the period marked by Thatcher, and the following analysis is centred on the ways powerful women were represented in three important women-authored plays of the seventies and eighties. Caryl Churchill's *Owners* and *Top Girls* emerged, respectively, at the beginning and end of the period, while Pam Gems's *Queen Christina* appeared in 1977. Only Marlene – the protagonist of *Top Girls* – can be considered a genuine Thatcherite; however, Marion – the ambitious property developer in *Owners* – exhibits character traits that prefigure the Thatcher phenomenon, since for both Marion and Marlene the desire for achievement motivates all other actions. It is equally important to stress that while Thatcher only became prime minister in 1979, she had been occupying high-profile posts for years before becoming Conservative Party leader in 1975. Moreover, reading *Owners* in the light of the Thatcher era, Churchill's visionary talent becomes increasingly self-evident, if not prophetic.

While Thatcher and Churchill's protagonists maintain their femininity yet deploy a consistent effort towards a certain intellectual and behavioural masculinity, Gems's Christina looks and behaves like a man, and, in her rare attempts at passing as a female, she resorts to performance and masquerade. Queen Christina is also a pre-Thatcherite figure, but unlike Marion she interrogates the internal contradictions within feminist discourses in the seventies. The issue of accommodating family life and careers arises in all three plays, but the dilemma created by the opposing choices is by far the strongest for Christina. In contrast to Marion's and Marlene's egalitarian feminism, Christina tackles and subsequently rejects radical feminism before briefly identifying as a socialist feminist. Eventually, she refuses to privilege any particular stance, thus echoing Gems's own reservations towards feminism. The end note, therefore, is one of ambivalence, re-formulating the question of whether women should build a separate culture or keep demanding access to a mainstream society identified hitherto with masculine values.

Queen Christina

Pam Gems has had a complicated relationship with feminism, and has not acknowledged any association with the labels 'woman playwright' or 'feminist icon'. Accordingly, she has maintained both her empathy with and distance from feminism as an ideology. Her main objection to feminist theatre was located in its alleged 'anti-men' stance, though she has addressed issues considered to be feminist.[11] In 1977 she claimed that the phrase '"feminist writer" [was] absolutely meaningless', because of its polemical implications.[12] Gems later amended this statement, specifying that she did consider herself a feminist in private, and acknowledged her work's feminist perspective. Gems also contended that her intention was 'to steer would-be dramatic writers away from the preaching-to-the-converted', 'that ha[d] been so prevalent in committed theatre'.[13] A major source of Gems's resistance to being labelled as feminist was her desire to present her plays as artistic interventions, rather than political statements. However, she often contested social and sexual as well as theatrical conventions (Figure 3).

Gems has shown ample evidence of experimentation with style and form, often combining cutting-edge dramatic techniques with realism. Her work is also permeated by a preoccupation with cultural icons, from the seventeenth-century queen of Sweden to Edith Piaf or Mrs Patrick Campbell. Most of her plays are focused around one central female protagonist, to whom the male characters are supportive figures. Susan Bassnett-McGuire has argued that plays such as *Queen Christina* ended up being patriarchal owing to their (limited) focus on one central character.[14] For Gems, however, the single protagonist who copes on her own in a patriarchal environment serves exactly the opposite end: to put across a woman's point of view. *Queen Christina* was originally commissioned in 1974 by Ann Jellicoe, in her capacity as literary manager at the Royal Court. Nevertheless, it encountered rejection a year later by the new, male management appointed after Jellicoe's departure. Gems was told that her play was 'too sprawly, too expensive to do [...] and it would appeal more to women'.[15] Despite the Royal Court's hostility to the subject matter the play premièred in 1977 at the original Other Place, the RSC's studio theatre in Stratford. *Queen Christina* became the first play by a woman to be staged at

Figure 3 Sheila Allen and Iain Mitchell in *Queen Christina* by Pam Gems, RSC Other Place, 1977 (credit: 'Joe Cocks Studio Collection © Shakespeare Birthplace Trust').

Stratford, and was also directed and designed by women: Penny Cherns and Di Seymour. The play has been revived on a number of occasions, including performances by Tricycle Theatre in 1982 and by Absolute Theatre in 1997.

The majority of Gems's characters are based on historical figures, as Gems revisits history by picking up on occasions when women had access to challenging roles. Though set in chronologically disparate moments, Gems's plays may be interpreted as a series of matrilineal texts, and as a way of reclaiming women's presence in culture and society. As she stresses herself, 'If you're writing as a woman [...] you want to explode some of the grosser myths that have been erected by men; the sentimentalisation of women and therefore the reduction of them.'[16] She points out the necessity of 'reparation' on behalf of women but – preoccupied by the question of truth, both in art and life – Gems does not treat her protagonists with positive discrimination. Queen Christina, for instance, is initially featured scorning her mother, deprecating femininity. Towards the end of the play, after having abdicated, she is shown mourning: yet not for her mother or for the throne she gave up, but for her missed maternal opportunity.

Christina does not give birth herself, yet her life constantly moves around the succession and the production of heirs. Gems has referred to this historical parable as a 'uterine play', stressing an essentialist view of sexual and gender identity. Though the play explores a case of transgression against conventional patterns, it takes for granted the connection between womanhood and reproduction, and the centrality of motherhood in (most) women's lives. As Gems explained, 'I was the pre-Pill generation that got married and had children – no choice – but this seemed to me to be the dilemma that women at this time were in.'[17] Nevertheless, Gems is also preoccupied with her subsequent experience of post-Liberation and post-Pill times, in which women have obtained economic and sexual liberties. According to Elaine Aston, Gems constantly negotiates a 'dual vision', bringing her '"before" and "after" experiences to bear on the complications which greater choice and opportunity mean for women'.[18]

The opening of *Queen Christina* shows Christina as a little girl, witnessing her mother give birth to a stillborn child. This event is the latest in a series in which the Queen has been trying to produce a male heir for the throne of Sweden. Finally convinced of the futility of trying for a male baby, the king proclaims Christina as the future heir: 'We're going to make a queen of you [...] not like your mother [...] like me, like a king.'[19] To Axel, the chancellor's objections that Christina is of 'the wrong sex', the king's firm reply is to make 'a man of her', by training and legislation.[20] In fact, this artificial interference with gender leads to a total alteration of Christina's existential choices; she is taught to behave like a man, and learns to hunt, fight and develop an interest in intellectual, political and military matters. As she assimilates the characteristic traits of masculinity, she finds that performing the acquired gender becomes easier than behaving according to the conventions of her original gender. For instance, she is metaphorically presented as handling the 'bloody [thirty years'] war' with great success, yet failing to cope with the monthly period, hence participating in another war: with her own body.

Unlike Greta Garbo's 1933 movie, where Christina appeared as a 'shining pale, intellectual beauty, who had romantically chosen freedom',[21] Gems wanted to call attention to the story's complex historic context. Gems's protagonist, like the actual historical figure, is a plain woman, in opposition to Garbo's attractive Christina. Gems's focus is on the confusion of Christina caught between the 'manly qualities of a king and the fecundity of a woman', or in Aston's words, 'the trappings of masculine power' and the 'disempowered body of a woman'.[22]

Garbo's character is also encouraged to marry and produce heirs, but her resistance is a result of not having found the right partner. Another crucial difference between the two versions is that while Garbo's Christina gives up the throne for passionate love, Gems's protagonist abdicates when she realizes the incompatibility between her own understanding and the public expectation of her gender identity. Psychologically identifying herself as a man, Gems's Christina is unable to switch to the traditional female function of reproduction, as she had distanced herself from the practice of womanhood. For Geraldine Cousin, in fact, the focus is on the switch from Christina's inadequate connection to femininity to her identification as a man. She argues that Christina's 'transformation into a man has been too successful', since the '"only truth" she knows is a man's, and she will not "pollute" it'.[23]

Thus, in the quid-pro-quo scene of Act One, Scene Two, Christina is taken for a man until she reveals her identity. Gems opens the scene from the male suitor's perspective and thus, the audience find themselves confronted with what seems to be the conventionally most appropriate outcome, and take the wrong person (a beautiful lady-in-waiting) for the queen. Even after the identity of the real Christina is revealed, she keeps on playing with expectations and suddenly switches to the role of the frail woman, taking the prince's 'nerveless arm' and standing beside him in 'wifely stance'.[24] Thus, Gems signals the opposition between Christina's biological sex and socially constructed gender; and using the device of cross-dressing, allows for a 'vision of fluidity of gender options [...], a utopian prospect of release from the ties of sexual difference'.[25]

The issue of Christina's looks is raised repeatedly, and it is Christina's overtly feminine mother who locates her daughter's ugliness as the reason behind the lack of male interest. Speaking from her own position as a woman who achieved status via her alliance with a man, Christina's mother is unable to understand the dynamics of Christina's cultural and intellectual identification or her unwillingness to yield to conventions. It is, in fact, Christina's awareness of her own physical repulsiveness that constitutes a major argument for refusing to breed: 'What sort of a litter do you think we'd produce', 'No! there's one freak on the throne [...] no need to perpetuate the joke.'[26] Christina's passionate resistance to motherhood conjures up Shulamith Firestone's radical feminist view advocating that women should give up bearing children altogether. Firestone's 'case for a feminist revolution' argued for the exploration of the links between biology and social conditioning: 'To free women from their biology would be to threaten the social unit that is organised around biological reproduction and the subjection of women to their biological destiny, the family.'[27] Doing away with the biological family, therefore, was suggested as the solution to women's oppression, since it was motherhood that had led to the first division of labour.

Aware of her inadequacy regarding the conventional feminine, Christina first reinforces the mind/body binary, and only later does she deconstruct this opposition, making explicit her challenge to societal expectations. Her extended conversations with Descartes – through which Gems underpins the interconnection between drama, theory and political practice – only fuel this impulse as she gradually learns not to pursue unattainable goals. This sudden shift in her attitude recalls Firestone's statement from 1970, according to which 'Love is the pivot of women's oppression.'[28] As an attempt to liberate herself from sexual oppression, Christina dissociates sex from love, and throughout the second act pursues her famously uninhibited and non-committed exploration of sexuality. This approach to sex as a source of pleasure, as well as a terrain where power relations are negotiated, can be viewed in parallel with the stance reached at the First National Women's Liberation Conference in London: 'We can't talk of sex as anything but a joke or a battleground.'[29] Gradually, in the seventies, the debate on sex transformed into a crusade against heterosexuality, claiming that only women who cut all ties with men could be taken seriously in the struggle against male domination. Gems does not position Christina as a representative of political lesbianism, yet she makes her consider and then challenge the idea and practice of female separatism. Unlike Christina, Gems has declared herself a believer in marriage as commitment and, in the play, places Christina's mother to contend that women do not 'need to understand theory' as they are too busy just 'keeping their families alive' under conditions of war.[30]

Christina's conflict between her sex and her gender is illustrated by an exchange with the royal doctor. At her protest against a diet she finds unsuitable for a queen, Christina is informed that it had been prescribed for the woman, not the monarch. This dual nature of Christina's identity is also emphasized by Axel. Having so far related to Christina as the man he has trained, Axel suddenly expects her to give birth to an heir. Christina's refusal, however, seals her transformation into a man. Passionately arguing against her social and political duty to give birth, she claims Axel's respect for the transgender being he has turned her into. Christina is aware that she represents but an intellectual companion for men; as for women, she has never identified as one, since following male role models led her to develop only contempt for women: 'I'm damned if I breed for them and be destroyed like my mother.'[31]

Though latently present earlier, Christina's genuine plans are sealed with her spectacular abdication. She offers her crown first to the chancellor and then her fiancée, and her diamond brooch to her mother, renouncing the emblems of femininity as well as social status. The scene ends with Christina's ecstatic departure from the ceremony, and hence the constraints of tradition and gender stereotyping. It is the metonymy of the dress, however, abandoned on the throne, that reiterates Christina's 'gender-based conflict between marriage, reproduction and disempowerment on the one hand, and monarchy, non-childbearing body, and power on the other'. [32]

Act Two follows Christina on her self-chosen exile, exploring new ways of life in France and Rome. These encounters act as the confrontation of two sets of ideologies (feminism and Catholicism), both of which she is tempted to consider though neither will eventually prove convincing for her. Her meeting with the French Bluestockings leaves both parties dissatisfied when they find that all they have in common is the refusal to marry and breed (further) children. There is a discrepancy between the almost brutal simplicity of Christina and the mannered style of the French ladies, an opposition that replicates the controversy between grassroots, practical and theoretical, academic feminism. Inspired by the seventies political lesbianism as a resistance to male oppression and the only solution for women's genuine liberation ('lesbianism was perceived as a feminist, political act by the burgeoning women's right movement, and there were many rules to the sapphic sex act'),[33] Gems's ladies advocate radical feminism. Christina, on the other hand, admits to having difficulties with adjusting to women. Though Christina's stance is a product of her conditioning, her attitude echoes a major problem associated with feminism as a movement: 'The idea that you had to choose between men and the women's movement was quite an oppression.'[34] Though she declares herself a sceptic, Christina's attraction to Catholicism – a religion dominated by paternal authority figures – introduces another gap between the positions of the two parties, placing her in an anti-feminist stance. When asked to demand the same freedoms for women as men currently have and, hence, enrol in a liberal, equality-feminist engagement, Christina declines involvement.

Discrepancies in opinion also emerge in her theological discussions. Christina finds that the pope's opinions on women's role in society and parenting are similar to the ones she has been defying in Sweden, including the same concern with the need for heirs and with women's destiny in procreation. Eventually, she tackles the question of love as the principle on which society should be organized. But she cannot dissociate the command to love, advocated by the pope as a biblical imposition, from the command to *be* loved – the desire Christina has always had, but has never explored. This approach can be read as Gems's questioning of the politicization of private lives. Although second-wave feminism began with the commandment that 'the personal is political', it has subsequently generated severe internal contradictions, especially as far as women's sexual orientation is concerned. A major source of such tension was provided by certain patterns of behaviour and identification, such as lesbianism, being adopted with an exclusively political scope. By liberating the realm of personal life from political interpretations Gems seems to be arguing for a new kind of feminism, characteristic of the nineties, that does not wish to colonize women's private lives and offer generalizing formulae.

For Christina, the commandments 'to love' and 'be loved' have never gone together, and 'being loved' was only achievable by recompensing the partner. In Christina's relationship with Monaldescho, female power is traded for male physical appeal. Christina has no illusions that Monaldescho is attracted to her as a woman; in fact she takes it for granted that he is aware of her former and potential future social status and that this is the source of his interest in her. It is his manifestation of affection that confuses Christina. Such an attitude has not been stipulated in their initial trade-off and, therefore, unbalances their power relations and needs elimination. Following the climactic scene of Monaldescho's execution, Christina's next move is one of seclusion, tormented by a deep guilt for the crime she committed more out of temper than conviction. For the first time the woman who has lived in the public sphere finds herself confined to the claustrophobic space of one room. Rejected by Rome, her sole opportunity for re-establishing contact with the political world is by contending for the throne of Poland. Christina is fully aware, however, that the offer is addressed to her male self who would secure the peace in the name of Catholicism. However, she also knows that any transgression she might commit to this role would be sanctioned to the biological woman in her.

This dilemma – between returning to the mainstream or maintaining anonymity – initiates her challenge not only to her previous contempt for women but also to her adoption into the male world. Gems captures her protagonist's discovery of the traditional realm of femininity in strong olfactory images. Gradually, she experiences sympathy for women and a sudden awareness of class inequalities gives voice to a note of socialist feminism through Christina's demand for all women to be on the same footing. In spite of her genuine wish to consider herself a woman from then on, however, Christina is also aware that she has missed her opportunity for giving birth. It is only now that she fully perceives the irrevocable nature of the choice that was taken on her behalf: 'I have been betrayed. [...] *(She slaps her abdomen.)* This has been betrayed.'[35]

Since contending for the throne does not satisfy her any longer, she tackles the question that, in fact, constitutes the central thesis of the play: 'In God's name, why must I choose?'[36] Reversing the well-known slogan demanding the availability of abortions, Gems makes Christina contemplate why a woman must choose between an independent life and giving birth. Christina is finally able to account lucidly for the fact that, by prioritizing the throne, all other choices have been rated secondary: 'I have been denied my birthright.'[37] Despite her discovery of the maternal drive, and despite being tempted by an essentialist understanding of sexual division reminiscent of cultural feminism, she suddenly asserts her belief in the social construction of gender. Ironically, it is the biological impossibility of enacting her so-far-repressed female side that leads her to acknowledge: 'We are nature! It is we who change and create change!'[38]

Unable to accept the whim of fate, the final scene captures Christina in a rebellion against this closure of choices, as she confronts Azzolino as the representative of patriarchal domination in both religious and political terms. This confrontation encapsulates her protest against having been a mere instrument in political machinations, and it acts out as physical violence her longing for the child she has never had. Her whipping of the male oppressor can equally be read as the tarantella dance of the female hysteric, who thus somatizes her subversive potential and claims her inner freedom. Through the appropriation of a severely gendered act, Christina emphasizes on yet another level – her break with her socially constructed gender and her availability for becoming a woman. The hysterical fit also signifies rebirth in Clément's and Cixous's radical theory; hence Christina emerges as a 'newly born woman', with a potentially stable gender and sexual identity.[39]

Queen Christina, therefore, does not end on a note of resignation; Christina being presented to demand an adequate answer to the need for women choosing between careers and family. In an attempt to legitimize the use of a seventeenth- century figure for the exploration of late twentieth-century situations, Gems acknowledges present-day women's wider opportunities for having children while still pursuing a career. She stresses, however, that what is still badly needed is the production of 'maps of the new terrain in which we find ourselves'.[40] In other words, choices no longer have to be as clear-cut as in Christina's time. Gems claimed that a large proportion of women today do not want to take an active role in the public domain or assume the responsibility of irreversible choices. According to Gems, women are less inclined than men to competitiveness: for her, Thatcher and the style she represented constituted 'the anomaly' not the norm.[41] The playwright also acknowledged that another segment of contemporary women, those who do want careers, still find it confusing to accommodate the often contradictory aspects of their various identities. Via the juxtaposition of extremes and by addressing the performance of gender, *Queen Christina* equally asks what it means to be female (or indeed, male). As Gems presents Christina's suppression and rediscovery of womanhood, she places this case study in a universal context, exploring the boundaries of individual freedom.

Owners

Owners (1972) was Caryl Churchill's first full-length play to be produced by a professional company. It also focused critical attention on the author in a new way, as until then she was known as a prolific writer of radio plays. The play was performed at the Royal Court Upstairs and constituted the first collaboration between the playwright and the Royal Court. This was followed by Churchill's 1975 appointment as the first woman Resident Dramatist at the Royal Court and the theatre's production of several Churchill plays. Although written in the heyday of second-wave feminism the play does not feature any obvious seventies feminist character. The issues that Churchill acknowledges are both social (the idea of ownership, involving landlords and tenants) and philosophical (the opposition between Western aggressiveness and Eastern passivity).

In lieu of using traditional gender stereotypes, Churchill centres her play on a gender role-reversal. Instead of having just two characters, however, Churchill operates with two sets of polar contrasts: the active force is a woman and the major passive factor is a man, while both are supported by other characters. For instance, there are two opposed women: one prefigures the eighties obsession with power and the other connotes a domestic, traditional sense of femininity. Similarly, there is a passive male at the centre, but there are active men as well. These examples illustrate that Churchill avoids a focus on biological difference. Women may take up values generally considered to be masculine, while men can feel attracted towards feminine ones.

The women characters – Marion, occupying the public domain of business versus Lisa, confined within her home – are connected via Marion's ownership of the flat that Lisa and her family inhabit. Churchill complements Marion's greed and thirst for power with a husband who has given up on career aspirations. Clegg, nevertheless, finds it difficult to cope with his wife's success. Lured by the fantasy that he will eventually dominate his wife via sexual subordination, Clegg advocates male chauvinism and misogyny. Eventually, it will not be Marion but Lisa whom Clegg succeeds in dominating sexually. Since Lisa is the wife of Alec – whom Marion is still in love with – possessing Lisa signifies the 'ownership' of something that belongs to Marion's object of desire, and hence leads to Clegg's indirect victory over Marion.

The strongest longing nevertheless is for succession, and for the transmission of one's fortune and name via the production of children. Ironically, the only fertile couple is the one that do not have much to transmit in material terms. Clegg's vision of the 'Clegg and Son' chain of butcher's shops has proved to be a shattered dream, while Marion can only aim at a successor by acquisition. Offering a critique of utilitarian exploitation, Churchill highlights Lisa's and Alec's financial insecurity as the foundation of Marion's blackmail. The couple's latest child becomes the object of a commercial exchange on terms and conditions imposed by Marion: they can remain in the flat provided they hand the newborn baby over to Marion and Clegg, who will raise it as their own. Towards the end of the play, this baby is returned by Marion's aid to Lisa, in a gesture prioritizing the biological mother–infant bond: 'It is not your baby, Marion, by any stretch of imagination.'[42]

As opposed to Lisa's family-centredness, Marion leads an independent life despite her marriage. She has concentrated on achieving success, a fact that translates into a certain willingness not to have or nurture children. However, surrogate parenthood – via Marion's sudden interest in Lisa's baby – takes up a major section of the play. Churchill turns to issues that have subsequently become central in the ethics of adoption and surrogacy, such as who is a child's real mother: the biological (birth) mother or the legal (adoptive) mother. Marion considers herself a legitimate legal mother to the child, and the exchange perfectly acceptable both morally and psychologically, although Churchill concludes the play with Marion's failed attempt at surrogacy, arguing for the prevalence of the biological bond. In Marion's surrogate parenting, for instance, the component of care is non-existent. Her desire to acquire a child is fuelled by the economic necessity of having an heir, but also by her rivalry with Lisa. As Marion is unable to obtain Alec or have his child herself, she settles for second best: appropriating Lisa's baby. Through this latter exercise Marion is symbolically transformed into a substitute for Lisa, not merely as a surrogate mother to the latter's child but also as a substitute partner to Alec.

The only character uninterested in possession is Alec. Even Lisa has moments when she is taken over by acquisitiveness; she is particularly upset after the burglary of their house and tries to save the home she considers theirs. It is her quest to regain their child given up for adoption, however, that makes her dependent on her instinct for possession. Lisa desperately wants the child she has lost in the uneven battle with Marion, partly owing to the operation of her maternal instinct, but also as the child's absence reminds her of their inferior social status. As Elaine Aston observes, '"Owning" and buying babies is a class and gender issue: economic privilege empowers one class of mothers and fathers to buy: [sic] economic deprivation encourages disempowered mothers to sell. Lisa, as Churchill's dramatic representation of the economically deprived birth mother is, therefore, as much a victim of her class as of her gender.'[43]

Though economic and social tension underpins the entire play, it is the final scene that establishes Marion as the ultimate victor, and where her materialist individualism is set most strikingly against the misery of the others. A fire triggers the death of the disputed baby and leaves Lisa and Alec without a home, yet for Marion it connotes achievement: 'I never knew I could do a thing like that. I might be capable of anything.'[44] This claim is emblematic for the excessive potential of liberal feminism. Churchill posits Marion's (and later, Marlene's) stance as extreme, and carries out a firm socialist-inspired critique of egalitarian feminism by juxtaposing Marion's 'achievements' with the fate of her victims. In Lisa's case, economic and sexual exploitation only amplify one another, and the most emphatic aspect of her victimization follows the moment of giving birth. Having witnessed the affair between Alec and Marion, she is the one who offers the baby to Marion; however, her legal co-operation is coerced when she is still under the influence of anaesthetics, Churchill thus emphasizing the unequal power relations between Lisa and Marion. Some of the highly publicized surrogacy and adoption cases in the eighties equally revealed a lack of balance in the economic backgrounds of the participating parties, thus revealing the prophetic nature of Churchill's work. In the Baby M case in America and the Baby Cotton case in Britain, for instance, underprivileged mothers offered to gestate a baby and then hand it over to the infertile, yet financially more established couple. Controversy arose in both cases, as the birth mothers were reluctant to hand the babies over according to the terms of the contract. The mothers felt that the agreements were drawn up without their being aware of psychological consequences and, hence, argued against the adoptions.

Unlike Lisa, who wants her own baby, unlike Clegg who needs a son to inherit his business, and unlike Marion who wants to possess the baby as a part of Alec, Alec does not show any interest in the ownership of a specific child. For him, the traditional politics of fatherhood based on the necessity of producing a male heir in order to transmit name and fortune is devoid of meaning. He is prepared to care just as much for anyone else's child, and in this respect recalls Germaine Greer's idea of 'organic families' where the relationships between biological parents and offsprings are destabilized: 'The child need not even know that I was his womb-mother and I could have relationships with the other children as well.'[45] In an organic family, children could 'belong primarily to themselves' rather than being 'the extensions of their parents'; [46] a principle Alec advocates when he rescues the neighbours' baby, and instead of exercising ownership simply offers the baby a chance for life. This idea of a chance for life also connects with Churchill's personal experience of motherhood, as her work on the play was interrupted by a sudden miscarriage: 'I'd just come out of hospital [...]. Into it went for the first time a lot of things that had been building up in me over a long time, political attitudes as well as personal ones.'[47] Thus, Churchill sublimated her own loss through her politicization of the personal. Immediate experience fuelled her identification with feminism, enabling her to switch from defining herself as a 'writer' to a 'feminist writer'.[48]

Top Girls

Despite the ten-year gap between *Owners* and *Top Girls* the correspondences between the characters of Marion and Marlene are prophetical. Marion demonstrated as early as 1972 that 'The capitalist impulse [was] not determined by the biological difference between male and female',[49] while a reviewer talking about the 1987 revival of *Owners* was startled by the parallels between the aggressive real estate developer in the play and Thatcher. According to John Vidal, through this correspondence the play 'has become starkly relevant, whereas once it was more a philosophical debate on the nature of individual power-sharing'.[50] In fact, the character of Marion works as a study towards the figure of Marlene. Although Marion is driven by an impulse for domination from the very beginning, she relies on a male aide who acts on her behalf. At an early stage in the play she refers to herself as a man of destiny, suggesting not only that she is prepared to go beyond gender stereotypes but also that she has long-term career plans.

This statement can also be interpreted as Churchill's rejection of female equality in a capitalist system because it 'transforms women into surrogate men'.[51] Both Marion and Marlene are emblematic for egalitarian, liberal feminism, a mould also dramatized by Louise Page in her mid-eighties dramas on female professional success and mother–daughter relationships, 'Salonika' and 'Real Estate', which are discussed in Chapter 3. Both Churchill and Page examine women who aim to minimize the difference between the sexes, who achieve success exclusively in the system, and for whom the concerns of the individual prevail over those of the group.[52] Indeed, Marion's approach to business is just as unscrupulous as Marlene's. For Marlene, success is rooted in the rejection of motherhood together with her former life. Marion does not need to escape her geographical setting as long as she has the upper hand in her marriage. She does not need to leave children behind either, as she has none: she is either on the Pill (according to Worsely) or infertile (according to Clegg). Clegg's longing for a son is of no concern to her, until the opportunity arises for the fulfilment of her own obsession too. Marion's interest in the baby, therefore, does not come from a desire for parenting; hence she never becomes a genuine surrogate mother the way Clegg becomes a surrogate father.

Top Girls not only confirms Churchill's prophetic vision in *Owners* but also engages with similar dilemmas as Gems's *Queen Christina*.[53] Utilizing historical parables, both plays investigate the negotiation of motherhood from the perspective of career women. Gems offers an accurate image of the Swedish queen, while Churchill presents an encounter of apparently random characters drawn from history, fiction and painting – in a surrealistic opening tableau that recalls Judy Chicago's installation 'The Dinner Party'.[54] For Churchill it is not historical accuracy that prevails as her characters gather at Marlene's dinner table; their presence is legitimized by their contribution to a tradition in transgressive femininity. The strategies Churchill uses in *Top Girls* also evoke the experimental and radical feminist theatre of the late sixties and seventies, including a certain preoccupation with the didactic. The play features an all-female cast in which cast members (apart from the actress playing Marlene) play two, sometimes three roles, thus suggesting (despite Churchill's critique of class and intra-gender oppression) the interconnected nature of women's experience.

Churchill, however, warned against emphasis on particular ways of doubling. The sheer fact of one actress playing several roles, nevertheless, connotes the multiplicity of experiences and ideological stances, also encountered by Queen Christina. In *Top Girls,* the juxtaposition of characters and of the three acts also invites a comparative analysis. The first act, disrupting the conventions of realism, is set in contrast with the following two, presenting scenes from everyday life, thus dissolving the boundaries between myth and reality.

Preoccupied by the theme of success, Churchill chooses the diners and their hostess for their claims to fame in conditions hostile to female emancipation. Unlike the feminism of the seventies, which was dominated by the 'tyranny of structurelessness' – celebrating non-hierarchical and consensual modes of organization – the eighties were legendary for prioritizing opportunism, individual decision-taking and independent careers.[55] Whereas *Queen Christina* was produced in 1977, towards the end of the Labour government's term in office, Churchill's 1982 play responded to the return of Conservative leadership and the rise of Margaret Thatcher. It is the presentations offered by the guests – invited to celebrate Marlene's promotion to managing director of the 'Top Girls' employment agency – that set up a context for her achievements. However, this 'dramatic genealogy of Marlene's historical community'[56] gradually builds up a picture that also contains compromises, just as Marlene's success will be revealed as rooted in intra-gender oppression, itself imposed by the competitive ethics of the capitalist system.

The fact that Marlene invites figures from the past emphasizes not merely her lack of personal relationships but also her uniqueness as a successful woman: 'The dream of the past reminds us not only of the historical weight of women's oppression but also of the futility of individual solutions.'[57] Marlene has appropriated masculine values to the extent that she organizes her party at a restaurant, the traditional location for business networking. As the juxtaposition of the guests' accounts unveils, most of their achievements (apart from Gret's) are linked to some form of submissiveness to men. The correspondences between the lives of the various women only demonstrate, in fact, that 'the changes in the position of women have been superficial: literally a question of costume'.[58] Some of the women, like Isabella or Pope Joan, reached fame by assuming roles so far reserved for men, others, like Nijo or Griselda, did so by emphasizing their archetypal feminine qualities, and hence by encouraging conformity to male expectations.

Isabella, Joan and Nijo are historical figures, while Gret and Griselda are fictional, invented by a male imagination. Gret, however, advocates a radical, non-compromising feminism, as opposed to Isabella and Joan – the closest to Marlene – who opt for equality-feminism, aspiring to achievements normally licensed to men. Joan also shares with Marlene the obsession with dominance, as well as the lack of ease with regard to pregnancy. The least vocal character (apart from her outburst at the end of the scene) is Gret. She identifies with women from her class and time, unlike the other guests who are captured as individuals. Gret gives the least evidence of submission to patriarchal domination by comparison with the others. An outsider to the party as a silent witness and in terms of status – like the waitress – Gret's presence suggests that the sense of community envisaged by Marlene as a background to her success is an imaginary construct. Gret's silence, therefore, acts as a metaphoric protest against Marlene's attempts at legitimizing her individual success in a male world. Uncomfortable at this staged reunion of contributors to a female tradition in achievement, Gret is, in fact, closer to the experiences of women excluded from the celebration. Like the waitress, she can be seen to 'personify in mythic fashion the stance represented by Marlene's sister, Joyce',[59] thereby connecting to the forthcoming sections.

Gret is also connected to Angie via their rebellions. They display the same intensity of outburst and speak intuitively. While Gret leads an army of women in battle, Angie's protest is only mapped out symbolically and is directed against Joyce, whom she perceives as the bad, denying and constraining mother. Apart from Angie's psychoanalytically motivated desire to kill Joyce, it is the menstrual blood-tasting episode that epitomizes her transgression, as a moment that revisits feminist celebratory rites. It is also significant that she involves her friend Kit in this ritual. This detail transforms Angie into the only genuinely feminist character in the play, in the sense of having understood the importance of female community. Since Joyce only theoretically embraces socialism and never does anything concrete to change her situation, she is positioned, in fact, to emphasize the impossibility of her achieving change. In this manner Churchill locates Joyce as a counter-figure to Gret, yet she also voices her socialist feminist-inspired reservation with regard to accomplishing change on an individual basis.

The pivotal character in Churchill's analysis of class relations is Marlene's working-class sister, Joyce. In opposition to Marlene, Joyce has remained in the country, leading the life women in their family have traditionally lived. Churchill captures the stark working-class realities in the scenes dedicated to Joyce and to Marlene's oppression of her sister, a theme she returned to in *Fen* (1983) where she examined violent power conflicts between women. It is the countryside of the Fens, the suffocating gritty world, that women like Marlene are passionately trying to escape from. There would be no contact between Marlene and Joyce in *Top Girls* were it not for the dialogue set up by the adolescent Angie, who despite being Marlene's daughter is raised by Joyce as her own child. Triumph for Marlene, thus, is only achievable at the expense of silencing her motherhood. When confronted by the archetypal family woman, Mrs Kidd, whose husband Marlene has beaten in the quest for promotion, the same mutual exclusion between the private and public comes to the fore: 'You're one of these ballbreakers/that's what you are. You'll end up [...] miserable and lonely. You're not natural.'[60]

Marlene, in fact, is an individualist who has achieved a career due to favourable circumstances. Without Joyce's adoption of Angie she could not have led an independent life, a fact that she has never acknowledged. Moreover, Marlene's acceptance of same-sex exploitation finds a powerful role model in Thatcher. Thatcher's major attraction for Marlene is the achievement of success in a male-dominated world, though Marlene subsequently becomes a supporter of Thatcher's economic policies as well. Joyce's hatred of the Thatcher government, culminating in the mock-hyperbolic 'Hitlerina' label, epitomized the disowning of Thatcher by the mainly socialist-oriented women's movement: 'If they can be called a feminist by dint of what [they have] achieved it makes a mockery of a word which embraces in its meaning support for other women.'[61]

By the nineties, however, a re-evaluation of Thatcher both as a political leader and as a role model for women had been initiated. She was not only Britain's first woman prime minister but also the only party leader in the twentieth century to win three consecutive elections. Her name has been encapsulated into a political doctrine, while the tabloid press has proclaimed her the new incarnation of Britannia. Despite her personal unpopularity some of her economic policies did prove popular, including certain aspects of privatization, and the rise in home ownership. Tony Blair was the first Labour leader to acknowledge Thatcher's economic importance, to which he posited himself as a 'natural heir'.[62] November 2000, however, witnessed the acrimonious end of this relationship, with Blair claiming that 'we are in a new era' and 'it is time we move British politics beyond the time of Margaret Thatcher'.[63]

Natasha Walter's 1998 feminist rehabilitation of Thatcher focused on the intersection of gender issues with economics and class. She highlighted her normalization of female success, her transgression of class and gender barriers, as well as her launching of the concept of the 'different-but-equal' powerful woman. Despite her constant references to her experience as a woman, however, Thatcher was often labelled 'a man', her success being viewed as non-representative for average women. For instance, in *Top Girls*, Joyce is a single mother forced to do cleaning work to make ends meet. For Marlene, however, Joyce's sacrifice seems to be perfectly acceptable in order for her to achieve success. Her justification uncannily resembles that of Howard Kidd, who keeps his 'traditional' wife at home while he builds a career. Thus, the 'ethics of competition', advocated by Marlene, is irrevocably opposed to and only achieved at the expense of the 'ethics of caring', represented by Joyce and Mrs. Kidd.[64]

Churchill creates a balance by emphasizing the conflict between Marlene and Joyce, as well as by getting both to assume responsibility for their existential choices. Churchill makes the point that Joyce is motivated by a profound sense of duty, whereas Marlene has deliberately opted out from family responsibility. Joyce is equally aware of Angie's inability to compete, but her stance is one of concern, rooted in affection. She reminds Marlene that it is the likes of Angie who are most exposed to the effects of class inequalities. Marlene, however, is a 'meritocrat', a believer in privileges not so much inherited but achieved through personal efforts: 'I don't believe in class. Anyone can do anything if they've got what it takes.'[65] Thus, Churchill prefigured Thatcher's infamous comment on the non-existence of society: 'We don't belong to society, we are all just individuals doing the best we can for ourselves.'[66]

Though Angie is present in most scenes of the second and third acts, there are few insights into her perspective. Churchill suggests that she is uninterested in school and still likes to play in her teenage years, but also that she did not develop a satisfactory relationship with Joyce. The first reference to any form of agency is her desire to get in touch with her supposed aunt wished-to-be her mother,[67] whom she phones and visits in her office. The latter especially, a contemporary, demythologized version of a journey to somewhere distant in pursuit of a tempting goal, is a particularly significant act of transgression for Angie. Despite her fear of the future, the power of seduction is stronger and she yields to the urge of biology that claims the retrieval of her mother. The glamour surrounding Marlene is also a temptation-cum-fake ideal, something Angie believes she too can have access to. In this respect she recalls Queen Christina, who is also confronted by the deceptiveness of a central yet unachievable bogus ideal. At the end, Christina acknowledges that she cannot bear children, whereas Angie is forced to confront the fact that her aspiration towards Marlene's lifestyle is going to remain outside her reach.

Churchill returns to Angie in the next act, which, in fact, chronologically precedes both others. In the last line of the play, Angie addresses to Marlene her most clearly articulated statement rooted in some kind of understanding of her circumstances: 'Frightening'. It is not accidental that Pope Joan's last word in the dinner scene is also the Latin term for 'frightening'. This repetition connects the most disadvantaged character with the one who has excelled through her intellect. Thus, Churchill contributes yet another parallel between the historical–surrealist opening and the realistic sections, but also offers solid support to Angie's call for help. Angie's call, in fact, is not an isolated moment. The previous scene, which features Angie at a later time, conveys her desire to kill Joyce, whom we then still believe to be her mother. She also manifests an attraction towards menstrual blood or vomit, traditionally associated with the concept of pollution. Thus, Angie acquires an indirect capacity of challenging long-held taboos in Western culture, and transgresses societal norms. However, her final cry of despair is ambivalent, opening up multiple explanations. It might have been triggered by a nightmare, but it may equally be the result of her so-far-repressed awareness of her biological mother's individualism. It may also be generated by her sudden sense of isolation or the consequence of her emerging uncertainties about the bleak perspective of her own future.[68]

Angie's lack of eloquence might also be read as a direct reference to her inability to adapt to the language propagated by Marlene, in spite of her attempt to join Marlene both in private and in public. Despite her repeated endeavours at re-establishing the bond with her birth mother, she fails to tune in to Marlene's point of view and unconsciously reiterates Joyce. Thus, she ends up emphasizing the viability of surrogate links above biological ones, even if all she is genuinely aware of is a sense of confusion and discomfort. Angie's desperate outbreak at the end might also be interpreted as metaphoric for the difficulties feminism encounters, as a result of critiques from other discourses. Despite Angie's outburst, Marlene enacts the abandonment of her daughter once again. Perhaps triggered by instinct, Angie repeatedly addresses her as 'mother' on this occasion, but Marlene invariably informs her that her mother is Joyce. Thus, the play's final tableau freezes on a daughter unwanted by her mother and a woman reiterating her renunciation of the maternal function.

Despite rejecting Angie, Marlene insists on the irrelevance of class. For Joyce, however, this terrain is not up for negotiation. With Joyce's refusal to include Marlene in the same social category as herself, a belated response to Marlene's abandonment of class and family roots,

Churchill questions not only the Conservative politics of the eighties but also the legitimacy of egalitarian feminism. Lou Wakefield, the actress who played Kit and the waitress in the original Royal Court production, contended: 'This is a feminist play in that it's self-criticism of the women's movement. [...] If women do get the top jobs, there's also a job to be done in reassessing that job in feminist or humanitarian terms.'[69] Janet Brown formulated a more precise reading in terms of a potential feminist intervention. In her view, Joyce and Gret acted as heralds of the so-called next wave in the Women's Movement, intended to fight towards the elimination of oppression via direct struggle.[70] Churchill was not that optimistic. She acknowledged the need for a feminist and socialist intervention, but also forecast the inadequacies and subsequent failures of the Left by stressing Joyce's inertia. While the original 1982 production of the play has been treated as a socialist feminist critique of liberal feminism, the 1991 revival, in the wake of Thatcher's departure from office in November 1990, was seen as a 'state-of-the-nation debate about the Thatcher legacy of a materially divided, "us and them" Britain'.[71] The play's 2001 revival, however, benefited less from alignment to current events and despite being staged by one of the most promising female directors, Thea Sharrock, young audiences did not herald the play as particularly relevant to their problems.

In another instance of prophetic vision, Churchill warned of a backlash inherent in the pursuit of success achieved on exclusively male terms. Marlene's – and Thatcher's – success can mainly be registered as individual cases that did not contribute sufficiently to the alteration of the average woman's life. In *Top Girls*, following the general emphasis in eighties society on women and work, women's career options are only presented as feasible if renouncing parenthood. By the nineties, this image had changed to the negotiation of the two spheres, although minimal arrangements have been made on behalf of the state to support women in this endeavour. In fact, juggling careers with parenthood has become a staple of nineties life for many women. Another central preoccupation has become the realization that there are biological, not only social, boundaries, and nineties theatre, as discussed in Chapter 5, has concentrated extensively on the representation of obstacles preventing the fulfilment of maternal desire.

Conclusion

Perhaps the most traditional aspect of these plays is that the playwrights focus on a defining choice, and the crucial choice in both cases involves an individual's acceptance or rejection of the biological fact of motherhood. Focusing on professional women's options for motherhood, both Gems and Churchill highlight the difficulties experienced by those wishing to combine the public and the private. In fact, not only do the playwrights emphasize the pitfalls of such an attempt in the seventies and early eighties, but they also warn of the compromises women had to make – whatever their history – when opting for either possibility. For neither Gems's Queen Christina nor Churchill's Marion or Marlene is public self-fulfilment compatible with a traditional private life.

Confronting two types of motherhood, in *Top Girls* Churchill makes a case for the viability of surrogate links as opposed to biological ones. Marlene's abandonment of Angie is ethically flawed not just because she disregards her daughter, but also because she constructs her success on the exploitation of her sister. While offering a socialist critique of Thatcherism and liberal feminism, Churchill warns of the difficulties of assuming a career while being a mother. She dwells on the mutual exclusion of most professions and parenthood, not only through Marlene, but also via Joyce who could not leave home because she had to care for Angie. The same idea is reinforced in reverse via the women in the opening scene, as all have given up motherhood for a vocation.

Queen Christina presents a protagonist who was denied her birthright, *Owners* shows a character uninterested in giving birth, while *Top Girls* features a woman who renounces motherhood herself. As for their location in the public versus private sphere, all three protagonists follow trajectories in both. Christina is transferred from the private to the public under Axel's surrogate care, in order to move back to the private on the occasion of her discovery of femininity. Marion and Marlene also pass from the private to the public; however, this is engineered by their own career aspirations rather than by external intervention. Situated throughout in the sphere of the home, Lisa, Joyce and Angie have the least access to choice. Joyce simply inherits Marlene's child (while Lisa loses hers to Marion), while Angie is entirely denied any potential for success. Thus, the playwrights signal possibilities of transgression regarding conventional perceptions of the feminine, yet they also highlight the cost at which it is often achieved (intra-gender and class oppression in *Owners* and *Top Girls*, reconstruction of gender identity in *Queen Christina*).

Christina overcomes her resignation, mapping out a fresh direction in life; Marion loses property, yet finds herself victorious over the more significant loss experienced by others; while Marlene re-enacts her abandonment of Angie and hence, symbolically returns to the start of her quest. The supporting characters, however, are not granted a voice at this stage either. Angie is shown in despair at Marlene's act of denial and the prospect of a bleak future, Joyce is not even present, while Lisa is left to contemplate the destruction of both her baby and home. Gems and Churchill – writing from different positions in terms of feminist involvement – acknowledge, therefore, the importance of addressing women's options for a simultaneous assumption of parenthood and career. They concentrate on cases in which motherhood and the achievement of professional success rule out one another, as a result of prioritizing either of the two alternatives. By contrasting instances of liberal, socialist as well as radical and cultural feminism, the playwrights signal both the complexity and the internal contradictions within feminist thinking. They also insist on the inadequacy of the current state of affairs in terms of employment opportunities and childcare provision, and urge a new negotiation of women's place in society.

3
Challenging the Bond: Mothers versus Daughters

The eighties and nineties have introduced a generation of women playwrights whose emergence is a direct result of the ground-breaking work done by their forebears. Especially Caryl Churchill is credited as a major influence, although Shelagh Delaney and Pam Gems have also been acknowledged as contributors to the opening up of new artistic pathways for women dramatists, and for younger writers, Sarah Daniels and Timberlake Wertenbaker equally join the ranks of those inspiring new work. Many up-and-coming playwrights started to write as a result of encouragement from women directors or theatre groups, but most would not have been able to consolidate their careers without the patronage of the (generally male) artistic directors of theatres like the Royal Court, where several plays discussed here premièred. The playwrights starting their careers in this period 'began to write different kinds of "feminist theatre"' in which, often, 'parts for men began to be replaced by all-women's plays' or in which the focus was predominantly on 'women's relationships to each other'.[1]

The latter theme is the focus of the forthcoming two chapters, charting the landscape of British women's theatre through the topic of mother–daughter relationships. Chapter 4 examines the teenage subject as mother, whereas this chapter looks at the complexities available within matrilineal bonds, via work as varied as Louise Page's *Salonika* (1982) and *Real Estate* (1984), Shelagh Stephenson's *The Memory of Water* (1986), Charlotte Keatley's *My Mother Said I Never Should* (1987), Winsome Pinnock's *Leave Taking* (1987), Diane Samuels's *Kindertransport* (1993), Phyllis Nagy's, *Butterfly Kiss* (1994) and Sarah Kane's *Phaedra's Love* (1996). Most of these plays have been produced by mainstream theatres, though often by women directors, while the subsequent sections feature fringe work as well as productions by touring women's collectives. All plays discussed have been published – some in Methuen's *Plays by Women* series, others individually or in collections of the respective playwright's work.

The dramatists included here represent different pathways in terms of identity politics. The authors emerging in the eighties continue to define themselves within the framework of particular kinds of feminism (such as socialist feminism for Louise Page, Sharman MacDonald, and Charlotte Keatley), or identification in terms of race (blackness for Winsome Pinnock, Jewishness for Diane Samuels); however, later playwrights refuse to apply categorizations to themselves (Phyllis Nagy, Sarah Kane). Kane has not even acknowledged the importance of writing as a woman. Considering that any subject can be of potential relevance to any writer, Nagy argued against the tradition in women's writing to address topics like motherhood, while Kane claimed that the examination of the gender struggle was uninteresting, as it was 'symptomatic of a much wider malaise'.[2]

In fact, one of the dominant characteristics of theatre in the nineties has been the absence of overt ideology. Unlike the state-of-the-nation plays of the seventies or the committed feminist dramas of the seventies and eighties, new writing in the nineties by both genders has focused increasingly on the politics of everyday life. Moreover, by the mid-nineties even playwrights with known political agendas have re-formulated their position, as Page contends: 'the strength of feminism' is that 'it changes and regroups and runs a constant guerrilla warfare'; it features its inherent contradictions while 'the debate continues'.[3] In parallel with embracing the idea of constant transformation, playwrights have expressed their concern regarding the ghettoization of feminism and indicated the pointlessness of preaching to the converted, advocating instead a theatre that aims to influence people.

Salonika and *Real Estate*

Louise Page's *Salonika* and *Real Estate* are often perceived as companion plays addressing different manifestations of mother–daughter relationships. Written just two years apart, both plays centre on a mother and daughter dichotomy, complemented by supportive male characters.[4] Through the latter, the mother–daughter bonds are re-contextualized, as they include husbands and fathers but also unmarried partners. Thus, Page moves her investigations beyond the confines of the nuclear family, and indirectly builds on work produced in the seventies as far as changing moral and sexual attitudes are concerned.

Page's plays, however, display elements that predominantly fit the liberal feminist agenda. Page's female protagonists are preoccupied with achieving some sort of equality with men, and favour careers as an alternative to private life. In other words, professional success appears as a major concern, not unlike the case of *Queen Christina, Owners* or *Top Girls* discussed in Chapter 2; however, Page does not oppose her protagonists' egalitarian position with alternative perspectives as in Gems's or Churchill's plays. Nevertheless, Page situates herself on the political Left and claimed that she was a 'socialist feminist' who 'writes about women because [she is] a woman'.[5] She insists on the importance of taking inspiration from one's own experience and focusing on 'minutiae', which are 'the moments that actually affect people'.[6] Most of Page's work centres on intimate domestic scenes and involves only a handful of characters, thus responding to financial strictures and appealing to studio theatres rather than main house spaces.

Salonika features two female and three male characters, who interact in various permutations with each other. Page elaborates on a love story, occurring later in life, to Charlotte and Leonard, examined as a digression within the mother–daughter relationship between Charlotte and Enid. The two women, in their eighties and sixties, respectively, have travelled to Greece to visit the grave of Ben, Charlotte's husband and Enid's father, who died during World War I. Crucially, however, they end up revisiting their own lives and re-evaluating their relationship. The two women have never separated: Ben died before Enid's birth and the adult Enid has always looked after her mother. So when Leonard proposes to Charlotte, the dilemma Page raises is not about the relationship between sexuality and ageing, but about separation versus loyalty. This bond between the two women, however, is as restrictive as it is unbreakable, and it is permeated by tensions rooted in differing world views. Charlotte can only see a woman's destiny in marriage, whereas for Enid an active professional life is of equal standing:

> CHARLOTTE: I never know how you didn't manage to get married in the war. [...] You'd have got the pension for it.
> ENID: I've got a pension. They've used me up just the same as a man would have done.[7]

Enid's defining trait is her sense of responsibility. In a reversal of the caring role, she considers it her duty to provide for her mother, and she claims to oppose her mother's marriage because, as a couple, Charlotte and Leonard would be more vulnerable. She sees this contribution of care as a central facet of their relationship and refuses to perceive the difference between marital and filial love.

In parallel with testing this mother–daughter bond, Page also examines a father–daughter, and, to a lesser extent, a husband–wife relationship. Despite not having known Ben (Enid) or having had only a brief relationship with him (Charlotte), the two protagonists have classified his death as a casualty of war and found relief in his heroism. Especially in Enid's case, this has constituted a dominant impact, the only major influence apart from Charlotte's. In fact, besides continuing to play the role of her mother's child well into her sixties, Enid also perceives herself as her father's daughter. For her he is as real as anyone appearing in the present, which constitutes the reason for her inability to liberate herself from under his influence. In fact, it is only when Enid finds out about the actual circumstances of her father's death that she can free herself. Learning about Ben's suicide demythologizes her hero, and this allows her to remove herself from under the shadow of the person by whose values she has lived. Instrumental in this new turn is Peter, who epitomizes freedom *par excellence* and is the only character who shows concern about Enid as a person rather than a provider. He also attempts to help her, in this sense assuming a surrogate parental role. As Peter informs Enid about Ben's death, he also prefigures his own death at the climax of the play. These two intertwined events finally sever Enid's bonds of parental dependence. Confronting the erroneous perception of her father, doubled by Peter's demonstration of human mortality, Enid glimpses her past inertia – able for the first time to see things for herself.

In contrast to the inseparable mother and daughter in *Salonika*, *Real Estate* features a mother and a daughter separated for most of the latter's adult life. Page initially planned this play as a two-hander, but later she added secondary male characters. Page is known for her sympathetic portrayal of men, and she contends that it is important for women playwrights 'to write men who are credible, men who can be perceived as patterns'.[8] Moreover, in 1985 she declared: 'I don't believe in female separation. [...] I can't write plays just to provide parts for women. [...] I write about things I want to discuss.'[9] In *Real Estate*, she focuses on two male protagonists committed to their partners, while the women run away from and search for each other. At the centre, there is Gwen, the mother figure, and Jenny, the daughter figure, complemented by Dick, Gwen's second husband, and Eric, Jenny's partner, father of a daughter from a previous relationship. The play opens with Gwen and Jenny, but unlike *Salonika*, this time the setting is Britain, and instead of detachment from spatial and temporal naturalism, the chronologically presented plot is a reunion at home. (Since Jenny left home, she has settled in London, while Gwen has remarried and started a business as an estate agent. In fact, this is the first meeting between Jenny and Gwen's husband.)

Despite the difficulties in communication between mother and daughter, Jenny's visit aims to end their separation. She is pregnant, and as a prospective mother, she sees family history in a fresh light. It is Gwen's maternal instinct, however, that opens the conversation on this topic and encourages Jenny to contextualize her new experience. Epitomizing concerns emerging in the eighties and continuing into the nineties, Jenny is expecting a baby by her non-cohabiting partner and aims to raise it as a single mother. She is also older than mothers dramatized in earlier plays, and thus prefigures the trend of thirty-something professional women's longing for parenthood that dominates Chapter Five. At 38, Jenny is facing possibly her last chance for a baby, and Page sums up the potential complications of pregnancy later in life. Jenny's circumstances, however, are not explored in detail as the playwright's concerns are not with fertility or pregnancy; rather, they are oriented towards the way in which the daughter's maternity impacts her relationship with her mother.

In parallel with Jenny's desire to re-establish the bond with her mother, Page unveils the extent to which Gwen has made a point about writing her estranged daughter out of her life. Being abandoned by her daughter signified a failed attempt at mothering for Gwen, and Jenny's unexpected appearance harks back to Gwen's worst experiences: her daughter's equally unexpected departure but also her miscarriage later in life. Transferring unsolicited domestic energies into professional success – Dick explains to Jenny – Gwen 'stopped being your mother and went into business'.[10] This type of dichotomy between the private and the public also characterizes *Salonika*'s Enid who renounces a family of her own in order to fulfil her responsibilities. Jenny, on the other hand, represents another pathway as far as the experience of motherhood is concerned. She aims to raise a baby while earning a living and to negotiate full-time parenthood with a career. Refusing to marry the father of her baby, she recommends an alternative arrangement in which Eric can play a part-time parental role.

Thus, when Dick prepares to welcome Jenny as a permanent resident in their home, Gwen hesitates: 'I don't want the responsibility for her life. Not any more.'[11] Unable to contemplate the possibility of being abandoned for the second time, doubled by the realization that she is excluded from Jenny's and Dick's strengthening bond, Gwen braces for a finale that rewrites yet again the power relations in the family. Moving full circle, she gives up the career that constituted her refuge between Jenny's departure and return, but instead of dedicating her time to her granddaughter and hence experiencing the motherhood she was denied, she replicates Jenny's original path and leaves everything behind. In Page's own account, this ending constitutes a real 'subversive' turn, as she allows the mother to be 'free to live her own life and not bring up the grandchild'.[12] In this way, she also opens up the possibility of experiencing parenthood for Dick, in place of the absent Eric who cannot accept a second part-time paternal role. Just as Jenny denies Eric full participation in the life of their baby, she has denied Gwen the chance of overcoming the trauma of the past. Refusing to accept her mother's offer of her childhood toys, Jenny implicitly rejects Gwen's admission of having always cared about her. Thus, Page ends on a note of collapse in the Gwen–Jenny relationship, engineered by the daughter and carried out in practice by the mother. This situation is the opposite of the outcome in *Salonika*, where the two women's bond is further consolidated by the elimination of supporting characters. In other words, Page suggests alternative pathways for the operation of mother–daughter relationships in *Salonika* and *Real Estate*, despite stating, in both, the potential for tension and frustration. She celebrates mutual dependence, but also warns of rivalries, in particular where female bonding is unbalanced by the presence of men.

The Memory of Water

The Memory of Water was first performed at the Hampstead Theatre, London, on 11 July 1986 under the direction of Terry Johnson. The production then transferred to the West End, where it won the 2000 Laurence Olivier Award for Best Comedy. This type of commercial success is rooted in the play's comic undertones, which secured its popularity with audiences, and it is a relatively rare phenomenon in British women's theatre. It is even rarer to find the topic of motherhood or mother–daughter relations attracting such attention. In this sense, Stephenson's work joins Charlotte Keatley's contemporaneous play in a category of one-off hits that, on the one hand, situate the playwright in a league of excellence, but, on the other hand, set a level of expectation that is almost impossible to fulfil.

Stephenson unites three sisters on the eve of their mother's funeral, thus exploring past conflicts between siblings and between the mother and her daughters. The title is derived from a scientific observation according to which water has a form of memory in the sense that when a curative element is added to it and then removed, the water retains the curative properties. This reference is the play's central metaphor, and the story explores to what extent the dead mother has impacted her children's lives. Utilizing memory and nostalgia, Stephenson makes an attempt at manipulating chronology, and she disrupts the linear flow of events with flashbacks to the past. All flashbacks in *The Memory of Water* involve the mother and only one of her daughters, thus conjuring up particular capsules in time and inviting the audience to witness their evolving relationship.

The play opens with such a case in point: Vi, the dead mother of the present, is pictured immaculately dressed in sixties fashion. She is the centre of attention, watched from the sides by her daughter, Mary. The scene draws attention to the tensions between the protagonists, and highlights Mary's already existent academic interests. This moment, calling attention to Vi as a sexually attractive woman, is conjured up at a later stage again, this time as a fragment of Mary's imagination. It seemingly prompts a discussion about standards of female beauty, but, ultimately, it reveals Vi's inability to relate to her daughters. They all have a story to confirm her inadequacy as a mother, from her insistence on female passivity in relation to men to her avoidance of addressing sexual education. In another flashback, it is Vi who explores her reasons for her lack of attachment to her daughters. She confesses to Mary how she 'never cared for women' and situates her daughters' lack of femininity at the root of her inability to relate to them: 'You've come out wrong, all of you.' [13]

Despite the play's non-linear structure, the dialogue is predominantly naturalistic – this feature, apart from allowing for strong roles for female performers, consolidates the play's connection with the tradition of bourgeois theatre. It is this latter association that explains the play's commercial success, and undermines its potentially radical aura by a theatrically conservative spectacle. Nevertheless, Stephenson's attention to intricate details of women's lives aligns her work with feminist concerns, as – in Gayle Austin's definition – feminism can refer to 'anything that pays attention to women'.[14] In fact, depending on various aspects of the play, several specific interpretations of feminism can be identified: the play's realist strand and plausibility in historical terms as well as the protagonists' professional success evoke liberal feminism, whereas the preoccupation with motherhood and sisterhood connotes cultural feminist concerns.[15]

The subject of mother–daughter reunions is central to radical feminism, on the one hand, and psychoanalytic feminism, on the other. Mary Daly has argued in *Gyn/Ecology* (1978) that the very aim of radical feminism was a reunion with the mother, and a transformation of the relationship between mother and daughter (the re-establishment of 'Mother-Right'). For Luce Irigaray, women – in being forced to distance themselves from the maternal figure – end up being alienated from themselves, a phenomenon that can only be counteracted by the economy of an 'inter-subjective' relationship between mother and daughter.[16] In Stephenson's play, of course, the mother appears as a problematic figure, towards whom her daughters display ambivalent feelings. By reconstructing the mother's past, however, the daughters re-live her and their own respective histories; and the play itself becomes a bridge of sorts to negotiate the fissure between mother and daughters.

Unresolved matters also come to the fore between the sisters, as they mourn their mother. A central area of divergence between the sisters is constituted by their varying degrees of contact with their mother, and Teresa, who looked after the mother at the end, resents the others' absence. Crucially, all three sisters re-evaluate their relationship with their mother and make statements about their position, ranging from Mary's medical observation about the naturalness of death to Catherine's rejection of both culpability and the actual person: 'I've nothing to feel guilty about at all. I didn't like her.'[17] A competition of sorts emerges in which the sisters try to establish the least favourite of the three. Ultimately, as Mary sums up, it is irrelevant to whom exactly a particular event did occur: it is the appropriation of the story that counts, as it potentially 'fits' more than one protagonist.

In the process of revisiting the past, the sisters not only re-evaluate events but also redefine memory as such. Besides simply wanting to re-live her own childhood, however, Mary's imaginary explorations are rooted in her desire for motherhood. She is in her late thirties and has been in a long-term relationship with Mike, but he is married to another woman by whom he has children. Thus, Stephenson dissociates between the nature of parental desire along gender lines, and signals the possibility of simultaneous alternative arrangements beyond the nuclear family. She also raises the increasingly topical question of ageing in relation to female fertility, as well as the implications of teenage pregnancy. It is revealed that Mary has given birth as a teenager and her baby was given up for adoption. Thus, protected from the stigma associated with bearing a child outside wedlock, Mary was able to continue her education and, as a result, achieve her present status. Therefore, imagining herself to be pregnant is an act of compensation for this renunciation that occurred over 20 years ago; however, Mary is to learn that her son has long been dead, a fact both Vi and her sisters agreed not to disclose. Mary is confronted with the details of this event in a final flashback scene with Vi. Again, the scene conveys the lack of genuine connection between mother and daughter: Mary cannot forgive Vi for having taken decisions on her behalf, even if these led to an easier life for her, and Vi resents Mary for preventing any intimacy from developing between them.

In fact, this concept of memory against all odds epitomized by the title, of persistence despite internal and external intervention, encapsulates the situation of all the protagonists. It is particularly relevant for Mary, especially when she puts on her mother's dress. Through this transformation, Mary is confirmed as looking exactly like her mother, a fact reinforced by the ensemble photo freezing the scene where not only Mary appears as Vi but Vi herself emerges in the line-up, this time in the spectating role occupied by Mary earlier. Moreover, in the flashback scene opening the second act, Vi talks about seeing herself in Mary. She situates Mary's earlier efforts at claiming a space in the patrilineal network of her family against biological factors of inheritance within the maternal line. As the play approaches its dénouement, it is this principle of unity within the female line that comes to the fore. Having exposed the resentment and pain rooted in inadequate mothering and sibling rivalry, Teresa, Catherine and Mary acquire a fresh generosity with regard to their mother. They finally understand her loneliness and frustration, and they also come to terms with the fact that the processes of memory operate independently of one's control: 'She goes through us like water. Whether we like it or not.'[18]

My Mother Said I Never Should

In 1987, Charlotte Keatley brought together four characters representing subsequent stages in a matrilineage. *My Mother Said I Never Should* focused on generational problems between mothers and daughters, grandmothers and grandchildren. Keatley's characters cover the span of the twentieth century until the time of the play's first performance at the Contact Theatre, Manchester in 1987. Apart from this naturalistic aspect, the play operates in a temporal frame of its own. The events are not chronological, yet neither do they occur in a simultaneous fashion. The result is something 'in between', especially in the scenes that unite all characters, with their age differences erased.

These scenes – acting as a kind of unconscious reservoir of repressed wishes and desires – are set in a space called 'The Wasteground', and feature the characters as children, interacting with each other as peers.

By starting the play with one such scene and interspersing childhood interludes throughout, Keatley offers opportunities for distancing from the realistic framework of the other scenes. Another effect these scenes help to create is a sense of *déjà vu,* reinforced by the daughters' re-enactment of incidents from their mothers' lives. Keatley's re-enactments, however, are not merely repetitions of the same story as 'moments occur again and again, differently for each'.[19] Whenever replaying events by and for the next generation, she alters the emphasis. Keatley highlighted the idea of interconnectedness between the lives of women across generations, though she also stated that one needed to 'switch back and forth in order to see the connections'.[20] Keatley presents four different pathways in life, defined not only by the social and class position of the characters, but also by the possibilities offered by disparate historical moments. She also experiments with the ways in which the women's lives are either moulded by or organized in opposition to their mother's expectations, and, thus, treats emotional baggage as both a limiting and inspiring factor.

Keatley wished to acknowledge the debt women owe to their forebears yet, ironically, the very conditions of this play's writing pointed to a lack of awareness concerning women's history. As Keatley admitted, she was not aware of the existence of other plays on mother–daughter relationships before she wrote hers, not even the Women's Theatre Group's *My Mother Says I Never Should* (1975); and one can only hope that the success of Keatley's own play has contributed to avoiding such an oversight on behalf of future generations. Keatley has often emphasized her socialist feminist position and called her own feminism and socialism 'innate'. She insisted recently, however, that she considered herself 'feminist' only in the terms defined by her. According to this definition feminism is primarily about the ability 'to achieve the role *you* want to play', 'to change the roles we [women and men] have been ascribed'.[21] Significantly, feminism for Keatley applied to men as well as women, and was interesting mainly at a practical level – as opposed to the theoretical approach prevalent in academia. Keatley has referred to her preference for learning her own feminism by communicating with working-class women in the North of England, and she has made a political point of residing outside London in order to lead a grassroots-oriented life in Manchester.

Just as she contrasts academic and pragmatic feminism, Keatley opposes theatre establishment and fringe theatre. She regrets the reservations frequently manifested towards new work by influential theatre directors and critics, calling attention to the potential danger of losing valuable experimental work. *My Mother Said I Never Should* was also initially turned down by several directors on the grounds that it was not a 'real play'. Eventually, Brigid Larmour recognized the play's intuitive nature and staged it at the Contact Theatre in Manchester. The play's subsequent run at the Royal Court in 1989 achieved the highest advance box office sales the theatre had experienced to that date, partly because the production also attracted a non-traditional audience. In this respect, *My Mother Said I Never Should* recalls the itinerary of *A Taste of Honey* three decades earlier: Delaney's play was also denigrated as a naïve text before being discovered by Joan Littlewood.

Keatley stated the importance of political commitment in the late eighties: 'One thing I hate is women writers not wanting to say that they're feminist. I know it's difficult [...]. But when it comes down to it, if you're a woman writing plays you have to acknowledge that a part of you, a part of the person that writes, is representative as well as individual, in a way which is not true for men.'[22] A decade later, however, she made a case against the category 'feminist theatre': '[It] is ridiculous. When men write plays they are not called masculine theatre. I use the word "female" as opposed to "feminist" because the latter has such political connotations.'[23] In alignment with the apolitical nineties, she stated that she was writing about life in general, although women may have been the characters through whom she chose to represent life. Despite Keatley's self-defined feminism – which does not integrate radical feminist ideas as theorized by Shulamith Firestone or Andrea Dworkin, for instance – *My Mother Said I Never Should* has regularly been associated with radical feminist theatre owing to its fluid sense of time and the experimental nature of the 'Wasteground' scenes.[24] Brigid Larmour emphasized the importance of assessing the innovative qualities of this play within the context of its first production and stressed its influence on subsequent authors.[25]

The idea of subverting linear time had predominantly been scrutinized in French feminist theory, fiction and drama, although it has become increasingly prominent in British women's theatre as well. Julia Kristeva associated linear time with an equality-feminist project, while connecting radical feminism with a cyclical and 'monumental' perception of time, situated outside the confines of time as a teleological progression and, hence, patriarchal domain.[26] In parallel with the symbolic relevance of Kristeva's divisions, Gillian Hanna of Monstrous Regiment highlighted some practical aspects of women's perception of time:

> It's precisely a refusal to accept [...] that life is linear [...] which has to do with male experience. [...] They are born into a world where they can map out life. [...] It has to do with a career. It has to do with your work. [...] Now for a woman, life is not like that. It does not have that pattern. For a woman life and experience is broken-backed.[27]

Keatley, in principle, has stated her ambition as far as aesthetic values are concerned. Theatre, according to her, should be practised as 'an art form, not a platform'.[28] Despite her initial support of feminism, she does not consider political writing adequate any longer, and she also rejects the intellectualizing nature of performance: 'The most powerful effect of theatre is the unconscious of the writer connecting with the unconscious of the audience'.[29] Such statements are problematic when considering the artistic and political potential as well as audience impact of theatre; however, the details of Keatley's play do make an attempt at achieving such a connection. The protagonists are featured in situations familiar to most audiences at crucial moments of their lives and, as befits Keatley's class thesis, are often involved with some sort of manual activity. The characters are folding sheets, preparing food or tea, and the conversations occur in addition to or in spite of the primary activity of 'doing' something immediately useful. While such a juxtaposition of activities can be read as dramatizing women's belief that their problems are not important enough in themselves, it also points to the difficulties women face in communication. As in the dinner scene of *Top Girls*, the women are talking yet not communicating. It is the inability to listen to others that explains most of the uncanny re-enactments of past events. For instance, characters often repeat lines spoken previously by another woman at a similar stage in life. Keatley's explanation of the phenomenon leads back to her preoccupation with the unconscious: 'I feel very strongly [...] that you open your imagination to connect way beyond to what you could know in your own life span.'[30]

In biological terms, in *My Mother Said I Never Should*, Doris is the mother of Margaret, who is the mother of Jackie, who in her turn is the mother of Rosie. In fact, the bonds between these women are far more complex, and often the direct mother–daughter relationships operate with most difficulty. There are moments rooted in emotional distance, even alienation, between mothers and daughters, though scenes of reconciliation often follow. A major example of the lack of solidarity is the silence surrounding the fact that Doris was born out of wedlock; instead of revealing this information in the context of the unmarried Jackie's pregnancy, both Doris and Margaret pretend that there have never been single mothers in their family. Keatley stresses that Jackie loves Rosie, yet financial difficulties and prejudice against single mothers force her to hand her baby over to Margaret, who, thus, simultaneously becomes mother and grandmother to Rosie.

According to the agreement between Margaret and Jackie, Rosie is to be told the truth about her mother on her 16th birthday. Due to Margaret's premature death, however, Rosie finds herself confronted by facts via the accidental discovery of her birth certificate. This leads to her revealing that she has always suspected that Jackie was more than a sister, although previously she mentioned how unmotherly Jackie was: 'You're old enough to be my mum. I'm glad you're not.'[31] Despite her earlier admiration for Jackie, reminiscent of Angie's fascination with Marlene in *Top Girls*, Rosie reinforces her rejection of Jackie but also of motherhood, claiming that she will not have any children. While refusing to come to terms with her immediate and literal past, Rosie nevertheless continues to be overwhelmed by memories of a more distant and symbolic past. Via an old solitaire game that used to belong to Doris's mother, Rosie establishes another connection with a tradition that runs back generations. Thus, in spite of failing to find harmony with her biological mother, solving the game implicitly entitles Rosie to a place in the lineage of her forerunners.

Rosie acquires the ultimate surrogate mother (Doris) when she is already past the age of needing one. Previously, Rosie has experienced a daughter–mother relationship with Margaret, based on mutual respect. The reason behind their lack of intimacy includes Margaret's concern not to accidentally reveal the identity of Rosie's birth mother, having a full-time job, and, crucially, Margaret's initial decision not to have children at all. She informs her mates in a 'Wasteground' scene that 'I'm not having any babies.'[32] The scene commemorating her engagement to Ken is overwhelmed by her enthusiasm for a future in which women do not have to 'waste their lives' as they can earn a living and avoid childbirth.[33] As far as Margaret's relationship with Doris is concerned, Keatley utilizes material poverty to suggest a lack of an emotional bond between mother and daughter. Doris endeavours to make her daughter the respectable woman she could not be; however, she fails to communicate with her on an intimate level. Doris's ambivalent feelings towards motherhood are synthesized in her rhetorical question to Margaret: 'What makes you think I wanted children?'[34] Previously, however, she was talking about the instinctive desire women feel for motherhood: 'I'm talking about the *desire* ... for little arms reaching up and clinging round your neck. *(She buries her face in the sheet, then holds it out to Margaret to do likewise).* Smell: lavender. From the beds, there. Mother nature is very hard to fight.'[35]

It is Margaret and Jackie's relationship, however, that is the most confrontational. While in the 'Wasteground' scenes Jackie expresses her anger, in the naturalistic scenes, she is unable to negotiate her relationship with Margaret, and the two women only establish mutual confidence following Rosie's birth. The scene in which Rosie is transferred from Jackie's Manchester housing-estate flat to Margaret and Ken's home is dominated by a powerful sense of women's solidarity at such key stages of life as birth. This instant female bond recalls another statement made by Kristeva, according to which pregnancy and childbirth can be experienced as reunions with one's own mother: 'By giving birth, the woman enters into contact with her mother; she becomes, she is her own mother; they are the same continuity differentiating itself.'[36]

In the matrilineage presented by Keatley, transformations between maternal and filial roles occur spontaneously. Margaret, for instance, is captured correctly calling the baby 'Rosie', yet the second time she asks: 'Did you have a bad dream, Jackie?'[37] Choosing to ignore for a moment the lapse of time, Margaret's substitution of the two names blends the separate characters of Jackie and Rosie into one archetypal child, while she herself emerges as the archetypal mother. Keatley suggests that Margaret develops an appreciation for her maternal role gradually, starting from an initial denigration of motherhood to a desire for further children, interrupted by a traumatic miscarriage. Doris stresses that the cause of the miscarriage was Margaret's haste to get a job – thus questioning the compatibility between professional careers and motherhood. The case study of the young Jackie has also highlighted the difficulties, social and financial, experienced by single mothers. Although Keatley does not present a version of the plot where Rosie is brought up by Jackie, she seems to suggest that Jackie, who embarked on motherhood in order to see 'if [her] theories worked', would have had entirely different prospects without Margaret's help.[38] However, motherhood and working for wages proves to be problematic for Margaret as well. She does not experience economic but psychological hardship, as she has increasingly less time to spend with her husband

and Rosie. For the mature Jackie, in contrast, professional and financial stability actually trigger a desire for maternity.

Keatley juxtaposes a range of options regarding the experience of motherhood, depending on historical moment, age, education or social class. 'Every play [...] is a capsule about society at a [given] time,'[39] she contended, and the matrilineage in *My Mother Said I Never Should* brings together harmonious relationships alongside silences and repressed tensions that have led to frustrations and misunderstandings. Despite the fact that both Doris and Margaret have considered avoiding childbirth, they have given birth to daughters to whom they did not get particularly close. In contrast, for the sixties rebel Jackie, becoming a mother constitutes a new adventure, but circumstances lead her to abandoning her child. Instead of being Rosie's mother, therefore, Jackie has become her elder sister, while both remain Margaret's daughters. Unable to forgive Jackie, Rosie celebrates surrogacy even after Margaret's death, as she moves on to another cultural bond with Doris rather than to her biological mother. Ultimately, it is the importance of genuine relationships amongst women that Keatley wishes to emphasize, as a necessary foundation to women's survival in society.

Leave Taking

A comparable trajectory of mother–daughter confrontations followed by reconciliation is dramatized in Winsome Pinnock's 1987 *Leave Taking*. Though Pinnock only features two generations, she also connects back to an imaginary female lineage against which the relationships in the play are implicitly measured. Pinnock's play, winner of the 1991 George Devine award, was first performed at the Liverpool Playhouse Studio in November 1987, staged at the Lyric Studio in 1990 and revived by the National Theatre in 1996. Although Pinnock's work is strongly grounded in the context of black British theatre and she has contributed to the landmark series of scripts by black British women playwrights edited by Yvonne Brewster, *Leave Taking* was published in a selection focusing on new writing, *First Run: New Plays by New Writers*.

This publication marked Pinnock's acceptance by the theatrical mainstream, reflected in the production of her plays by the likes of the Royal Court and the National Theatre where, in fact, her work was predominantly seen by white audiences. Pinnock herself contends, however, that the attention her work received was circumstantial: 'There was a lot of interest in my work when I first started because it was a time when the black woman writer was sexy.'[40] In her view, it has been the Women's Playhouse Trust that offered the most consistent support to her career. In fact, she calls attention to the precarious nature of dependence as a playwright on the judgement of others, often men, and observes that theatre is governed by fads: 'The trend really is for a particular kind of play at the moment and that marginalizes every play that doesn't fit the trend.'[41]

Pinnock, like Jackie Kay, belongs to a generation of black playwrights born in the United Kingdom who made their artistic debut in the mid-eighties. For both, an intense preoccupation with origins was a staple of their early writing, exploring a nostalgia of sorts for their ancestors' past and coming to terms with their ethnic origin. Pinnock, however, comments on the difficulties of negotiating her political and artistic agendas. As one of the few prominent figures in black British women's drama, she has been aware of being expected to speak up for an entire race and sex, as well as generation, often to the detriment of artistic creativity. Overall, however, Pinnock finds the 'conflict interesting', and takes every opportunity to assert her right to work on her own terms. Like her protagonist Viv, who undermines her academic success to make a point about agency, Pinnock does not want to be successful following standards set by others: 'The whole act of writing the play is about me saying [...] "This is the playwright I am. These are the terms on which I write, within the tradition of European playwriting, but about subjects that take in my own heritage, my own past."'[42]

Leave Taking examines the relationship between a mother (Enid) and her two daughters (Del and Viv) involving two other protagonists with strong associations to their black heritage: Mai, the *obeah* woman, and Broderick, a male relative who like the mother came to Britain as a young adult in the fifties. Both Broderick and Enid have concentrated, since their arrival, on integration into British life; Enid making significant sacrifices towards her daughters' social and professional success. She invests particularly in the education of Viv, thus aiming to prevent her younger daughter replicating her own life. As Pinnock contends,

> One of my things in all the plays is examining the idea of the victim. To be black was always to be in the position of victim. [...] I play with the idea of what a victim is and none of the characters accept that definition of themselves, because they all take action. [...] Enid [...] is trying to do something for her daughters, trying to save them from the fate of victimhood.[43]

Enid insists on Viv's education as a route of distantiation from the past of women in their family, while her other strategy, aimed at Del, is to prevent her replication of early motherhood. In the opening scene, Enid takes her daughters to Mai for a reading of their future, clearly aimed at finding out about Del's pregnancy. Mai, however, sensing Enid's intrusion into her daughters' lives, refuses to reveal anything. In fact, instead of delving into the daughters' past, present or future, Mai invites Enid to revisit her own life and her relationship with her mother left behind in the Caribbean. For Enid, the past has been precisely what she intended to forget, considering repression the best way of coping with an unsatisfactory life: 'England been good to me. To all of us. I love England an' I bring up the girls to love England because they English.'[44] For Broderick, on the other hand, familiarity with the past is crucial. In his view, Enid's daughters are bound to get mixed up if only taught English values as they have 'Caribbean souls'. Like Mai, he conjures up the image of Enid's mother whom he labels a 'heroine' for fighting colonialism: 'Strong. That why black women so powerful. Is in the blood. Look at you mother.'[45] Confronted with such strong women in her line, instead of gaining confidence, Viv voices concerns of inadequacy. Ironically, from Enid's perspective, strength and confidence are associated with education rather than with the maternal qualities, but while Viv acknowledges Enid's efforts, Del opts for defiance.

In parallel with Del situating herself in opposition to her mother, Enid's memories of her own mother become increasingly vivid. In her conversations with Broderick, she evokes their Caribbean past and after decades of repression allows herself some nostalgic relief. Del's severing of links with her mother replicates Enid's departure and loss of contact with her mother decades ago. It is her mother's death, however, that unleashes a profound sense of guilt in Enid, for having been an inadequate daughter and for not having provided sufficient financial support. In fact, not helping her mother more was Enid's greatest sacrifice, which she conducted at her mother's request. Being asked to deny her heritage was the ultimate rejection for Enid, and her current resurgence of guilt conveys pain as much about the present as the past. Enid's guilt also transfers to Viv who, although unaware of Enid's initial commitment, senses a responsibility for family in need, and instead of financing her own education, she offers the money received from Enid to her pregnant sister. Thus, against their mother's will, both daughters find themselves perpetuating precisely the route their mother would have wished them to avoid. This route gains different connotations once viewed from Del's perspective. As Del puts it, it is not the baby that she wants but the associated agency, as she perceives pregnancy as a way of gaining attention and recognition.

Besides the mother figures of Enid and of her absent mother, Mai emerges as an alternative maternal icon. As an *obeah* woman she caters for needs that English culture is unable to accommodate, and although she repositions herself and her services into a new context, she operates in a ritualistic realm. She is presented, however, as both an individual and professional woman, signifying on yet another level Pinnock's preoccupation with hybridity: as an individual Mai aims, and succeeds more than Enid, at integration into Britain, while as a professional she harks back to the culture left behind in Jamaica.[46] Through the latter, she carries out an archetypal mothering of sorts, appealing particularly to Enid, whereas through the former, she literally reaches out to Del, in place of her distant son. Moreover, as she accepts Del as her surrogate daughter, she also prepares to pass on her professional skills to her. By the end of the play, Del becomes Mai's assistant, in a symbolic transformation that simultaneously removes her from mainstream British culture and makes her embrace the traditions of her racial heritage. It is, however, her decision to have a baby as a single mother at a young age that positions her firmly in the female line of her family, and ultimately helps her recapture her sense of self. As Del and Enid reconcile, they reassess their mother–daughter relationship. By re-living her mother's life, Del is finally able to perceive Enid's needs, while Enid, confronted with the failure of her own bond with her mother, learns to accept that it is up to each generation to configure their own route.

Kindertransport

Diane Samuels's *Kindertransport* was co-winner of the 1992 Verity Bargate Award, and winner of 1993 Meyer Whitworth Award. It was first produced at the Cockpit, Soho Theatre Company, in 1993, directed by Abigail Morris. The play was also performed at the Manhattan Theatre Club in New York in May 1994, and it was revived at the Palace Theatre, Watford, in 1996, transferring to the West End. Other productions have taken place in several European countries, and the play was dramatized for radio and aired on BBC Radio 4 in November 1995. Rooted in the life stories of Holocaust survivors, the play dwells on the evacuation to Britain of over 10,000 Jewish children from Nazi Germany. Samuels, herself of British Jewish origin, researched her play by interviewing survivors, and she highlights the fact that 'actual experiences are woven into the fabric of the play'.[47] As Samuels recalls, she was prompted to write the play by a friend, a descendant of someone who had been part of the Kindertransport and who was haunted by the guilt of survival. This element appears strongly in the character of Evelyn, whereas another factor that impacted on the writer – learning by accident about someone who had been in Auschwitz, but had never spoken about this experience – is transposed into Faith's and Lil's accidental discovery of Evelyn's childhood memorabilia. A final incident that Samuels cites as having influenced her writing was a survivor's rage at her parents for having abandoned her, despite being aware of the potential consequences of staying in Germany. This attitude underpins Evelyn's encounter with her birth mother years after their separation, and leads to her inability to reunite with her.

To further emphasize the play's factual roots, the published play text is prefaced by a selection of 'personal accounts' – reminiscences by survivors of the Kindertransport. They touch upon issues like the separation between children and their parents, the children's first encounter with their foster parents, the survivors' ambition to integrate as much as possible into British life and the identity crisis resulting from such a cultural transfer. Anne Karpf has argued that *Kindertransport* marks a turning point in dealing with Jewishness in Britain, where 'consciousness about the refugee and survivor communities is a very recent phenomenon':

Until very recently, the second generation of both survivors and refugees has followed in the footsteps of the first – deferential, mute, acutely sensitive to the British culture of embarrassment [...], so perhaps it's not surprising that the psychosocial effects of the Holocaust only really came into public view with Diane Samuels's recent *Kindertransport*.[48]

In Samuels's view, however, this overt examination has to do with ageing and looking back on one's childhood. Moreover, she stresses that 'the reason most British people were interested in the play was because it is about mothers and daughters not because it is about Jewish experience.'[49]

In fact, Samuels clarifies that she is not writing about the Kindertransport, but using it as a metaphor: 'What the play is about is separation. It's about separation between mothers and daughters.'[50] *Kindertransport* concentrates on three generations in a female line coming to terms with personal as well as public history. It takes place in the storage room of Evelyn's house in a London suburb, in what Samuels terms recent times. Evelyn is described as an English middle-class woman in her fifties, and she is occasionally doubled by her younger self, Eva. Eva's appearances span the ages 9–17, and she is Jewish German, becoming increasingly English. Eva is one of the children destined for the Kindertransport who ends up being adopted by an English family. In an aim to avoid naturalistic theatre, Samuels constructs her play through a range of flashbacks intertwined with present events, thereby constantly transposing the audience to another reality. Eva's story is often mediated by the other characters: Evelyn as she recalls her younger self, but also Evelyn's foster mother Lil, and her daughter Faith. The latter, unaware of her mother's past, accidentally learns about their Jewishness while looking for items to take away to her new home. Thus, the imminent departure of one daughter leads to revelations about another departure decades before; but while the twenty-something Faith intends to move house as a gesture of independence, Eva aged nine leaves Nazi Germany as a result of her parents' decision on her behalf.

Eva first appears at home in Hamburg in the late thirties. The play's opening scene sets up two of the key parameters for Eva's destiny: a children's story book entitled 'The Ratcatcher', and the importance of autonomy. Helga, Eva's birth mother, is preparing Eva for her journey, teaching her to look after herself. As Eva succeeds at sewing a button on her coat she praises her: 'You don't need me. It's good.'[51] This attempt at severing the bonds of dependence between daughter and mother are replicated on a number of occasions in the play. As a child, Eva is sent away, albeit for her own good, by Helga, whereas, in the play's present, it is Faith who is urged to make up her mind, by her mother Evelyn. Samuels switches regularly between the theatrical present and past, and at times characters belonging to the present are able to 'see' protagonists from the past onstage, although they never interact. Moreover, the Eva/Evelyn divide is one of the crucial conceptual and structural features of the play, marking the split between past and present, as well as the opposition between the retention of identity and assimilation.

The play is constructed on a number of symmetries, most obviously the mother–daughter links between Helga and Eva, and Evelyn and Faith. Snapshots featuring the two pairs alternate at a fast pace in Act One: for instance, Helga picks up Eva's suitcase and then Faith finds it, tentatively opening it. The toy train she pulls out of it leads to the image of the actual train taking Eva away, and it is paralleled by the mouth organ in Eva's luggage – smuggled in by Eva despite her mother's advice, almost confiscated by the German boarder guard, and eventually found again by Faith. In a flashback scene, the last item Eva receives from her mother is a pair of shoes, with a gold watch and jewellery built into its heels. Replicating values transmitted down the family line, particularly the perpetuation of life through children, Helga claims: 'You are my children. You are my jewels. We old ones invest our future in you.'[52]

Juxtapositions between Eva and Faith continue in the section where Eva meets Lil, her English foster mother, under whose care she gradually transforms into Evelyn. Lil appears both in the present and via past reminiscences, and has, in general, a conciliatory role. For instance, she immediately senses the intrusive potential of Faith rummaging through Evelyn's boxes. Just as the young Eva resents being sent away from home, Faith feels excluded from the history of her family. She perceives Evelyn's – and indeed Lil's – reticence to talk about the past as a personal affront, and she is unable to relate to her mother's attempts at transforming ambiguity into seemingly clear-cut categories, such as her adoption of Christianity and anglicizing her name. Eva's integration has been gradual rather than abrupt, however, and included a number of significant stages, such as first referring to England as 'home', or selling her keepsakes symbolizing her Jewish origin in an emblematic effort of distantiation from her foreign past. Eva's assimilation can be seen as Samuels critiquing the circumstances of social acceptance in post-war Britain. In this sense, it is central that Eva is adopted by the English Lil and not a Jewish family, for it reflects 'the heavy pressure to assimilate' exerted by the representatives of Anglo-Jewry who are anxious to maintain the harmony between the Jewish and non-Jewish population.[53] In June 1939, the Board of Deputies and the German-Jewish Aid Committee even issued a booklet entitled 'Helpful Information and Guidance for Every Refugee', which propagated the use of English and urged people to refrain from using German.

Despite Lil's advice, Faith confronts Evelyn and asks about Eva. Continuing her strategy of repression, Evelyn insists on privacy, which only exacerbates Faith's sense of exclusion. Instead of clarifications, therefore, the climax is overt mother-daughter conflict as Faith also questions Evelyn's mothering skills. This confrontation causes unease in Evelyn's relationship with both Faith and Lil. Evelyn finds Lil too intrusive, both in the present and in the past, and she articulates her resentment for having been adopted by Lil and, hence, made to betray her birth mother. She labels Lil 'murderer' and 'child-stealer', but in Lil's definition of motherhood it is she who was right: 'being there where it counts'.[54] Evelyn and Faith finally reconcile following another revelation, this time only shared between the two of them, as Lil has never learned about Evelyn's birth mother surviving the war and reclaiming her daughter. This 'return from the dead', as Beate Neumaier argues, not only 'threatens to annihilate the hard-won new British identity', but also forces Eva to re-live her mother's rejection, which she has not yet managed to fully overcome.[55] Thus, on the eve of Helga's departure to America she chooses stability instead of dislocation, and she interrogates the parental right to take decisions on their children's behalf: 'Why did you send me away when you were in danger? No one made you. You chose to do it. Didn't it ever occur to you that I might have wanted to die with you?'[56] As far as Evelyn is concerned, Helga's approach is a case of inadequate mothering, in the past for giving her up, and in the present for intruding into her life after years of absence. Helga's appearance, for Evelyn, is synonymous with an overt punishment for her survival and, therefore, it cannot lead to reconciliation. As an ultimate metaphor, she equates Helga with the Ratcatcher, encapsulating the haunting and inescapability of guilt.

'The Ratcatcher', a German fairy tale known in its English incarnation as 'The Pied Piper', was the story Eva requested upon her departure to England, and its recurrence throughout the play reiterates a sense of guilt and fear of punishment. The image appears in association with a variety of characters, including Nazi and British officials, but also Lil, the foster mother taking Eva away from her actual parents, and Helga, the birth mother returning after years of absence to dislocate Eva now turned Evelyn from the shelter of her new identity. As Faith continues searching in her mother's attic, itself a space associated with repression, it is a copy of 'The Ratcatcher' that she comes across in its original German version dated 1939 – an indication that it was sent to Eva after she left for England. At the end of the play, after Faith and Evelyn reconcile and details from the past are clarified, the shadow of the ratcatcher takes over the entire stage. Thus, Samuels closes by calling attention to the haunting of the past over the present, and stresses the inadequacy of denial as a survival strategy.

Though Faith resents not having been offered the chance to know her real family line, it is the emergence of a context for her own biography that she cherishes. This includes considering the implications of her Jewishness, despite her mother's conversion to Christianity, her willingness to share her mother's sense of guilt for survival and, unlike Eva/Evelyn, her desire to strengthen their mother–daughter bond. Thus, Samuels articulates 'the necessity to know and take care of the past', as well as the need for a relationship based on mutual trust between mothers and daughters.[57] In several Samuels plays, in fact, mothers play a crucial role. Rosa in *Mrs Gorsky* celebrates her motherhood to five children while, conversely, the protagonist of *Mata Hari* abandons her family to pursue her career-cum-sexual interests. These pathways complement the mother–daughter avenues in *Kindertransport*, as Samuels explores different aspects of being a mother. In her view, women have to deal with motherhood whether they are mothers or not, as they are all daughters. Samuels's ambition is 'to let the witches [...] and the magic back in', since she perceives British theatre as dominated by patriarchal models, and her aim is to bring female emotional energy alive in theatre:

> I will continue to do this through the rest of my life. And if I do not get produced because of it, that's not going to stop me. I've got a real mission here. I think it's time to reconnect the relationship [...] between theatre and healing, the performing arts and healing arts, medicine, community, creative arts and communal arts.[58]

Butterfly Kiss

Butterfly Kiss was Phyllis Nagy's second play produced in London, and it premièred in April 1994 at the Almeida Theatre, directed by Steven Pimlott. A New Yorker, Nagy arrived in the United Kingdom in 1992 for a brief exchange at the Royal Court. She decided, however, to make her stay permanent, and her work has since been regularly perceived as integral to British as well as American theatre. Nagy's subject matter, however, is predominantly rooted in US reality; for instance, *Butterfly Kiss* was staged as a comment on the American Dream, emphasizing the dysfunctionality of the all-American family. Another staple of Nagy's work has been a preoccupation with redefining gay and lesbian characters in theatre. She insists on fully rounded individuals, including flaws as well as positive traits, and this ambition has occasionally led to severe criticism from the press for what they believed to be unsympathetic characters.

Butterfly Kiss, in fact, has scandalized some people, as they were puzzled equally by the play's innovative structure and content. As Aston contends, unlike Keatley's 'three-generation-mothers-play, that typifies the acceptable face of bourgeois-feminist mother-daughter theatre – Nagy's *Butterfly Kiss* represents the filial/maternal as a site of violence'.[59]

In the latter case, a lesbian kiss was overshadowed by the play's climax in matricide, as were previous instances of anti-chronological structure by Nagy's reinterpretation of the memory play. Like Stephenson or Keatley, Nagy also switches between past and present. However, Nagy's protagonist, twenty-five-year-old Lily Ross, remembers rather than acts out her past (according to the stage directions, no attempt should be made to 'play' the characters' younger selves). The play is set in Lily's jail cell, where she has been imprisoned following her charge with the murder of her mother, Jenny. Intercut with moments in Lily's past, involving her mother, grandmother, father and her first lover, are scenes of her current lover, Martha, searching for a motive to the murder. Besides the constant transfers between past and present, the play also negotiates the opposition of reality and fantasy, involvement and detachment, 'in an open-ended examination of form'.[60]

Nagy's plays have been perceived as provocations, and the playwright has confessed her fascination with violence. She featured an act of aggression in her debut play, *Weldon Rising* (1992), whereas *Butterfly Kiss* addresses violence at a personal level. In Aleks Sierz's words, Nagy's sense of violence 'raises questions about individual responsibility' and, in Lily's case, about 'murder being a loving act'.[61] This interpretation of death as a gift and of murder as an act of service is supported by Lily telling Martha that 'My mother asked me to kill her', and according to this scenario agency is instantly transferred from Lily to her mother.[62] Ultimately, however, the murder is left unanswered, and the play does not end with a restoration of order: 'What is subverted [by Nagy] is any idea that a simple explanation is possible. Lily's murder of her mother is meant to be inexplicable because that way it stays disturbing, praying on the mind.'[63] The play, however, is not only disturbing as a result of its puzzling nature; it is taboo-breaking in terms of accepted behaviour norms between members of a female line. This deviation ranges from lack of chemistry between mothers and daughters (Sally to Jenny: 'I shrivel [...] just thinking how could I have given birth to something like you'), via the rejection of viewing oneself in the context of established domestic structures (Lily: 'I'm not part of an American family'), to physical elimination of one another.[64] In other words, Nagy's preoccupations are rooted in the psychological, but they are ultimately political, aimed at subverting current structures of kinship. As Michael Coveney states, 'Lily's decisive act of matricide' is 'an ultimate statement in social and domestic defiance'.[65]

According to Nagy, 'when a son kills his mother, it can be seen as understandable and even heroic. A man can break with his mother symbolically and it's a rite of passage. [But] when a daughter does it, it's seen as fundamentally unnatural, a violation of the sacred bond between mother and daughter.'[66] Nagy indicates the abundance of the theme in literature and theatre: 'I'm so tired of seeing mother-daughter plays where they're all so nice to each other. [...] for every step forward a female dramatist takes writing a mother-daughter play that is actually honest, or tries to grapple with the issue, you get ten of those (the dishonest plays).'[67] However, she claims that despite the exploration of the topic in a variety of forms, the bond is always reaffirmed in the end. In this sense, *Butterfly Kiss* re-formulates the perception of the family as a structural unit, and, also, it situates itself outside established patterns in theatre history. On this level, in fact, it breaks with the very organization of this study as well, constituting a fresh point of reference in the dramatic negotiation of mother–daughter relationships. On another level, the play can be safely inscribed into the paradigm of mother–daughter plays examined throughout this book. It addresses the issue of care, as far as needing and providing it is concerned, and Lily's final act is an instance of taking care of her mother. Paradoxically, care in this case metamorhoses into murder; however, Lily's attempts at providing care locate her in a surrogate maternal role of sorts, as Nagy also reverses the caring roles between mother and daughter. The play blacks out to this reversal amplified to a literal level: Lily brushing her mother's hair, even after she substitutes the brush with a gun.

Nagy has also established a connection between subject matter and particular plays by women that got produced by male managements. She claimed that such plays 'were all about the process of being a woman, as filtered through the eyes of men'.[68] In other words, only works that conformed to male expectations concerning the treatment of topics like motherhood or pregnancy got produced, and then these, by being in the public view, perpetuated a particular mould of writing on these subjects. Nagy has clearly wished to situate her own contribution against this trend and to claim the right for a different style. In 2002, she referred to the case of Caryl Churchill, liberated by her ageing, who as a woman in her sixties finally achieved a kind of 'sexless' status, which allowed her to tackle any subject, not just the ones traditionally 'allocated' to female writers.[69] Nevertheless, in an interview given at the height of laddism in late nineties theatre, she emphasized the importance of a supportive artistic climate:

If things carry on the way they are currently, with [...] this ridiculous promotion of men and bad plays and misogyny, then I, for one, will

stop writing plays. I will no longer be a playwright in that sort of theatre culture. I will find something else to do instead.[70]

Her latest play *Neverland* opened in 1999, while her first film as a
director, *Mrs Harris,* premièred in September 2005 at the Toronto Film
Festival.

Phaedra's Love

Phaedra's Love was first performed at the Gate Theatre in London on 15
May 1996.[71] It was directed by Kane herself, after she fell out with the
initial director, Cath Mattock. The play was commissioned by David
Farr, then artistic director of the Gate, whose interest in Kane stemmed
from his reactions to *Blasted.* In his initial meeting with Kane shortly
after the controversy at the Royal Court, it was protection from malig-
nant criticism that Farr offered Kane in exchange for her opting for the
Notting Hill studio theatre as a venue for her next production. Farr
meant genuine support in dealing with potential attacks, but also,
implicitly, indicated less exposure owing to the Gate's fringe status. Farr
invited Kane to write for a season of new British plays based on ancient
stories, preferably Greek or Roman tragedy. Thus, Kane took immediate
inspiration from Seneca, and in her play tests the boundaries of dramatic representation and revisits the very tradition of tragedy as a genre
and theatrical practice. She interrogates the concept of tragic character,
and reconsiders the dynamic between protagonist and supporting roles.
She also edits out established figures in earlier versions of the various
plays based on Phaedra and Hippolytus and adds new characters, thus
modernizing the myth to suit the late 20th century. As Kane indicated
herself, she wanted 'to keep the classical concerns of Greek theatre –
love, hate, death, revenge, suicide – but use a completely contemporary
urban poetry'.[72]

Graham Saunders argues that while 'previous plays based on the
Phaedra myth rely on the conflict' arising out of the 'opposition
between desire and repulsion, *Phaedra's Love* shows the consequences
that consummation brings'.[73] In fact, the very title of Kane's play repositions the focus from a key protagonist, as in Seneca's or Racine's
Phaedra, to a relational situation in which one character is located as the
object of another's longing. Kane insists on Phaedra's role as an agent
and calls attention to her desire as a phenomenon, before she invites
the audience to identify its object. Kane opted not to name Hippolytus
in the title, acknowledging that he undergoes a significant transformation

in the course of the play, and is, in a sense, Phaedra's invention. The play, however, dedicates considerable stage time to Hippolytus. It opens with him, and he is the only character to be onstage alone. There are also a number of situations where the various protagonists discuss Hippolytus and, hence, indirectly make him the focus of attention. The doctor is the one who first raises the question of Phaedra as a (possibly inadequate) surrogate mother while also indicating his awareness of her obsession with Hippolytus. As a next phase, Phaedra's daughter, Strophe, tries to persuade her mother to lose interest in Hippolytus, while Phaedra articulates the lack of blood links between herself and Hippolytus, and reveals the intensity of her feelings.

Instead of the nurse offering a maternal role, Kane features a daughter. She stems from Phaedra's first marriage, and is thus no blood relation to either Hippolytus or Theseus. In this respect she is the most independent of all characters, and, further, she is free of the ballast of classical connotations. She is also most concerned with keeping up appearances, emphasizing the importance of secrecy over Phaedra's love. Despite aiming to protect Phaedra, and, therefore, arguably, the institutions of monarchy and matrimony, it is Strophe who reveals the most in terms of sexuality. Having had sexual experiences with both Hippolytus and Theseus, she has not only committed adultery and incest, but, crucially in contrast with Phaedra, she has dissociated sex from love. For Strophe, as for Hippolytus and indeed Theseus, sex is just sex, without further ramifications into commitment or affection.

Phaedra is not only unable to separate sex from love, but she cannot displace love from the very centre of her preoccupations. In David Greig's words, the play maps out 'the landscape of love', to complement Kane's other landscapes in earlier and later works: 'the landscape of violation, of loneliness, of power, of mental collapse'.[74] Love takes over Phaedra's being and situates all other relationships secondary. It makes her re-evaluate her role as a wife to Theseus, but, more imminently, to reconsider the implications of being a mother to Strophe and stepmother to Hippolytus. In Strophe's case, Kane simply reverses the situation, opposing Strophe's matter-of-factness fuelled by experience with Phaedra's hesitation rooted in innocence. But it is not just sexual kudos that establishes this status quo between mother and daughter. It is also a matter of confidence and the ability to contextualize events that locate Strophe in a caring role. She is in a position to expertly advise Phaedra, aware, like the confidantes in classical tragedy, of the potential outcomes inherent in illicit desire. It is also Strophe who first names Hippolytus as the object of Phaedra's love, though she insists on keeping this passion secret, from the public as well as from Hippolytus himself. Crucially, despite seeming comfortable with the reversal of the caring role in their relationship and her own position of control, she voices her dissatisfaction with Phaedra abandoning her maternal role altogether.

Hippolytus, on the other hand, seems to sarcastically reiterate the family links between them, as 'an ancient tragedy transforms itself into a modern soap opera'. He challenges Phaedra on her reluctance to allowing him to call her 'mother', and deliberately insults her by thus attracting attention to her age.[75] However, he then goes on to explore the different bonds he and Strophe have with Phaedra, highlighting the differences between biological and cultural parenthood. As Greig contends, in Phaedra and Hippolytus, 'Kane marked the two poles that are the extremes of the human response to love' – one 'total self-abnegation', the other 'total self-preservation'.[76] In a sense, it is a vulnerability of sorts that they share, translated into the total rejection of emotion for Hippolytus and an irresistible urge to abandon herself to desire for Phaedra. Crucially, for both protagonists, 'moral choices are expressions of personal freedom',[77] and Hippolytus's understanding of Phaedra's sacrifice will be the ultimate bond that connects them. Committing suicide is the only way forward for Phaedra, and turning himself in to justice is the only acceptable way for Hippolytus when recognizing in Phaedra's act the gift of her life to him.

While Phaedra has arguably the least stage time and Hippolytus the most, Strophe connects the various threads of the plot together. It is she, who, after Phaedra's suicide, tries to establish what has actually happened, interrogating Hippolytus and trying to maintain her mother's reputation. As details come to the fore, Phaedra's present to Hippolytus becomes increasingly clear, leading to his obligation to own up to the accusation of rape. This confirms to Hippolytus the intensity and purity of Phaedra's love, and concludes his pursuit of honesty. This act finally constitutes an event worthy of his expectations, as it redefines the boundaries of what is human. All the rest is irrelevant, including the perception of others, subsequently altered by Strophe's last minute revelation of Hippolytus's innocence and thus her withdrawal of loyalty to her mother. As far as Hippolytus is concerned, he can only destroy himself – and through this all others, including the monarchy itself. As he conveys his desire for experiencing similar moments at the play's climax, the purity of Phaedra's feeling is finally matched by Hyppolytus's honesty and his equally pure self-hatred.[78]

Kane's theatre has epitomized the emerging 'in-yer-face' move-ment. According to a 1997 interview, the problems Kane addresses are 'the ones we have as human beings', adding that an 'over-emphasis on sexual politics is a diversion from our main problem'. Formulating a position taboo to women playwrights until the nineties, Kane re-appropriates the right to dramatize whatever subject she chooses in a gender-neutral way:

> My only responsibility as a writer is to the truth, however unpleasant that truth may be. I have no responsibility as a woman writer because I don't believe there's such a thing. [...] I don't want to be represen-tative of any biological or social group of which I happen to be a member.[79]

Claims like this as well as Kane's embracing of violence in her early plays undermine easy categorization indeed. Feminist theatre criticism has pointed out, for instance, that Kane's tendency for violence 'aligns her more with the political writing of Edward Bond than any of the established women political writers of the senior generation such as Caryl Churchill or Wertenbaker'.[80] Despite being reminiscent of earlier traditions, however, Kane's work has also synchronized drama with youth culture, thus having attracted new audiences to the theatre. Kane has equally appropriated a belief prevalent in feminism, that is, of aim-ing to make a lasting contribution through interventional means: 'If we can experience something through art, then we might be able to change our future, because experience engraves lessons on our hearts through suffering.'[81]

Conclusion

The dramatists discussed in this chapter illustrate divergent political and artistic agendas that are emblematic of the shifts in ideological posi-tioning from the mid-eighties onwards. Playwrights writing in the eighties preface their work by formulating their particular political loca-tion, whereas those emerging in the course of the nineties refute the very legitimacy of such underpinning. Instead of focusing on major political subjects, the latter celebrate the politics of the everyday in a post-modern attempt of distantiation. Throughout the nineties, in fact, even earlier playwrights with previous allegiances redefine their current location and wish to nuance their particular brand of feminism, while as far as the label 'feminist theatre' is concerned, most dramatists express reservations. Chapters 5 and 6 elaborate further on the perspectives of authors and practitioners working at the turn of the third millennium, aiming to establish a relationship between women's writing for performance and feminism today.

In terms of artistic agendas, the majority of dramatists aim to position their work as artistic interventions first and foremost. They also emphasize ambitions such as making sense of the chaos (Page), connecting to the collective unconscious (Keatley), bringing female emotional energy alive in performance (Samuels), as well as gaining the right to address any subject matter of their choice (Nagy, Kane). The majority of plays discussed subvert linearity and include flashbacks to the past, and thus emphasize the role of memory. Despite this unifying factor, however, the plays vary considerably in terms of formal originality, and range from relatively conservative pieces where the central strand is rooted in realism to instances without an ambition of correspondence with actual events. As all plays focus on some sort of a female lineage, however, even the theatrically conservative strands can be accounted as radical, owing to the playwrights' intense preoccupation with women's experience.

Most plays problematize biological parenthood and specify the intricacies of mother–daughter relationships. Keatley and Page, for instance, offer a celebratory support to surrogacy and treat it as a metaphor for the viability of human relationships. Parenthood is often associated with caring, at times in a reversal of roles (Stephenson, Kane) or in paradoxical situations, such as Nagy's matricide. Pinnock, on the other hand, explores a case study in excessive and intrusive care, leading to distantiation in the first instance, and ultimately, to a replication of patterns in the maternal line. In some form or other, all the playwrights interrogate the often taken-for-granted harmony inherent in women's communities, and emphasize selfishness, rivalry and difficulties in communication instead.

The playwrights also address parenthood as a non-exclusive realm. Page highlights men's inclination for parenting, irrespective of biological bonds, while Keatley and Samuels negotiate the task of mothering across women belonging to different generations and bloodlines. In several plays, there are references to men who have fathered children, in association with illegitimacy or inadequate relationships. Nagy, Kane and Page include a balance between male and female protagonists, the latter making a point about writing adequate roles for men as well as women. Keatley, Samuels and Stephenson, on the other hand, prioritize female casts, aiming to revisit the gender-power ratio on stage, and offering an insight into female bonding in the absence of men.

4
Daughters as Mothers: The Teenager as Potential Parent

Motherhood in situations where the protagonist is not yet an adult, and consequently needs to negotiate becoming a parent while, often, dependent on parents herself, is dramatized in a broad range of seventies and eighties plays. This preoccupation reflects ongoing changes in societal attitudes concerning the timing and circumstances of parenthood; but plays about teenagers emerge at this particular time also as a result of significant transformations on the social, political and legal terrain. Adolescents gradually emerge as subjects in their own right in the wake of the late sixties and seventies counter-cultural protest movements, and I test this claim by examining a number of case studies from the British women's theatre scene, such as the Women's Theatre Group's (WTG's) *My Mother Says I Never Should* (1975), Grace Dayley's *Rose's Story* (1984), Sharman MacDonald's *When I Was a Girl, I Used to Scream and Shout...*(1984) and Trish Cooke's *Back Street Mammy* (1989). These plays examine various contexts in which young protagonists take centre stage, and in particular address situations where teenage pregnancy arises. As the playwrights and practitioners interrogate some of the options available to the adolescent subject, they also react to the changing legal and ethical climate in this period, especially regarding contraception and abortion.

The 1967 Abortion Act heralded a new start not only as far as unwanted pregnancies but also the assumption of motherhood at a specific moment in time was concerned, while the 1969 Divorce Reform Act paved the way for an equitable separation between partners. Following these two key events, the 1970 Women's Liberation Conference at Ruskin College in Oxford formulated its equality-seeking demands on pay and education, requiring 24-hour access to nurseries and free contraception and abortion on demand. Following pressures by the

Women's Liberation Movement, a number of other legislative events emerged to ameliorate women's unequal status in society, including the Equal Pay Act in 1970, the Working Women's Charter in 1974, and the Sex Discrimination Act in 1975. Despite all these contributing to a sense of change, as Bart Moore-Gilbert argues, 'the 1970s can be seen as a decade of only partial success for the Women's Movement'. He indicates flaws in the implementation of some of the acts, especially regarding equal pay, and charts the rise of the Pro-life Movement to restrict women's newly acquired right to control their reproduction: 'Moral panic about the collapse of the family and the increasing number of single mothers suggest a backlash was well under way by the end of the decade'.[1]

Theatre groups active in the seventies tapped into this changing territory, sensing the discrepancies between day-to-day practice at the grassroots level and the legal and political framework. The WTG, for instance, was at the core of the wider British counter-cultural and alternative theatre movement, and identified as its mission to call attention to imminent issues developing in society. Thus, they shared an agenda with other touring agitprop groups, while they also identified with the aims of Theatre in Education. These values were often shared by individual playwrights of the period as well, such as Grace Dayley, whose debut play replicated concerns explored earlier by the WTG, although from a black British perspective. Dayley was also writing as a young, somewhat naive author, who did not benefit from being nurtured by a supportive director or theatre group. Trish Cooke, on the other hand, another black author emerging only a few years later, was able to collaborate briefly with both the socialist feminist and black theatre scene, and hence present her work to larger audiences. Among the case studies included in this chapter Sharman MacDonald appears to be the least affiliated with a particular theatre scene, as she has written for mainstream as well as fringe theatres in England and Scotland alike. She focuses on individuals negotiating personal problems, often in white middle-class contexts, but since these situations include a clash of generations and rivalries between mothers and daughters, besides reclaiming the right for agency on behalf of the teenage subject, her work too acquires political undertones.

My Mother Says I Never Should

As a feminist theatre company, the WTG had 'an important collective, counter-cultural history to narrate'.[2] Its policies included a focus on an accessible and entertaining theatre by, for and about women, reaching out to as many women as possible – not just regular theatre-goers, encouraging new writing by women, reclaiming through performance women's history and recording women's condition, offering role models and positive discrimination to lesbian and black women. The group started off as a socialist feminist organization and was managed collectively until the late eighties, when financial constraints forced them to appoint a management team. The company took its cues from everyday conversation and activities, and responded to the impact of television and popular culture. There was a preoccupation with the immediacy of experience, wanting to recreate a slice of apparently real life, including facts but also trivia and gossip: 'realistic elements have a didactic purpose, and this purpose is sharpened by the non-realistic elements, such as music, stylization, and direct contact with the audience.'[3]

In 1975 the WTG produced *My Mother Says I Never Should* specifically for teenagers, a seldom targeted section of the non-theatre-going public.[4] The company aimed to perform the play for this audience in their own spaces, such as youth clubs and schools, and to address a topical issue through which to provoke a dialogue. The topic was contraception and abortion, and the context the experiences of teenage girls and the sexual double standards operating in society. Influenced by political theatre, the play features an all-female cast and takes a consciously partisan pro-women perspective. Like other issue plays of the seventies, *My Mother Says I Never Should* is based on case studies and juxtaposes two alternatives: a girl wishing to experiment with her sexuality and consequently taking risks (Wendy), and another hesitating, not necessarily as a result of personal conservative attitudes but not yet emotionally ready to embark on this route (Terri). In both cases, the company wanted to present their protagonists as independent agents, making their own decisions whether good or bad.

The play also integrates older women's views on sexuality. These include an emphasis on bourgeois morality (Terri's mother: 'Nobody wants to marry a girl with a reputation')[5], the position of a teacher trying to negotiate tolerance with responsibility, as well as the unapologetic celebration of pleasure. The latter view is represented by two protagonists coming from either side of the age divide. According to Terri's grandmother the pill is 'for stopping babies, so you can enjoy yourself', while for the twenty-something Diane sex is something 'you fancy [...] as much as he does.'[6] Crucially, however, both qualify their statements – the grandmother pointing to the naturalness of sex and Diane indicating the importance of responsible behaviour. The play also addresses the issue of career opportunities available for women, and again, there are significant divisions according to generation. The mother perceives marriage as the best career choice; for the teenage Terri, however, neither negotiating paid work with housework nor being a full-time housewife appear as viable alternatives.

Framing the realistic details, a singer introduces and concludes the play. The integration of music was important to women-centred performance, as Gillian Hanna of Monstrous Regiment – besides WTG the other major feminist company of the decade – pointed out: 'we had to have the music to smash that regular and acceptable theatrical form'.[7] In *My Mother Says I Never Should* this device reiterates the title and links the play to the well-known skipping song, and hence to the audience's immediate experience. It also establishes a direct contact with the spectators:

> We've been talking to you about choices
> 'Cause some day we think you'll find:
> If you don't control your body
> Somebody's gonna screw your mind.[8]

WTG wanted to address this topic as a result of the scarcity of adequate literature on the subject. Thus, they focused on a sympathetic doctor who not only helps the protagonist in a particular situation, but also draws attention to the broader context of decision-taking in matters of sexuality and parenthood. The company also intended to challenge the legal age of consent and the idea of responsibility attached to a particular age barrier. They made the two protagonists 15, just under the age of consent, pointing to the anomaly of the assumption that teenagers cannot have sex just because they are considered to be too young to have children. In other words, the company and the play argued for the dissociation of sexuality from parenthood, and for the location of women, irrespective of their age, as independent agents of their own will.

The play was informed by significant research: discussions with teenagers, teachers and parents and the examination of contraceptive advice available for young people at the time. The company was aware that their target audience had practically no previous experience of theatre-going, being the first generation predominantly influenced by television, and thus they capitalized on the familiarity of TV-style storylines. It was equally important to create characters the audience could identify with, an ambition carried forward in post-performance discussions where participants were encouraged to imagine themselves into the roles addressed in the play. This technique not only made the points raised in the show more emphatic, but also allowed for audience feedback to be incorporated into the performance.

The play's initial reception was warm, attracting school groups via the Inner and Greater London Education Authority (ILEA and GLEA, respectively). The ILEA Health Inspector even contended: 'Excellent, really excellent. Covered all the issues. I wonder if your next play could be teeth.'[9] There were, however, dissenting voices as well, which found the open style of discussion subversive and felt that it could encourage sexual promiscuity, while the play's recommendation of the pill also triggered criticism from the Women's Liberation Movement. The backlash culminated in an article published by a teacher in the *Evening Standard* in December 1978, entitled 'Incitement to Sex in a Film for Schools'. In it, the teacher claimed that the disproportionately large number of teenage pregnancies in London could be attributed to a propaganda film shown in schools: a video version of *My Mother Says I Never Should*. Thus, the use of the play as a teaching resource was discontinued; however, in 1980 the text appeared in a collection bringing together emblematic works from the socialist theatre scene in Britain. The volume, edited by Michelene Wandor, was published by Journeyman, an independent radical publishing house (the collection was rejected by both commercial and feminist publishers earlier); and therefore the plays included became available for performance by other groups, besides constituting a valuable social document of the period.

When I Was a Girl, I Used to Scream and Shout...

Sharman MacDonald's *When I Was a Girl, I Used to Scream and Shout...*was first performed at the Bush Theatre, London, in November 1984, and was directed by Simon Stokes. The production transferred to the West End, won the *Evening Standard*'s Most Promising Playwright Award and brought MacDonald overnight success in the UK and abroad, prompting her to give up acting for playwriting. MacDonald is generally categorized as a Scottish playwright, although her work has been mainly seen outside Scotland, in major venues in London (National Theatre, Royal Court, Almeida) as well as Leeds (West Yorkshire Playhouse). Most of her plays, however, have Scottish settings and 'touch on issues deeply resonant in Scottish culture: complex mothers in strange and even destructive relationships with their children (particularly their daughters), absent or problematic fathers, confused adolescents, an immediate and deeply affecting physical world, and the nature of memory, nostalgia, and regret'.[10]

When I Was a Girl, I Used to Scream and Shout... is, for instance, set on the East coast of Scotland and explores an almost 20-year period in the lives of a mother (Morag) and a daughter (Fiona). It starts and finishes in the present, 1983, but frequently delves back to the past. It also involves two key relationships for the daughter: with her best friend Vari and her boyfriend Ewan, but while Vari appears both in the present and the past, Ewan emerges only through Fiona's reminiscences. The play's present features a reunion between mother and daughter, engineered by the former to revisit their life together and to address the future. Anticipating subsequent concerns in nineties theatre, MacDonald addresses the issue of ageing in relation to motherhood; however, instead of raising the matter from the perspective of the protagonist concerned, she dramatizes an external view: a mother concerned about her daughter being still single at 32, and hence jeopardizing her chances for having a child. Morag invokes the imagery of the female biological clock as well as a case of early menopause in their family to put pressure on Fiona, and underpins her argument with an axiom of patriarchal values, also replicated by an adolescent Vari: 'Every woman needs to have a child.'[11] As it happens though, Fiona has had a child as a teenager, but in Morag's words 'that doesn't count'; what she means is 'a proper child. Of my body. Of your body',[12] and distinguishes between having had a baby and having been a mother, stressing the differences between biological and nurturing motherhood.

MacDonald chooses not to explore the whereabouts of this child further; what she concentrates on is the examination of the mother–daughter relationship, both in the present as adults but primarily in the past, at various stages of Fiona's adolescence. In both categories, however, this relationship is mediated by an external participant, Vari. Morag has even invited her to their reunion, to replicate Vari's crucial presence in events past. It was Vari who acted as Fiona's first confidante, and who first learned about Morag's happiness with a man after years of single life. Vari is also an emblem for a different avenue in female existence: married with three children she is precisely the model Morag would have liked for herself and would wish the independent Fiona to follow. Examined from Vari's perspective, however, motherhood entails drawbacks as well as advantages, such as having no time for privacy, as well as acquiring a 'mother's body' as opposed to Fiona's youthful slenderness.

In contrast to scenes set in the present, the flashbacks invoke moments in the fifties and sixties. MacDonald calls her style of writing 'female structure', emphasizing its cyclical nature. She refers to the resistance still prevalent among critics and audiences as far as this style is concerned, but has manifested her disbelief in existing conventions: 'I don't think there are any rules.'[13] In an interview published in 1997 she was optimistic if not visionary about the future: 'There will be a woman who breaks through it all and will be accepted for the plays she writes'.[14] The flashbacks in *When I Was a Girl, I Used to Scream and Shout...* often capture dialogues between Fiona and Vari and deal with the exploration of teenage sexuality. Thus, they unite two central facets of feminist theatre: a subversion of chronology and an investigation of bonding between women. Although, as in Stephenson's and Keatley's case discussed in Chapter 3, elements of bourgeois feminism are constantly present through the play's historically accurate setting and plausible dialogue, MacDonald also invokes cultural and radical feminism via her focus on the maternal and on the timelessness of female friendship. In fact, according to Trevor R. Griffiths, 'the play's strength lies in its delineation of female sexual awakening in the flashbacks' (rather than in the contemporary scenes 'which lack social contextualization or plot development').[15]

The flashback scenes oppose Vari's relative ease with regard to matters sexual to Fiona's repression, rooted in her puritan education. MacDonald details Fiona's lack of intimacy with Morag, and indicates not only the daughter's rejection of her mother's lifestyle but also of the very standards of femininity imposed upon her: 'I don't want to be a young lady.'[16] This rejection of her mother's expectations is reiterated once again at a later stage in the reunion as adults, as Fiona articulates her position: 'I just don't want a baby.'[17] As opposed to Morag's unconditional support to mainstream society's equation of women with mothers, Fiona is childless deliberately, as a result of her preference for a career but not necessarily due to lack of a permanent relationship. For Morag, on the other hand, being left by her husband equalled unfulfilled maternal desire, as motherhood outside marriage was socially unacceptable for her generation: 'When your father left I was thirty-seven. I was very grateful to him I wasn't forty. [...] At thirty-seven I had another baby in me.'[18]

MacDonald suggests the ambivalence of the mother–daughter relationship from its early days to the present; however, she chooses a scene in 1966 to illuminate its origin. Set in a bathroom, the scene indicates a certain transgression of taboos from the very start, and delivers two defining confessions from Morag. On the one hand, she reveals to Fiona her love for a new man, and on the other – in reaction to her daughter's reticence to her new-found happiness as well as her resentment for Fiona's earlier bond with her father – she lays bare her true feelings for her: 'I didn't like you then and I don't like you now.'[19] Thus, MacDonald articulates the boundaries of maternal love, and suggests the possibility of dissociating between duty and genuine affection. As Morag renounces her maternal role (in parallel with acquiring the role of a sexual subject), she transfers her caring duties to their ever-present confidante, Vari – turning her into a surrogate mother for Fiona. As a reaction to this denial, Fiona's plans include the same strategy the mother plans for herself: having a baby; but while for Morag a child in her late thirties represents the last chance for fulfilling a long-term desire, Fiona's motivation is to make sure that her mother does not abandon her. Unlike Morag who waited for years for the emergence of a suitable partner, Fiona simply utilizes a 'donor' (Ewan, a neighbouring lad); in the aftermath of the act, however, she realizes the responsibility involved in parenthood – as well as in interfering with someone else's destiny – and decides on having an abortion.

One of the key concerns of the Women's Liberation Movement has been women's right to control their reproductive processes, via a variety of methods including abortion. Campaigns for women's rights to safe abortions have been central to second-wave feminism, and the topic continues to be a sensitive issue to this day. Not all feminists agree with the legitimacy of abortions, however; certain radical feminists such as Adrienne Rich argue that abortions are further instruments of male domination over women. Most feminists, nevertheless, even if they are against termination, are likely to put the safety of the mother first, as opposed to the focus on the unborn child practiced by the medical profession, in agreement with the Pro-life Movement and religious organizations. Often, male partners or family members are also in support of Pro-life aims, as evidenced by Ewan, the so-far-absent father, in MacDonald's play. His brief involvement at a crucial time in Fiona's pregnancy raises the issue of decision-taking on parenthood along gender lines. Ironically, his intervention only extends to preventing termination – and not to a responsible, long-term parental responsibility; however, MacDonald's' sheer signalling of paternal rights is an important thematic innovation.

Ewan is less interested in practising fatherhood than he is in establishing a contact between Morag and Fiona. Instead of projecting himself and Fiona in the role of prospective parents, he reiterates the necessity of their dependence on parental figures. Through this intervention, he also perpetuates the trend of mother–daughter communications being facilitated by external agents, and, as Fiona has initially planned, he achieves the desired effect. Morag's staying behind, however, occurs at a stage when Fiona was ready to let her go, and takes place at the price of denying agency to both women: the mother forces (unwanted) parenthood upon her daughter, while, in her turn, she is being denied – and denies herself – the chance of opting out of motherhood. As MacDonald recalls, she was 'in touch with what was going on' at the time of writing the play, and she hated the idea that 'feminists were putting women up on a platform' declaring women 'good' and men 'bad'.[20] Aiming to redress the balance within mainstream perceptions on gender relations, as well as on the generational power structure, she indicates complexity and rejects categorizations. In her words, 'what Fiona did [to her mother] was absolutely appalling' but 'what the mother, in turn, was doing and had done was equally appalling. They were repressing each other'.[21] Despite the playwright's arguable impartiality in this sense, there was criticism of MacDonald being unfair on the mother by denying her a chance for happiness and forcing her to locate personal future secondary to that of her daughter's. In a later play, *All Thing Nice,* where MacDonald examines three generations in a maternal line, she tackles an even stronger taboo: the grandmother almost prostituting her granddaughter. In both cases MacDonald's interest lies in exploring possibilities and pushing these to their limit, deliberately transgressing expectations.

As far as feminism is concerned, like most dramatists speaking in the nineties, MacDonald also addresses the importance of change. She situates herself in a different phase to her mother's generation, and indicates the shaping up of yet another stage for her daughter's age group: 'I wasn't allowed to be angry when I was growing up [...]. I encourage my daughter's anger and her spirit and assume [...] that the generation coming up will be astonishing. [...] But not fighting for feminism, that won't be it; they'll simply do and they'll simply be, which is fantastic.'[22] This approach clearly builds on and benefits from the achievements of previous generations, without needing to worry about ghettoization. In an ideal case, it will finally succeed in treating women as human beings *par excellence*; in the opposite, it will simply deny credit where it is due and require yet another generation to emerge and stake up their claims.

Rose's Story

Teenage sexuality and pregnancy has featured extensively in the work of black British women playwrights, including Grace Dayley's *Rose's*

Story (1984), Trish Cooke's *Back Street Mammy* (1989) and Christine George's *Family Bliss* (1989). Several plays examine the issue of unplanned pregnancy – in the context of broken marriages and generation conflict in *Family Bliss*, and of an ultra-religious background in *Rose's Story* – and the family becomes a site for conflict, often with open confrontations and estrangement between the generations. A well-known example in this sense is Winsome Pinnock's *Leave Taking* (1987), a play scrutinizing the generation gap between a mother and her daughters in a British family of Caribbean descent discussed in Chapter 3. Apart from family issues, here Pinnock also explored double cultural identity – British and Caribbean – another major concern for black and ethnic minority playwrights. In Pinnock's words, for British-born playwrights who had inherited a West Indian cultural tradition, 'issues of identity were of pressing concern, the idea of being trapped between certain dualities: migrant/native; 'black' culture/'white' culture; being caught between two cultures and belonging to neither'.[23] However, Pinnock equally called attention to the fact that such plays 'would have some political implication whatever they were about', since so few plays by black playwrights were produced: 'The play becomes representative, and it could not be otherwise when there is little to complement or contradict it'.[24]

The relatively small number of black-authored plays staged in Britain, especially in the seventies and eighties, is a direct reflection, on a cultural terrain, of the absence of a nurturing environment, and on the social and political terrain, of persisting racial tensions. Despite increasing attempts at political correctness, colour has constituted an unresolved issue, being primarily addressed in the media in the context of violent riots and crimes. Racially motivated incidents, such as the 1981 riots in Brixton and Liverpool's Toxteth, and the murders of Stephen Lawrence (1993), Damilola Taylor (2000) and Anthony Walker (2005), have particularly called attention to the inadequate negotiation of inter-racial exchange. Although the legal inquiries into these cases have not necessarily led to an explanation of facts, they have created a precedent for an intense debate on the matter in the public domain. For instance, following formal conclusion, the Lawrence case has continued the discussion of race relations via the medium of theatre. A dramatized version of the events was staged at the Tricycle Theatre, broadcast on prime time television as *The Colour of Justice* (2001).

Topical social and political issues were equally at the centre of the WTG's agenda, often in relation to a younger audience. Companies continued throughout the late seventies and early eighties to encourage young playwrights to give voice to their own immediate experiences. Thus has emerged for instance Andrea Dunbar, whose work is emblematic for white Northern working-class culture of the decade, and Grace Dayley, whose *Rose's Story* illuminates young black women's experience from a metropolitan perspective. As Susan Croft argues, 'family reaction to the discovery of sexuality is central to a number of black women's plays, some of which, like Grace Dayley's *Rose's Story*, examine the dilemmas of unplanned pregnancy.'[25] Unlike a number of other cases where the young female protagonist contemplates pregnancy on her own as a route towards individual freedom or social integration, Dayley allies her protagonist with her boyfriend, and the two of them set up a united front against society and authority. *Rose's Story* was published in the *Plays by Women* series edited by Michelene Wandor, and was first produced by the Drama Society at the Polytechnic of the South Bank on 25 January 1984, directed by Dayley herself. As a result of the production the Royal Court offered Dayley a 12-month internship, including the possibility of staging the play in the Theatre Upstairs. *Rose's Story* also featured among the handful of black plays referenced in Wandor's one paragraph on black authors in *Carry On, Understudies* (1981), where Wandor emphasized the 'stark, direct and naturalistic account of the impact of a young West Indian woman's pregnancy on her and her family'.[26]

The play was written while Dayley was still a student, and its style epitomizes this youthful vitality and emotional rawness. The play also reflects the lack of an adequate supportive context at the time for the emergence of minority women's voices in the theatre. In this sense, the play can be viewed as a 'survival story' on multiple levels, conveying not only Rose's personal journey towards independence, but also the quest of black women playwrights towards freedom of artistic expression. *Rose's Story* is also the chronologically earliest play by a non-white author discussed in this study, and constitutes therefore a landmark as far as the dramatization of black women's experience in relation to motherhood is concerned. Dayley writes in a frank and direct way, offering a slice-of-life of black working-class traditions in eighties Britain. Like subsequent playwrights, such as Winsome Pinnock and Trish Cooke, Dayley documents not only particular aspects of daily life but also carefully records her protagonists' cultural and linguistic markers. Thus, she juxtaposes various forms of English, ranging from the strongly accented patois of Rose's parents and boyfriend to the standard English spoken by the white representatives of authority. The protagonist mediates – like Cooke's Dynette in *Back Street Mammy* – between the two worlds, by having access to both registers and occasionally blending them into a unique linguistic mix.

Like Shelagh Delaney, who wanted to rectify the representation of homosexual characters onstage in *A Taste of Honey* (1958), Dayley was also attracted to playwriting by the desire to improve the 'unimpressive black productions' she saw.[27] She asked Caryl Phillips to help with her initial script, and consequently reconsidered the play's structure and added a monologue. Despite encouragement from black and fringe companies, however, she could not find anywhere to produce the play and, as a result, set up the Drama Society at the Polytechnic of the South Bank. Even having her own organization did not make it particularly easy to put on the play, though, but after many hurdles the play did première. It was very well received, despite the short run, and both cast and audience were able to make analogies between the play and their own lives. Like Dayley herself, many cast members were unmarried mothers, who recognized their personal experiences duplicated by the characters onstage. This focus on young single mothers also reconnects to Delaney's earlier treatment of the subject matter, although it primarily draws attention to the 'single teenage mum syndrome that has, in fact, a long history [...] of racialization, stigmatizing Black women as sexually promiscuous.[28]

Rose's Story is structured in two acts, and follows a linear story line in the life of fifteen-year-old Rose Johnson. It opens with a scene set in a doctor's surgery that establishes Rose's pregnancy as a fact, and starts off speculations as far as subsequent possibilities are concerned: 'Well, Miss Johnson, you are definitely pregnant... Do you want the baby?'[29] Owing to Rose's age, all representatives of authority, including the doctor and the social worker, suggest either abortion or adoption, and present these options as the most suitable alternatives. They claim to have her personal interest in view, but they refuse to consult her about their recommendations and rather than granting they actually refuse her agency.

In parallel with the various events in the plot telling a story, Rose also acts as a storyteller of her life. Departing from the naturalistic framework in operation in the rest of the play, at times she interrupts the flow of action and comments on events, directly to the audience. Griffin sees this device as instrumental in Rose's journey towards agency: 'her assumption of subject status depends on distinguishing her current self – assertive, independent, determined – from her past self – withdrawn, dependent, unassertive'; and claims that 'distinction is accomplished through the insertion of another body – that of the foetus – into her life history'.[30] Thus, for instance, Rose introduces herself and confirms her pregnancy in the opening scene, providing a context for her decision to leave her family for her boyfriend. She highlights her loneliness, the paradox of coming from a religious background where people spend all their time together without genuinely communicating with each other. Dayley conveys the lack of emotional connection between mother and daughter. Even when Rose is hoping to discuss her pregnancy with her mother, their conversation is hijacked by external figures, members of the religious community. In this respect, Dayley indicates the lack of responsibility Rose's mother assumes in this matter, effectively signing off her own agency as well, together with that of her daughter.

Unlike the representatives of white authority, Rose's family cannot contemplate abortion on religious grounds. From their point of view having the baby in unavoidable; however, they are less concerned with Rose's well-being than with their reputation. As Rose's father contends: 'De girl go weh a defile her body, she naw have no abortion [...] all life is sacred. But me noh whan notten fe do wid dat baby.'[31] In this respect, their agenda replicates that of the doctor or the social worker in denying Rose agency, and finding a solution on her behalf. Rose, however, is extremely vocal about her opinions and insists on her right to decide for herself: 'I'm not going to kill my baby, I'm not giving to any white couple who can't produce and I'm definitely not going to sign it over to the council.'[32] Like Pinnock's protagonist, Viv, Rose is also adamant 'to find herself and then to succeed on her terms. Not to feel that she has lost herself, or denied who she is, in order to fit in, or fit her mother's idea of success'.[33] Initially she also benefits from her boyfriend Leroy's support, who perceives fatherhood as a route towards achieving adult male status. For him, however, the prospect of becoming a father does not involve financial or moral responsibility, which ultimately leads to Rose opting to become a single mother.

Imminent motherhood also connotes adulthood for Rose, as she perceives this process as integral to growing up. Pregnancy equips her with a new motivation, and consequently strengthens her quest for agency: 'I now feel that I have a reason for living'.[34] As she is underage, however, she has no legal right to pursue her plans. As devised by the social worker and in agreement with her parents' wishes, Rose is eventually taken to a home for young unmarried mothers. This move seemingly undermines Rose's earlier aspirations towards independence, but it also suggests her ability to understand that she needs support to complete her education and look after her baby. Crucially, however, instead of laying the blame on black women's sexual promiscuity, Dayley points out the lack of an adequate family environment to protect young women. In other words, *Rose's Story* is part of 'a wider socio-cultural pattern which signals young women's vulnerability to sexual advances by men and resultant in pregnancies – a vulnerability that comes out of emotional rather than sexual needs'.[35] Although the play's ending does not lead to immediate access to agency as it signifies moving from parental to social authority, Rose nevertheless posits it as a fresh start and a genuine beginning to her story. Like Rose's new start in life, Dayley's play has contributed to the emerging tradition of black British women's drama and performance. Although Dayley did not carry on writing and directing, her work – present in the public domain through publication – has paved the way for subsequent generations of black women playwrights who have continued in the theatre to this day.

Back Street Mammy

Originally directed by Paulette Randall for the Temba Theatre Company at the Lyric Studio, Hammersmith (1989) – after a staged reading at the Half Moon – Cooke's *Back Street Mammy* was revived by the West Yorkshire Playhouse's Courtyard Theatre, in a season of 'contemporary' plays (1991). An actress as well as a writer for television, radio, theatre and film, Cooke has produced a body of work at the intersection of different genres and media. She wrote three plays for the stage – *Back Street Mammy, Running Dream* and *Gulp Fiction* – before taking the decision to only write for the theatre when chances for getting the work performed are relatively high. Though women's writing for the stage intensified, interest in staging this work dwindled throughout the nineties: 'The really scary thing [is] to realise that as a writer, you are dependent on individuals to make the work happen. It doesn't matter how much you write, it has no power if people don't allow it to be heard.'[36]

Back Street Mammy was a play Cooke felt she 'needed to write', in response to an offensive article about the statistics of young, single, black mothers in Birmingham: 'The figure was alarming but the section which irritated me most was the part that suggested these women had purposely gone out to get pregnant. I found the whole article racist and derogatory and I could not understand why the survey had been made in the first place.'[37] Despite being prompted by a debate involving racial bias, however, the play does not detail its protagonists' racial identity in the list of characters. As Griffin argues, names like Dynette operate as 'markers of difference' together with specific accents and culturally specific references; however, what is crucial is that 'the subject, rather than being set into a racialized frame that denies her subject status within a

Britain that has "no black in the Union Jack", is re-figured as a subject who is constitutive of the Britain depicted in the play'.[38]

On balance, the play generated a positive critical and audience response, and was hailed as 'new blood in the theatre' since Cooke looked at 'old issues through the eyes of a British-born black generation'. It was greeted as a 'surprising' play – 'poetic, tolerant and optimistic' – that rediscovered 'preoccupations that have not been fashionable in the theatre since the sixties: the guilt of sexual awakening, the oppressive burden of the older generation, the strength the child needs to fly the nest'.[39] Thus, Cooke's theatre returns to the basic issues of identity and self-expression that marked the fifties, but in the context of a changing multicultural society where these concerns are more complex.

Alongside re-figuring issues of content, Cooke also reinvented the teenage female protagonist in contemporary British women's theatre. Apart from Jo in *A Taste of Honey,* there have been hardly any landmark young female heroines in plays by post-war British women, and Cooke emphatically acknowledges the influence of Delaney's play on her work: 'It was one of the first plays that I ever saw; a touring company came and presented it at our school, and I was so inspired by it. This obviously shows in my work – I could just relate to it because it was Northern and the character felt real.'[40] Angie in *Top Girls* (1982) is not a protagonist in the conventional sense: she is a catalyst for the opposition between Marlene and Joyce, and Rosie in *My Mother Said I Never Should* (1987), while being such a figure, is not the sole heroine. In most plays by the British women playwrights I studied, the dominant female characters are, like their authors, mature women, carrying a large baggage of personal experiences.[41] Their present usually mediates between an intensely lived past and a challenging yet equally complicated future, and often they are unable to live the future as they would wish, as a result of the past.

With regard to the generation split, Cooke's play is structured along two strands. One features the teenage Dynette (aged 16) – discovering the facts of life, getting pregnant and going through a termination; and the other her mature self (aged 30 and mother of a child) – who reminisces about her termination while witnessing a childhood friend's longing for a baby. Although the two time-strands are clearly differentiated, Cooke's play conforms only partially to the norms of naturalist theatre. A number of scenes crosscut the two strands and could take place in either – subverting chronology – and she brings in a Greek-influenced chorus that reflects on events.

The mature Dynette's invocation of her aborted baby together with the teenager's prayers constitute the emotional thread of the play. In fact, the brief yet extremely powerful relationship between Dynette and her terminated baby is the most rewarding inter-personal bond she has experienced. Dynette's interactions with the chorus – acting in succession as a manifestation of social pressures, the voice of Catholic morality and a key to Dynette's own conscience and subconscious – constitute a similarly powerful though not equally intimate relationship. Starting from a naturalistic environment and a plausible protagonist, Cooke then introduces devices characteristic of presentational rather than representational theatre, thus opening up the dilemmas encountered by Dynette the individual, and granting them broader significance. By overlapping past, present and future and getting a choral voice to respond to the protagonist's concerns, the play attains symbolic dimensions, and transposes Dynette's story into the domain of the universal. This aesthetic approach indicates another feminist inheritance displayed by Cooke: in terms of an anti-naturalistic theatre language that Jellicoe helped create and which can now be taken for granted by playwrights.

Although Dynette belongs to a large family, she finds that genuine communication is almost impossible along blood links. Cooke claims that, lacking her mother's co-operation, Dynette is forced to look elsewhere in her quest for answers – to her elder sister Jan and her school friend Jackie. Jackie's outgoing nature as well as Jan's early motherhood, however, will prove misleading for Dynette who reads every statement literally. Her experimentation with casual sex is a mere reaction to what she thinks all her friends are doing and conveys her desperate attempt to act like the norm, as the chorus states: 'She wanted to know what she was missing. She wanted to know what IT was like.'[42] Despite her above-average intellect, Dynette does not establish a direct connection between the one-night stand and pregnancy. In a sense even on the terrain of sexual encounters all she really wants is knowledge, finding out what it is all about. Thus, the major goal she is after is the gathering of experience and the achievement of a certain sense of liberation resulting from cognition. In Cooke's words, all Dynette wants is 'to grow up and to be knowing'. 'It seems to her that 'everybody knows something about sex, about being grown-up and she is just innocent, and she wants to lose that innocence. By losing that innocence she unfortunately gets pregnant, and hence she is in the same situation her mum was.'[43] Thus, the temptation to discover motherhood extends her desire for cognition even further, as after having experimented with sex now she hopes to have an insight into giving birth.

By becoming a mother she also expects to be recognized as an adult. However, instead of welcoming her re-enactment of the standard fate of women in the community her mother (Maria) keeps on urging her to study:

MARIA: [...] Don't do like me.
DYNETTE: Mum I [...]
MARIA *(not letting* DYNETTE *interrupt)*: But you smart, *you* wouldn't be foolish like your modder.[44]

Cooke also investigates the limits faced by the individual female subject in decision-taking. Dynette is only granted agency when she appropriates her pregnancy (in its early stage): neither before – when getting pregnant – nor after – when being taken for an abortion – is she guiding her own actions. In other words, the teenage self of Dynette is a site for acting out the will of others, while she is denied her own voice. This denial is exercised via silence by her mother, via lack of sufficient attention by Jackie, via seeming support (yet, in fact, psychological pressure) by Jan and finally, via clinical intervention by the medical profession.

The play is permeated by an extremely lively, immediate atmosphere, echoing the authenticity of *A Taste of Honey*. Here is another Northern working-class environment, yet Cooke features a Caribbean family settled in England and confronts two generations. The older generation's vernacular is opposed to the regional accents of the younger characters, thus intersecting the strong accents of West Yorkshire and the Caribbean. Dynette also speaks in a register closer to Standard English, which is the linguistic note of the chorus. Thus, Cooke marks on yet another level the difficulties in communication between generations. The chorus acts as a 'commentary to underline Dynette's adolescent awakening as, in the context of a Catholic upbringing, she is torn between her conflicting desires and the opinions of friends and family'.[45]

The second strand features Dynette at age 30, having fulfilled her professional ambition, married and the mother of a one-year-old child. This self displays a range of post-feminist reminiscences, although Cooke does not find such a label helpful. She emphasizes that she is a black woman writer, which for her 'suggests from its very nature being a feminist writer'.[46] As for her kind of theatre, she is uninterested in definitions such as 'feminist theatre'. Her major preoccupation is in storytelling and in character portrayal, often achieved as a result of observation and personal experience. Ironically, it was Jackie whom Dynette tried to imitate as an adolescent; in the second strand it is Jackie who craves Dynette's maternal happiness. But while in the teenage section Dynette chased a fake ideal, Jackie's longing is rooted in the irreversibility of time: 'We're thirty Dynette! Thirty!' 'I can't wait any more!' [...] 'I want a baby!' 'I want a kid now!'[47] Although Cooke thus calls attention to women's desire for parenthood in various contexts of external denial, she only follows in detail Dynette's trajectory. She deliberately leaves Jackie's path open-ended, suggesting the possibility of motherhood later in life, but also the subsequent loss of interest in this obsession. What is ultimately crucial, according to Cooke, is coming to terms with one's decision, and she illustrates the importance of this fact with another flashback to Dynette's teenage pregnancy and termination.

In fact, it is the mature Dynette's prayer addressed to her 'little God' – her aborted baby – that evokes events that happened in the past. Through storytelling provided by the chorus, Cooke details the intensity of Dynette's repentance after her sexual encounter. Cooke also adapts a popular rhyme – previously utilized by the WTG and Keatley – to convey Dynette's sense of guilt and to transmit the power of surveillance of one generation above another. This rhyme also complements the presence of song – and rap, in the original production – and choral elements, emphasizing a ritualistic dimension. Cooke follows the heightened emotional intensity of Dynette's rite of passage that reaches its climax in the moment of abortion and complete loss of illusions. In fact, it is not the termination as such but Dynette's coming to terms with its moral acceptability that transforms her. Having realized that she cannot achieve the peace of mind she was hoping for (via knowledge and passage into adulthood), she acknowledges the need to reorganize her priorities and claim another right of agency. However, to do so she and the play must revisit and re-evaluate her multiple cultural belonging, which has both shaped and inhibited her life. In other words, the complex network of her roots – as a Northern, working-class, second generation West Indian and especially Catholic woman – requires an urgent re-negotiation of her position. As she puts it herself, she is 'changing' – first in a physical and then a spiritual sense – and realizes that she has found a new governing principle, her own access to intervention.

Thus, it is agency and choice that will ultimately grant her knowledge and passage to adulthood. The fact that she eventually achieves a career and is able to give birth, at a moment when she is prepared for motherhood, only reinforces the adequacy of this new regime. In Dynette's words, she has only 'postponed' the baby's birth, since throughout the entire period between the termination and the birth of her actual child she has found refuge in the special bond with her aborted baby. Cooke clarifies what Kate Harwood called the strong moral complexity of the text:

> To her the baby, herself and God are all one, but she is also able to separate them. It is a thought process that she goes through that helps her to forgive herself in a way. She knows that she has done wrong, but this is the only way she can live with that, by saying that she has just postponed, rather than killed, anything.[48]

Although Dynette has the strength to prioritize one option above others, she needs to justify this option to the inquisitive chorus:

> CHORUS (2 and 3): So you think you have the right?
> DYNETTE: To determine my own life, yes.
> CHORUS (All): You are forgetting the life of the baby.
> DYNETTE: There is no baby.
> CHORUS 3: The 'baby' will always be there. You will always be a back street mammy. A mother without a child. An orphan mother...
> DYNETTE: I thought I had a choice.
> CHORUS 3 (All): You have a choice. What is your decision?[49]

This passage of intense question-and-answer exchanges is clearly influenced by Greek theatre, while also establishing a parallel with Roman Catholic rituals. The analogy with a non-European tradition is also crucial: 'It is similar with African theatre, as well. It gives more strength. I thought that the chorus in *Back Street Mammy* acted as Dynette's conscience, [...], she cannot get away from it, she cannot do anything in private. It is guilt, and using the chorus was a good way of getting that across.'[50] Cooke also juxtaposes the ideas of abortion as an ultimate form of transgression in terms of Catholic morality and of confession as a route towards forgiveness and regained innocence. Ultimately, the acknowledgement of choice prevails, leads to an acceptance of past events and institutes termination as a mere fact of life: 'My body. My life. There was never a child involved. I had an abortion'.[51]

Conclusion

Spanning the seventies and eighties, the plays united in this chapter address the question of agency associated with pregnancy and the prospect of underage motherhood. The plays bring together different approaches in theatre making, and include a feminist theatre company based on collaboration (WTG) and several playwrights working either independently (Sharman MacDonald, Grace Dayley) or as a result of artistic commission (Trish Cooke). In fact, the works under discussion here are first plays for both Dayley and MacDonald, but while MacDonald has continued to produce other commercially successful plays, Dayley has withdrawn from the theatre world despite critical interest in her debut. Cooke has also discontinued writing plays, working instead in other media and as an actress, while the WTG, regularly threatened by lack of funding throughout its activity, re-emerged under the name Sphinx in 1991 and is still in operation in 2006, albeit following a different artistic platform. This state of affairs is far from arbitrary and reflects the challenges of long-term survival for women playwrights and performers in British theatre. Owing to precarious funding and the difficulties of having work accepted by theatre managements, even formerly successful authors may choose to re-orientate themselves, either to other media or to theatre work that potentially appeals to broader audiences.

The WTG had devised *My Mother Says I Never Should* to make a clear point about sexual education, and illustrates the best tradition of didactic theatre. It has deliberately targeted a teenage audience and performed the play in venues familiar to this particular segment of the population. Dayley's *Rose's Story* also circulated in a non-conventional theatre space, a university venue, but this decision was a result of the reluctance of theatre companies to take the play on board rather than the playwright's artistic or political preference. Dayley did not explicitly aim to practice didactic theatre; however, her lack of experience and youth have replicated the rawness and immediacy of agitprop. Though wishing to situate her work in a tradition of black theatre, Dayley's play emerged without the supportive context of a dedicated theatre scene or company. Her play, however, through publication, has become one of the earliest records of black British women's theatre surveyed in this study, and in this sense is integral to an emerging canon. Cooke, writing just a few years later, for instance, had the chance to collaborate with both the black women's and socialist theatre scene in Britain, and thus reached out to these scenes' regular audiences. Through the revival of *Back Street Mammy* at a major regional theatre, she also accessed mainstream venues, bringing her contribution to black women's theatre to the centre of attention. MacDonald's plays have been staged in mainstream theatres from the beginning of her career, although she also favoured fringe venues, in England as well as Scotland. Consequently, her work had the potential of reaching out to a truly heterogenous audience; however, the white middle-class bias of her plays, as well as their lack of overt political engagement, have more than certainly homogenized this variety.

In terms of style, the plays range from linear storylines to attempts at subverting chronology. Via the replication of real life in *My Mother Says I Never Should* and *Rose's Story*, the WTG and Dayley wish to respond to existing topical issues for their target community, and write from a passionate political platform. But while the WTG produced their piece as a result of collaboration, Dayley wrote mainly independently, and while *My Mother Says I Never Should* had been briefly integrated into the school curriculum, *Rose's Story* existed at the margins of the theatre scene and received only a limited run. MacDonald in *When I Was a Girl, I Used to Scream and Shout...* and Cooke in *Back Street Mammy* experiment with cyclical timeframes and include flashbacks to the past, thus juxtaposing their characters in the theatrical present with alter egos. In both cases, the identities of the protagonists have changed considerably over time, together with their perception on motherhood and their own relationships with their respective mothers. MacDonald and Cooke alike situate their young protagonists in the context of a defining friendship, and both revisit this friendship decades later. There is a contrast between the protagonist's and the friend's experience in both works, in the present as well as in the past, but while MacDonald addresses deliberate opposition, Cooke considers replication, and hence the perpetuation of female experience not only across biological but also alternative lines of succession.

Despite reflecting different positions as far as social class and race is concerned, the WTG, MacDonald, Dayley and Cooke locate the agency of their adolescent subjects centre stage. Teenage sexuality and pregnancy connote empowerment, and a route towards adulthood in all cases. Thus, in spite of generally replicating the fate of their forerunners, the various protagonists see their first sexual experience followed by pregnancy as a defining stage in reaching independence. In opposition to this view, the respective plays discussed situate alternatives on behalf of adult society: the WTG calls attention to responsible sexual behaviour, while MacDonald, Dayley and Cooke concentrate on generally negative parental attitudes. In all instances, it is adult control over teenage sexuality that is in focus, together with attempts at depriving adolescents of their newly claimed agency. As MacDonald's and Cooke's protagonists reflect on their teenage past from the vantage point of their present adult selves, adoption and abortion emerge as emblematic for external interference, not only as forms of actual intervention but also of psychological intrusion, with long-term traumatic effects.

5
Maternal Desire Against the Odds

In parallel with social and legal changes, as detailed earlier, the period between the mid-seventies to the mid-nineties is also emblematic of subsequent strands in feminism. Michelene Wandor writes from the perspective of seventies socialist feminism, Sarah Daniels embraces radical feminism in the eighties, Jackie Kay addresses the relationship between identity and equality in society, whereas Claire Luckham and Timberlake Wertenbaker comment on the problems of ideological affiliation in the nineties. Despite their different cultural and political locations, however, these playwrights share a preoccupation with women's choices with regard to maternity, and highlight the emotional, sexual, medical and political importance of this issue. The playwrights also investigate agency embodied in the desire for parenthood and the ways this agency is temporarily handed over to others – members of the medical or legal profession, friends or the family.

The plays examined cover two major clusters in terms of subject matter: on the one hand, they look at the possibilities of non-heterosexual parenting, and on the other hand, they analyse the options available for those unable to conceive or gestate spontaneously. Legal and societal resistance to lesbian parenthood is mainly discussed in the seventies and eighties, while reproductive technologies, ageing, reduced fertility and adoption feature predominantly in plays of the eighties and nineties. Thus, Daniels and Wertenbaker critique the male control of assisted reproductive technologies in *Byrthrite* (1986) and *The Break of Day* (1995), Luckham concentrates on a medical climate hostile towards imperfection in *The Choice* (1992), Kay and Wertenbaker address inter-racial and cross-continental adoptions in *The Adoption Papers* (1991) and *The Break of Day*, and Daniels and Wandor celebrate lesbian motherhood in *Neaptide* (1980) and, respectively, *Care and Control* (1975) and *AID Thy Neighbour* (1978).

110

The issue of who is in control of birth has become a central component of the debate on parenthood since the advent of artificial reproductive technologies. Britain has been at the forefront of such research since the late sixties and early seventies, and was 'responsible' for the world's first test-tube baby, Louise Brown, born in 1978. The success was engineered by Robert Edwards and Patrick Steptoe using in vitro fertilization (IVF), although the Browns were not aware of the fact that they were involved in the experimentation of a new area in science.[1] Following this case, further developments such as research on surplus human embryos or the implantation of eggs from one woman to another were achieved. British genetic engineering became particularly widely known after another scientist, Robert Winston, participated in a lengthy public debate over the merits of artificial reproduction with the Conservative MP Enoch Powell.

A fervent opponent of reproductive technologies, Powell attempted to ban all experiments, being motivated by what he termed the failure of the decisions reached by the Warnock Committee (1984). This committee examined the ethics in alternative ways of parenting, including IVF, adoption and surrogate parenting, and after prolonged consultations with experts, patients and parents-to-be published its decisions.[2] A clear aim of the Warnock Report was the preservation of the traditional family pattern; surrogate parenting (especially in commercial circumstances) was outlawed and artificial insemination or IVF were only authorized for heterosexual couples. Lesbian or gay parenting continued to be regarded as unacceptable, and could not be supported by institutions affiliated to the NHS.[3] From the perspective of scientific research, however, the Warnock Report agreed to a compromise, allowing experiments on embryos until they reach 14 days of development.[4] Later research shifted the focus from offering wider chances for birth to monitoring the 'quality' of newly born babies. In the United Kingdom, no definite ethical or legal measures have yet been taken with regard to the technologization of reproduction, despite repeated attempts. Following the success of animal cloning, research has turned towards the possibilities of applying this technique to humans. Owing to the strong ethical taboo and regulation by the Human Fertilisation and Embryology Authority (HFEA) and the Human Genetics Advisory Commission (HGAC), to date only cloning for medical purposes, such as treatment for Parkinson's and Alzheimer's diseases, has been authorized.

January 2000 saw the lifting of the ban on freezing and storing eggs. As a result of this procedure women can potentially delay motherhood for decades, not being rushed by the age-related decrease in fertility.

Fertilizing previously harvested eggs appears especially advantageous in the case of women suffering from illnesses like cancer, as thus they can have the opportunity to mother their genetically related children, though it may also help career women to delay starting a family. The early twenty-first century has witnessed several attempts at both options, and while the ethical debate is ongoing, scientific arguments favour such procedures. Also at the turn of the millennium, the previously controversial 'stem cell research' was given a green light (Human Tissue Act, 2004). According to this technique, cells can be removed from either embryos up to 14 days old or from the placenta of newly born babies, and used in the regeneration of diseased tissue. Although the technique has been used successfully, the moral taboo against the so-called designer babies continues to be extremely strong. While certain scientists plead for growing embryos outside the womb, testing that they do not carry genes for disease, the HFEA and public opinion, including the disabled community, is sceptical about women's routine screening for genetic disorders. The debate has also focused on reproductive tourism, whereby infertile women, generally from the affluent West, travel to countries with relatively relaxed legislations to acquire eggs from women in financially precarious situation. Replicating patterns in sex tourism, the burgeoning globalized fertility travel signals that the issue of economics in reproduction has slipped out of control, and harks back to the surrogacy scandals of the eighties, also marking the onset of another colonial practice that further reinforces hierarchies that disadvantage women. This phenomenon also underlines the fact that science is running ahead of the bioethical framework, as neither the use of eggs nor of sperm for reproduction outside the body has yet been adequately regulated.[5]

This emerging discipline of bioethics has not been sufficiently theorized either, although feminist scholarship has concentrated extensively on established facets of reproductive technologies. Major categories, such as the control of fertility through contraception or termination, technologies utilized in childbirth, technologies aimed at monitoring the health of the foetus and technologies that assist conception have been established; and while all aspects have generated extensive scrutiny, it is the issue of overcoming infertility that has most contrasted liberal and radical feminists.[6] The former have viewed science as a progressive medium that offers choice and autonomy alongside the possibility to extend parenthood beyond biological obstacles, while the latter have seen technology as a source of danger, enabling scientists to manipulate life itself. The pressure to not be childless, according to radical feminists, is rooted in the patriarchal association between barrenness and failure. It is this construction that, in the popular imagination, locates infertility as a social stigma and leads to emotional despair. Also, despite numerous cases of male infertility, the condition is predominantly perceived as a female problem that requires intervention. Radical feminists also protest against the fact that men dictate reproductive decisions despite women wanting fewer children than their partners, and consequently, against the mobilization of women's gestational abilities for patriarchal ends. A representative of one of the most vocal pressure groups – FINRRAGE (Feminist International Network of Resistance to Reproductive and Genetic Engineering) – declared that reproductive technology was a violation of 'human rights', while another view stated that all research was carried out at the expense of women.[7] Gena Corea argued that the rise of genetic engineering was rooted in man's obsession with creating a human being by himself – another reason for the linguistic invisibility of women, as scientific discourse seldom includes references to 'women' or 'mothers', focusing instead on 'parents', 'the couple' or 'the egg-donor'. She equally emphasized the medical profession's aspiration to reduce women to their reproductive parts, and protested against the relative availability of egg donors and surrogates, whom she labelled as 'reproductive prostitutes'.[8]

Other theoretical debates intersected with ethnographic accounts as well as investigations into philosophy, the arts and sociology. Ann Dally, for instance, emphasized the self-fulfilment inherent in mothering.[9] She also saw it as a maturing experience, an ambition that marked genuine adulthood. Sara Ruddick aimed her principle of 'maternal thinking' at the establishment of a utopian harmony, and associated childbirth with a potential for hope. She described mothers as peacemakers, and stressed their suspicion of violence and willingness for reconciliation. Mothers' work had the potential to create what she termed 'women's politics of resistance', inspired by the act and symbolism of birth as well as the responsibility for care. As for future gender relations, Ruddick made a commitment concerning the involvement of male partners: 'There will be mothers of both sexes who live out a transformed maternal thought in communities that share parental care – practically, emotionally, economically and socially.'[10]

Tuula Gordon claimed that it was not equality that should be sought, but rather one should wish for a society where 'the experience of having children could be a pleasure to all parents, male and female'.[11] As far as the sexual division of labour in parenting is concerned, conditions have not changed in a decisive manner since the debate was started in the early seventies. Most feminists have emphasized that as long as childcare is women's responsibility, women's position will be of subordination in society. In Joyce Trebilcot's words, a strategy for feminist activists should be to work at the institutional level and restructure childcare, so that this would not any longer be 'the primary responsibility of mothers and their female relatives'.[12] It is especially younger feminists who have favoured such an alternative, connecting it to a broader-scale negotiation of women's claims in relation to men: 'A new feminism is needed that sees the possibility of rapprochement between the sexes.'[13] Opening up the possibility of parenthood for everyone, though, needs to include the constant monitoring of any potential child abuse and harassment.

Writing in 1985, the radical lesbian feminist bell hooks voiced her ambivalent response to the resurgence of interest in motherhood.[14] She acknowledged the need for researching female parenthood, yet she warned against the romanticizing tendencies of the so-called motherist movement. Terms that came up in the course of the eighties on this special, nurturing quality of women included 'caring ethic', 'contextual thinking' and the idea of the 'different voice' initiated by Carol Gilligan.[15] According to maternal or cultural feminists, motherhood was the supreme route towards a woman's emotional fulfilment, whereas childless women were not only selfish but also failed with regard to femininity.[16] 'Maternal revivalism', in Lynne Segal's view, emerged as part of a process of withdrawal from public struggles where women did not achieve sufficient satisfaction.[17] Segal, in fact, offered a critique of the tendency to ignore motherhood, and located maternity as a source of power and pleasure. Sheila Kitzinger took it for granted that women would want to give birth and then dedicate time to nurture. She was one of the first British writers to offer an ethnographic analysis of motherhood, and her observation preceded an entire literature on the objectification of women by the medical profession:

> Grateful as most women are for all this care and awed by the advanced technology, it is not difficult to understand how a women can feel that she is merely a container for a foetus, [...] that her body is an inconvenient barrier to easy access [...] that if she were not around the pregnancy could progress with more efficiency.[18]

Negotiating motherhood and careers, however, led to a double-load for many women, resulting in exhaustion and frustration. Erica Jong highlighted this internal backlash, contending that by having attempted to be successful on all terrains women 'have won the right to be terminally exhausted'.[19] Natasha Walter, on the other hand, rejected giving up anything that a woman considered important for her self, career or family, claiming in 1998 that professional women should not have to pay an extreme price in terms of their careers to have children. As opposed to this tendency, older feminists and social scientists conveyed a different picture. According to LSE researcher Catherine Hakim two-thirds of women wanted to be homemakers. Hakim, in fact, established polar opposites between the model of the 'homemaker' and the 'career woman'; the former perceiving 'wage work as an *extension* of her homemaking role, not an *alternative* to it', and the latter seeking gratification through paid work and 'competing on the same terms as men'.[20] Margaret O'Brien observed that children of full-time working mothers were doing less well at school than those of women working part-time, and Sheila Kitzinger warned of the problems women might experience when getting back to work too early after childbirth. A way out, according to Melissa Benn, would be to remind everyone of the need to take a responsible attitude to parenthood: 'Feminism must not, along with government, forget that bringing up children is a form of work; neither motherhood nor fatherhood should need so much justification beyond itself.'[21]

At a time when most second-wave feminists revisit their positions and when many younger feminists voice a belief in post-feminism or the joys of housewifery, there is still a long way to go until consensus is reached. Post-feminism, in fact, parallels some of the claims formulated by backlash theories, and shares its preoccupation with highlighting the failure of feminism to amend women's social position, together with the claims that feminism has not represented women of all social classes, that feminism is a language of victimization, and that feminism neglects the personal and social significance of the family.[22] A number of writers and theorists born in the late sixties – such as the American Naomi Wolf, Rene Denfeld, Katie Roiphe or the British Natasha Walter – consider that feminism needs to acknowledge more the considerable gains it has already made. Advocating a liberal agenda centred on the individual rather than the community, they claim that women are no longer facing genuine discrimination, and since feminism now operates from within the power structures, it should interfere less with women's private lives.

When interpreted as a successor – rather than opponent – of second-wave feminism, however, post-feminism represents theoretical diversity and encapsulates a range of political and philosophical stances. As Ann Brooks contended, by the mid-nineties post-feminism had turned into a 'conceptual frame of reference encompassing the intersection of feminism with a number of other anti-foundationalist movements', including post-modernism, post-structuralism and post-colonialism.[23] This understanding of post-feminism has emerged as a result of the multiple trends that developed within feminist discourse and the intersection of these approaches with other disciplines, and includes an aim to destabilize fixed definitions of gender and sexuality, and to deconstruct authoritative practices and paradigms. Responding to both internal and external critiques of feminism, post-feminism represents a phase of maturity in the development of feminist consciousness, as 'it is able to subject its own premises to an ironical, skeptical and critical mode of analysis'.[24] Following the intense research on mothering and motherhood in the seventies, neither feminist scholarship nor governmental institutions have since granted sufficient attention to the practical details of this matter: 'It seems a pity that [feminism] still is not able to be a political voice that reflects the experience of motherhood, motherhood as both the affirmation of, and one crucial metaphor for, all that really matters for life!'[25] In such a situation the contribution of women playwrights has become especially important. Though theatre may not engineer overnight change, it reflects ongoing and anticipates forthcoming phenomena. As there is no overarching feminist standpoint, there is no ultimate artistic direction; on both terrains there are mutations and diversity: emblematic of multiplicity and continuous transformation.

Making a claim for lesbian motherhood

Care and Control

Michelene Wandor utilized *Care and Control* and *AID Thy Neighbour* to examine the biological, political and social complexities of lesbian motherhood on the one hand, and surrogate parenting on the other, and stressed the necessity for an explicit and immediately effective theatre. For her, feminist and socialist interventions should be intertwined to transmit a clear political message, and she stressed that the political analysis was 'absolutely essential' in understanding 'what writers have been doing in the 1970s and 1980s'.[26] Wandor's career is unique in the context of playwrights examined in this study, owing to her active role in the Women's Liberation Movement: 'I can't separate the way I try to look at things from the way I write, so I'd say I'm conscious of trying to incorporate a feminist way of looking at things in my work.'[27] Janelle Reinelt claimed that it was Wandor – more than any other single person – who helped to elucidate the relationship between theatre and the

Women's Movement in Britain,[28] and posited Wandor's career as a 'prototype' for the experiences of women who started in British theatre during the sixties. Reinelt singled out Wandor's middle-class, university background and socialist affiliations, but also her successful combination of career and parenthood, while Wandor reflected on the period in the following way:

> The general raising of the political temperature meant that all playwrights, even those who did not see themselves as 'political' or who tried to keep their distance from various political ideologies, were influenced by the public nature of the political debates and the visibility of political activism – socialist and feminist – at the end of the 1960s and the first part of the 1970s.[29]

Care and Control was scripted by Wandor for Gay Sweatshop, and was based on ideas researched and devised collaboratively by the company. In fact, Wandor was emphatic about her not being the 'author' of the play, and noted that her scripting it should be differentiated from 'writing'.[30] The play, directed by Kate Crutchley, was first performed at the Drill Hall in London in May 1977, subsequently recast for the Edinburgh Festival the same year. Women's personal experiences were at the root of the play; it integrated personal testimonies and was regularly juxtaposed with audience feedback in post-performance discussions. As Crutchley and Nancy Diuguid, one of the original performers and researchers, contended: '*Care and Control* is based on the experiences of lesbian mothers in their fight for custody for their children. The situations in the play are taken from life and have been adapted to preserve the anonymity of women who are still struggling in the court.'[31] This statement also sums up a number of key factors regarding Gay Sweatshop as a political company interested in addressing differing points of view, including the fact that a writer like Wandor was able to participate in the company's work without declaring an allegiance to lesbianism on a personal level.

The play was a response to audience suggestion in the wake of Gay Sweatshop's first women's show, Jill Posener's *Any Woman Can*, and constitutes 'the first feminist play requested by a specific audience'.[32] It was, therefore, an issue-based piece, presented in an agitprop-meets-social-realist style, and was well received by audiences who identified with its subject matter. Divided into two parts, the play juxtaposes a range of different living situations encountered by women in Act One, and a collage of court custody cases in Act Two. It brings together lesbian and heterosexual women in addressing common concerns: women seeking independence from men and the role of economics in establishing social status. Thus, for instance, heterosexual women wishing to have children outside marriage are presented as facing prejudices similar to those faced by lesbian couples, and financial status is shown as a key factor in being able to start and/or maintain a family. Throughout the play the voice of authority – moral and legal – is punctuated in opposition to the protagonists' perspectives, thus establishing a contrast between mainstream views and those of the avant-garde in sexual politics.

The play also addresses mainstream society's reservation at the time to integrate lesbianism, despite being first produced ten years after the Sexual Offences Act was amended. In a court scene, for instance, Carol is confronted by the judge on account of her sexuality, and is told that by adopting a 'homosexual way of life' she was 'flying in the face of what took place in the marriage ceremony'.[33] The representative of authority refuses to take any note of observations regarding the fallibility of marriage as an institution, and exclusively lays the blame on women for its failure. One husband, Gerald, locates his wife Elizabeth's affiliation with the Women's Liberation Movement as the cause of their marriage problems, and later sparks off a custody battle to prevent his son sharing a house with what he calls 'two bent women' 'living in a female brothel'.[34] Apart from proving his wife an unfit mother on sexual grounds, he obtains custody of their child on account of his impending new marriage and hence the ability to offer a financially secure and morally safe home.

Even where the lesbian couple succeeds in winning custody, lesbianism is only tolerated if silenced and kept invisible from children and society at large. This successful verdict, however, is also significantly qualified by the issuing authority, and reiterates hierarchies in economics and social status: unlike Gerald, the father in this case is in a financially inadequate position and is still single; in other words unable to provide a surrogate mother for the child. In this situation, the court decided to disregard the mother's lesbianism, claiming that it did not affect their judgement on the custody. It would be an oversight, therefore, to interpret this decision as an indicator of a sudden exercise of liberalism; it was simply a situation where the father 'could not offer physically adequate care which could replace that of the natural mother'.[35]

In other words, this decision perpetuates the age-old status quo as far as the gender division in parenthood is concerned. It inscribes childcare into women's realm, whether substantiated by biological links or not, and in fact, it is the pioneering of surrogate bonds on par with direct bloodlines that constitutes the truly cutting-edge aspect of the play. As one of the protagonists contends, there is still a long way to go until motherhood and fatherhood achieve equal status: 'I'll believe society takes fatherhood seriously when the Gents in the motorway services has a babies' changing room, just like the Ladies has.'[36] The play does not speculate on men's parental inclinations, but features previous partners of the women protagonists, who insist on their paternal rights only to prevent the women from taking control of the children. As the voice of authority in one of the off-the-record scenes admits, 'Sexual choice doesn't necessarily have anything to do with whether one wants to be a parent, or whether one is a good mother,'[37] thus linking twin concerns of feminist and gay movement agendas. Raising public awareness about women's right to exercise their maternal function irrespective of sexual orientation was a major necessity in 1977, and though it has since been removed from media scrutiny, it deserves due recognition.

AID Thy Neighbour

AID Thy Neighbour also interrogates radical issues on the seventies agenda. The play was part of a mini-season centred on feminist and lesbian issues, initiated by the Women's Project Group and directed by Kate Crutchley at the Theatre at New End in London in 1977. As in other Wandor plays, there is an exploration of the relationship between the personal and the political, presenting a strong case for the audience to associate with. The play was 'the first feminist play about Artificial Insemination by Donor (AID)',[38] and Jill Davies included it in the 'issue based' (as opposed to the 'coming out') lesbian canon, alongside *Care and Control* and Sarah Daniels's *Neaptide*.[39] Like *Care and Control*, *AID Thy Neighbour* is aimed at consciousness-raising and responded to a cultural context: the reactionary condemnation of lesbian motherhood and artificial insemination in the tabloid press of the time.

AID Thy Neighbour combines elements of agitprop and social realism with the tradition of the English comedy, but it was the play's content and not its relatively conventional form that contributed to its première at a small fringe venue and not in a mainstream space. For Wandor, however, it was important that audiences should be able to concentrate on the message of the play, and to facilitate that she preserved a familiar form. In a sense, therefore, the play demonstrates the possibility of renewal within a traditional framework: while the comic devices offer the audience an entertaining night out, the political message challenges potentially biased views on sexual politics. However, the play did not achieve commercial success and had a fairly short stage-life, without transferring. It did not receive significant critical attention either, a fact that Wandor attributed at the time to its subject matter and political attitude: 'There's still enormous resistance to anything with overt feminist consciousness, let alone a lesbian feminist one.'[40] Looking back on the play, however, it was the dissociation of parental desire from sexuality that she emphasized: 'The whole idea about who you expect to have maternal instinct or desire for children does not necessarily fall into predictable patterns.'[41]

Symmetrical in structure, the play is centred on a heterosexual and a lesbian couple, both desiring a baby, who experience emotions that do not observe conventional gender stereotypes. Most of the references to the couples in *AID Thy Neighbour* are given in tandem, building up a parallel between the lives of Sandy and Georgina, and Mary and Joseph. For instance, Scene One starts by locating a member of each couple in the relevant section of a semi-detached house separated by a dividing wall, while the play blacks out on the information that the wall will be demolished, as the characters have decided to live communally.[42] Mary is portrayed in domestic terms, wearing an apron and making preparations for dinner, while Georgina as having feminist inclinations: she is reading Adrienne Rich's *Of Woman Born*. Wandor opposes Sandy's feminine look (in a neat dress) to Joseph's stereotypical male image (he carries a briefcase and a bottle of wine); as soon as they start singing, however, she subverts the associations they transmit by their physical appearance. By inverting the male and female roles within the song and appropriating the text designed for the opposite gender, they both reveal tendencies for experimentation with identity that is explored further.

Wandor accentuates the similarities between the couples' day-to-day routines, thus undermining the assumed supremacy of the nuclear family above alternative family arrangements. In both cases the employee is the centre of attention and ignores the unpaid work of the stay-at-home partner. For Sandy career is crucial, yet despite her openly gay private life she conceals her sexual orientation in public – a fact emphasized by her distinctive dress code according to the work/home dichotomy. Sandy admits that she has no desire to give birth ('God, I wouldn't [...] want to have a baby myself. I'd feel I was being invaded'),[43] though she is willing to share the experience as Georgina's partner. Following a miscarriage, they contemplate adoption, but eventually they settle for artificial insemination by donor (the acronym of which is encoded in the play's title). Thus Georgina is granted the opportunity to live out the desired experience of giving birth, while the anonymity of the father prevents Sandy from feelings of exclusion.

While having a baby for the lesbian couple is complicated by societal resistance, for Mary and Joseph it is made difficult by physiological malfunctions, and both trigger interactions with fertility experts. Unlike Wertenbaker's and Luckham's later plays, where the physical space of the clinic amplifies the alienation, Wandor locates the couples' encounters with the medical profession in their own homes, and instead of featuring a patronizing male consultant, Wandor's is a sympathetic female specialist. She recommends the use of reproductive technology for both couples, and thus, for Sandy and Georgina the next challenge is the legal status of parenting, for Joseph it is his exclusion from the process of creation. Aiming at the legitimization of lesbian motherhood, Wandor presents Georgina's conception as unproblematic, versus the heterosexual Mary's medical complications and eventual failure. Thus, Wandor suggests that neither the desire for a child, nor the ability to conceive are matters to be taken for granted or to be associated exclusively with the traditional nuclear family. Her rhetorical question – 'Isn't science wonderful?'[44] – welcomes medically assisted reproduction as a means of contributing to parental fulfilment, beyond the boundaries of sexual identity and fertility. Wandor's celebratory approach gains extra importance in the light of Britain's first IVF baby, born in 1978. Writing at the dawn of a new era in the politics of reproduction, the issues of power and manipulation had not yet become as central to the debate for Wandor as for the playwrights of the nineties. Beside her celebratory tone, however, Wandor stresses the social expectations of the era in relation to motherhood. Georgina's interview with the nurse elicits prejudice, ranging from opprobrium towards unmarried mothers ('NURSE: Here at the ante-natal clinic we call all the Mums "Mrs". Saves the embarrassment all round') and control over their reproductive capacities ('NURSE: Go and see the social worker. / GEORGINA: Social worker?/ NURSE: To discuss having it adopted') to ageism (NURSE: Age? / GEORGINA: Thirty-three. / NURSE: Oh, dear').[45]

In parallel with recording Georgina and Sandy's parental achievement, Wandor makes a final attempt at easing the way for Mary and Joseph via their replication of an archetypal parental arrangement. As they bear the names of the biblical couple providing a family for Jesus, Wandor's heterosexual couple is connected not only to the Holy Family but also – in Julia Kristeva's terms – to the first artificial family. Mary finds herself located on par with the Virgin Mary, the most famous surrogate mother;[46] and in both cases pregnancy is dissociated from the 'natural' – including the sexual and the biological – and conception is linked to the spiritual (in the case of the Virgin Mary) or the medical (via assisted reproductive technologies, in the case of Wandor's Mary). As opposed to Georgina, however, Wandor's Mary not only keeps failing to conceive but gradually loses interest in motherhood altogether, emerging as neither a biological nor a surrogate mother. Consequently, Wandor revisits both a key canonical text and Kristeva's feminist interpretation, making a case for the legitimacy of individual choices, either for or against reproduction, irrespective of sexual orientation or fertility.

AID Thy Neighbour offers a celebratory support to lesbian and surrogate parenting. Unlike the sheer submission to the patterns of female biology (as in Delaney's work), Wandor starts off from a premise of longing and investigates instances of self-conscious intervention to circumvent physiological impediments and societal resistance. While *A Taste of Honey* connected male caring with homosexuality, Wandor presents a married man who longs to be a father as deprived of his paternal potential by a wife who does not have a 'vocation' for children. Wandor's political message is intertwined with comic moments, as she over-amplifies stereotypes conventionally associated with lesbian behaviour. Wandor makes fun of the familiarity of the stereotypes but also of the audience's predictable reactions to them. In this manner she calls attention to the negative constraint of stereotyping while simultaneously re-appropriating it for feminist purposes.

Neaptide

Sarah Daniels also turned to the subject of lesbian custody rights; however, instead of producing her play at a fringe venue, she wrote *Neaptide* for the National Theatre. It premièred on 26 June 1986 at the Cottesloe Theatre, directed by John Burgess, having won the George Devine Award in 1982. The play was Daniels's first work for the National and the second piece by a woman ever to be presented there, and the commission reflected her reputation, in the wake of *Masterpieces,* as a major new voice in British theatre. Daniels has also often been perceived as the face of radical feminism in the theatre. She claimed, however, in her introduction to her collected plays published in 1991 that she 'didn't set out to be a "Feminist Playwright"'.[47] Daniels acknowledges having been a feminist when she started writing, but she has also felt the need to call attention to the shifts in perception regarding feminism. Through such a presentation of her politics, Daniels maps out a different itinerary than Wandor, who has publicized her intention to explicitly address socialism and feminism in her work. As Lizbeth Goodman argues, Daniels makes a distinction between being qualified as a 'feminist playwright' and being a playwright who is feminist; in other words, between 'the intent' and 'the interpretation or political valuing' of her work.[48]

In her recent reservation to declare her political intentions, Daniels points to the constraining effect of labels, and points to the nineties trend in political distantiation. In the mid-nineties Daniels defined feminism as the 'awareness that we live in a patriarchal society, with a desire to challenge and hopefully change it', and formulated her idea of feminist theatre in the following way: 'A feminist play is something that isn't just about women, but challenges something to do with patriarchal society, or that actually pushes it one step further and challenges the status quo.'[49] Thus, she insists on opening up her sphere of examination to protect herself from being relegated to a thematic ghetto, and relocates her concern to challenging institutions of male authority over women. As Daniels points out, her plays are 'not about hating men' they are 'about putting the focus on women'.[50]

Despite Daniels's caution concerning the acknowledgement of her feminism, in the eighties she did make political statements. She went on record claiming not to wish to work with male directors (she revised this view since and has worked with several, including John Burgess on *Neaptide*), or insisting that theatres in receipt of public subsidies 'have an obligation to produce work which reflects a cross-section of themes about different experiences in society'.[51] She also revealed the pressures she felt when addressing lesbian motherhood, conscious of the fact that she was writing on behalf of so many women:

> Claire suffers slightly from [...] authorial self-censorship. For, like Radclyffe Hall, *vis-à-vis* her heroine in *The Well of Loneliness*, I was so aware of the prejudice which exists against lesbians that I made Claire a bit too good and/or 'right on' to be true. I was determined not to provide anyone with an excuse for thinking 'Perhaps her ex-husband should have got custody anyway.'[52]

In Mary Brewer's view, Daniels's approach is hardly surprising 'when one considers that her task is to challenge feminist mis-representations of mothering as much as men's'.[53] After all, Daniels's aim was to raise the profile of lesbian parenthood, not in the least by associating herself with one of the most emblematic figures of the British lesbian literary scene. Unlike Hall, with whom she shares the desire to portray lesbians as morally impeccable, Daniels chose not to perpetuate the sense of doom associated with Stephen Gordon but to allow for a celebratory ending that locates lesbianism as a successful route in life.

Neaptide is set in 1983, in a London suburb. It features two parallel strands focusing on the lesbian Claire and the heterosexual Val. They are sisters and daughters of Joyce, but while Val suffers from severe depression, Claire is a high achiever and has a satisfying private life until she gets involved in a custody battle. As in *Care and Control*, the husband has remarried and argues that a heterosexual family is a more suitable background for a child than a lesbian relationship, even if it is kept under cover. Claire is a closet lesbian, initially intending to change the system from within, and whose coming out only takes place halfway through the play, triggered by a student who in true seventies fashion declares her freedom to identify as she chooses: 'I am a lesbian. [...] Women should never again have to apologise for loving each other. [...] I am a lesbian and I am not alone.'[54] It is this model of moral stance that makes Claire unable to continue leading her dual life and to risk her career and motherhood in order to serve her politics. As it happens, Claire's replication of the student's coming out is further amplified by the headmistress of the school, who also turns out to be gay despite having attempted previously to eradicate any dissent from mainstream norms.

Thus, Claire's case for custody brings together two strands of lesbianism: the outspoken young generation of the students and the closet lesbians of old who had no alternative but to seemingly conform. Despite their support, however, custody is granted to the husband, Daniels leaving the current social order intact. In fact, in *Neaptide* – as well as in *Care and Control* – 'lesbianism itself goes on trial, not just lesbian motherhood' and 'lesbianism is never affirmed within a lesbian community', Daniels relegating lesbianism to the status of an 'alternative lifestyle'.[55] By refusing to romanticize the situation Daniels accurately taps in to the *Zeitgeist* of the time as far as the status of lesbian motherhood is concerned. Ranging from the uninformed to the outright homophobe, the views represented by Claire's colleagues signal mainstream society's inability to treat homosexuality as a facet of normal sexuality and to allow for its spontaneous association with parenthood. Crucially, however, Daniels also stipulates the lesbian community's awareness of this status quo and its resilience to work against the grain: 'You're not being judged on the quality of your parenting but on the basis of your sexuality.'[56]

Moreover, as a *deus ex machina* device, Daniels introduces a dénouement with a simultaneously political and escapist undertone: she allows her protagonist and her daughter to flee the small-minded community unable to view parenthood independently from sexuality, thus offering them another lease of life for their arrangement as mother and daughter. Hope, however, is associated with America and hence elsewhere – suggesting the pointlessness of resistance here. But the idea is Joyce's: despite her previous reservations concerning her daughter's lifestyle, Joyce, as a mother herself, understands the importance of maternal bonds and is prepared to revisit her beliefs. This outcome replicates the play's earlier references to the Demeter–Persephone myth, then cementing the bond between Claire and Poppy, now also integrating Joyce. Through the archetypal image of a mother saving her daughter, Daniels engineers two coups: Claire keeping her child despite losing her legal custody, and Joyce reviving her bond with her adult daughter.

Neaptide constitutes not only one of the most important interventions of the eighties on lesbian motherhood, but it is also the first play presented on a major British mainstream stage to feature lesbian protagonists. Crucially, however, at the time the play was not billed as a lesbian play. In fact, the play was often interpreted as an advocate for mothers' custody rights in general, and as a play about depression. Although Daniels made it clear that the play was about lesbian custody, it is the character of Val that connects *Neaptide* most explicitly to Daniels's other work in terms of challenging key institutions of male authority.[57] Val's speech sets up the power relations in society concerning the medical profession – and by extension, the legal profession – and patients/clients. She links these divergences in hierarchy to the medieval witchcraft trials, thus evoking an entire history of female disenfranchisement, seen to be perpetuated via contemporary medicine and legal intervention: 'The powerful male Doctor-Inquisitor. In the wings, the subservient female Handmaiden-Nurse. Stranded on a mud flat, myself, a Witch-patient.'[58] In other words, the judge in *Neaptide* is a direct kin not only of the Doctor-Inquisitor but also of the doctor in *Byrthrite* and the subsequent fertility experts in a range of nineties plays, all fixated on their dominance over female patients longing to overcome ageing or infertility in their desperate quest for motherhood.

Adoption, infertility, technology

Byrthrite

In *Byrthrite* Daniels wanted to address the implications of reproductive technology for women, and decided to set the play in the seventeenth century – when the 'role of the healer was taken out of the hands of women and established in the (male) profession of doctor' – in order to 'give poignancy to the ideas expressed in the play'.[59] As Daniels contended, such an opposition of two historical and cultural frameworks led to an over-ambitious project; however, the confrontation between male medical expertise and women as patients and practitioners of alternative ways of healing was an aspect as topical in the seventeenth century as in the twentieth century. Daniels was adamant for the play to be received as an intervention on concerns of the eighties and not a period piece, and encouraged references to then contemporary debates. The published text, for instance, was framed by an introduction highlighting key stages in the development of assisted reproductive technologies and assessing its merits and failures. The introduction points to factors such as 'efficiency, speed and control' inherent in biotechnology and posits that in 'human reproduction research women, our bodies ourselves, are the experimental material'.[60] As evidence, government bodies such as the Committee of Inquiry into Human Fertilization and Embryology are invoked, as they use scientific discourse for discussing reproduction and are elusive about the fact that it is women's lives that are involved in the process. In agreement with voices in both feminist theory and dramatic representation, the introduction notes that women are reduced to relevant body parts – wombs, ovaries etc. – and are only addressed within the context of the family or the heterosexual couple, thus being denied full personhood.

Daniels's work, therefore, wishes to challenge the premise that situates women's existence solely in biology or in relation to men. *Byrthrite* was first staged at the Royal Court Theatre Upstairs on 21 November 1986, directed by Carole Hayman, and constituted Daniels's third play for the theatre. It was received with considerable attention and reviewed extensively, generating controversy for her polemical tone from both male and female critics. Some wanted to merely argue back, while others took issue with Daniels's affinities with radical feminism, claiming that certain passages read like dramatized versions of feminist theory. Furthermore, Daniels was also accused of essentialism, in the sense of having reversed the patriarchal concept of fundamental differences between male and female, and simply celebrating the latter. Soon after writing *Byrthrite* Daniels declared her lack of interest in writing 'safe' plays, and posited her engagement with artistic and political challenges: 'I don't like plays where the audience goes out feeling purged. [...] I like challenges. [...] I write issue plays.'[61]

Byrthrite shares the agenda of other Daniels plays in the reclamation of forgotten voices in women's history and in dramatizing women's contribution to ideas of their times. The play is structured into two chronologically successive parts, and the action is episodic, shifting the focus between the individual and the collective. Owing to the interpolation of songs throughout, however, the play is lifted out of its historical – and by extension, its naturalistic – context and is brought in line with then contemporary concerns regarding medical and scientific approaches to reproduction and women's bodies. In both frameworks power and control is associated with the male sphere, and the playwright's ambition is to undermine and re-claim this power for female subjects.

Through a dense plot, Daniels addresses major aspects of the debate on reproduction. She locates power as its key component, in relation to a quest for agency. Thus, she equates medicine with a new religion and its potential to counter involuntary childlessness, and invokes the view, increasingly dominant at the turn of the new millennium, that connotes medical intervention with perfection. This sense of eugenics, aimed to eradicate illness or disability, is paralleled with the traditional association between barrenness and social unacceptability. The latter runs through the subtext of most plays on unfulfilled motherhood, most strikingly in two rewritings of Lorca's *Yerma*: Ruth Carter's *A Yearning* (staged by Tamasha, 1995) and Anna Furse's *Yerma's Eggs* (produced by Athletes of the Heart, 2003). For Daniels it is men's fascination with women's ability to give birth that fuels all endeavours, and the play concerns itself with men's experiments to extend this ability to themselves – via medical and technological development. On the one hand, Daniels depicts women's awareness of this process of displacement and their resistance to it, and on the other, discusses women's co-operation with the male medical system. The latter for some represents hope in times of infertility, but for others it is associated with exploitation and humiliation: 'My sister died in childbirth last week and the babe was torn limb from limb in the name of their science with these barbarous instruments.'[62]

Daniels traces the transfer of power from midwives to obstetricians leading to the consolidation of reproductive science. Phrases like 'we're here to stay' and 'replacement' indicate long-term ambition, together with the elevation of the doctor as the 'father of the future, perfect nation'.[63] She envisages, however, a similar trajectory of power being re-claimed by women, culminating in the creation of a school of midwives 'to buy back [their] birthright'.[64] In her radical denunciation of medical science Daniels calls for a united front among women to defy further exploitation: 'We must make certain that we be the last generation to bear witness to the wrongs done to us in the name of science.'[65] In a dramaturgically most innovative scene that forecasts subsequent preoccupations in disability theatre, as discussed in Chapter 6, Daniels reiterates this verbal denunciation meta-theatrically via the integration of sign language and taped voiceover. Through a 'dumb show' featuring the symbolic elimination of an archetypal eighteenth-century oppressor, the drowning of a model pricker, Daniels condemns and literally eliminates male authority, thus re-claiming women's rights to decision-taking and, by extension, to reproduction as a female realm.

The Adoption Papers

Jackie Kay's *The Adoption Papers* was initially a radio play aired on BBC Radio 3 in 1990, and then published by Bloodaxe in 1991. The collection was warmly received and won numerous prizes, including a Scottish Arts Council Book Award. The volume deals with an adopted child's search for a cultural identity, and addresses topical issues in the politics of adoption, kinship and family. Kay's work narrates a black girl's adoption by a white Scottish couple, and is written for three voices – a daughter, an adoptive mother and a birth mother – whose identities, despite the different typefaces in the printed text, are never entirely distinct. According to Kay, the fusion of voices was suggested by the radio producer, whereas the typeface changes for each voice were recommended by the publisher, despite Kay's preference for keeping these three identities intertwined.[66] This device of manifold yet interconnected voices also enables Kay to investigate with equal intensity the three characters' different points of view, without a bias attached to the persona modelled on herself. The daughter of a white Scottish mother and a Nigerian father, adopted as a baby by white working-class communist parents, Kay 'is the self-confessed paradigm of multiplicity' and her unusual background 'has sensitized her to the effects of cultural alterity on identity and imagination'.[67] As a result, her work is an outstanding contribution to several genres: from autobiography to fiction, poetry to theatre, feminism to race relations.

Kay was pregnant at the time of writing *The Adoption Papers*. She addressed the topic as a search for origins, and wrote it prior to meeting her birth parents.[68] Kay situates her investigation of inter-racial adoption in a childhood context, combining the process of growing up with coming to terms with ethnic and racial difference. Only the three protagonists mentioned above are given a voice of their own, but there are constant references to the opinions represented by the white Scottish community as well. It is, in fact, this indirectly featured community that first alerts to the non-conventional adoption of a black girl by a white couple. Till then both the daughter and the adoptive mother perceive their situation as normal, and only after this normality has been undermined do they start addressing the unorthodox aspects of their arrangement.

Kay follows key stages in the lives of her protagonists, for instance, the adoptive mother's torment at her inability to conceive and her attempts at hiding signs of her radicalism so the adoption agency does not consider them unsuitable as parents, or the racism the daughter experiences as a result of being raised as a black child in a predominately white Glasgow. She also juxtaposes the differing perspectives of the adoptive and birth mothers, opposing the (unfulfilled) desire for natural parenthood ('I always wanted to give birth/Do that incredible natural thing/That women do') to negotiating the consequences of having an unwanted child: 'I cannot pretend she's never been [...]/My own body a witness.'[69] Like Wandor earlier, or Carter and Furse some years later, Kay establishes a connection between infertility and failure, and draws attention to the resulting social stigma: 'There was/ something scandalous about adopting,/telling the world your secret failure.'[70] Both the daughter and the adoptive mother dedicate significant effort to defining what constitutes a 'real mammy', and the daughter interrogates her adoptive mother 'why aren't you and me the same colour', though she seals her affection for her by pointing out the irrelevance of actual blood links: 'But I love my mammy whether she's real or no.'[71] The adoptive mother, as a token of generosity, acknowledges the triangular relationship involving the birth mother, the daughter's 'other' mother, and indicates her support for her daughter's coming to terms with her own history. Kay also interrogates the circumstances in which the term 'mother' is available for use. For instance, as the title indicates, the birth mother relinquishes her maternal role by signing a document, which process, conversely, grants mother status to the adoptive mother.

The Adoption Papers dwells on the daughter's desire 'to know' her 'blood', as Kay explores the challenges involved in having 'parents who are not of the same tree'.[72] Kay emphasizes that birth links are not the only measures of legitimacy; in the adoptive mother's phrase, 'all this umbilical knot business is nonsense'.[73] In other words, for Kay identity is not a given: it is a matter of negotiation, involving categories such as race, gender, sexuality and class. For example, the adoptive mother reconstitutes how she was told that there were no available babies until she specified that colour was of no concern. Starting from this premise she moves on to a phase of denial with regard to racial difference: 'I brought her up as my own [...]/Colour matters to the nutters.'[74] Colour, however, matters above all for everyone else, and it is via the typical teenage endeavour of identifying role models that the daughter is confronted with addressing her racial make-up. None of her choices – Bette Davis, Katharine Hepburn, Elizabeth Taylor – are considered adequate for her and she loses out at an audition to a less talented but racially corresponding girl. In fact, the only association she is not sanctioned for is the one with Angela Davis, imprisoned at the time for her black rights activism. Davis instantly becomes the icon, and indeed the emblematic surrogate mother, the daughter has been looking for. The striking physical similarity between them establishes the strongest bond the daughter has experienced so far, gradually leading towards a conscious identification with Davis's political agenda as well. Despite the fact that Davis is unknown to her pals, for the daughter she constitutes the ultimate platform of belonging, in which she can – both literally and figuratively – recognize herself.

As a writer with strong Scottish allegiances, Kay has stated her reservations to the label British as far as identity was concerned. It is crucial for Kay though – as for Daniels – not to get too entangled in labels: 'I prefer as much wide open space around my works, and around the reading of it, as possible.'[75] Kay's work, therefore, does not invite or indeed allow straightforward answers. Speaking in 1995, Kay considered the term post-feminism 'a complete anachronism' when 'very simple, basic women's rights' did not exist.[76] For her, feminism was about equality, and in order to define feminism one had to go back to its basic roots. Thus, her 'outlook', 'feminism', 'socialism', 'awareness of own race and country and age', and 'awareness of being adopted' affect practically all her writing.[77] In her view feminism has impacted most strongly on British theatre in the early to mid-eighties; and nineties theatre, though more sophisticated, did not have the rawness of Gay Sweatshop (with whom she collaborated) or Monstrous Regiment. Kay also claimed lately that drama, as a medium, stopped satisfying her needs for artistic expression.[78] She contended that 'plays are the most difficult thing to get right', as they 'have to work on so many levels [...] visually, emotionally and intellectually'.[79] Having to date mastered poetry, fiction and drama, Kay is likely to search yet again for the most suitable genre for her artistic expression. As she intersects issues of race, gender, sexuality, nationality and class, Kay advocates a multifaceted identity, together with hope in a greater acceptance of difference.

The Choice

Claire Luckham's seventies plays – *Scum* (1976), written in collaboration with Chris Bond for Monstrous Regiment, and *Trafford Tanzi* (1978), featuring a man-beating woman wrestler – associated her name with feminism. Luckham wrote this play for a working-class audience in Liverpool aiming to establish immediate audience involvement; in a sense, therefore, the play compares with Trish Cooke's attempts at reaching out to a Northern working-class environment in the wake of Delaney's success. While for the majority of viewers and critics Tanzi's quest signified an interaction between liberal and working-class feminist commitments, the play was also read as a reinforcement of patriarchy, since it appropriated some of the latter's principles. *The Choice*, performed in 1992 at the Salisbury Playhouse directed by Annie Castledine, continued to be preoccupied with women's powerlessness. However, instead of locating women in situations where they are able to take 'responsibility for their own lives and challenge [this powerlessness]', *The Choice* investigates the ways in which women are denied responsibility.[80]

As her protagonist, Luckham now created an independent woman, with a career of her own, who is taken over by the manipulative power of the medical system in the course of her pregnancy with a potentially disabled baby. Originally someone with very strong opinions – on women's careers, family, babies – she is gradually eliminated from discourse and ends up reduced to a mere object for scientific scrutiny. Devoid of agency, she finds herself acting out the decisions taken on her behalf and, consequently, aborting the baby labelled unfit for survival. Rather than being interpreted in feminist terms, *The Choice* was perceived as a play about disability and was instantly categorized alongside other contemporary plays that addressed mental or physical handicaps.[81] Reasons for this appropriation included the fact that Luckham's own brother was diagnosed with Down's Syndrome, and the case of a paediatrician who was charged with allowing a baby with Down's Syndrome to die. Luckham discovered this case while researching the topic and integrated some of its details into her play. Nevertheless, Luckham warned that this play did not conform simply to the label 'play on disability'. *The Choice* was in fact, wrongly categorized as a case of a feminist writer giving up on the task of writing about issues arising from women's experience: 'It is not just a play about Down's; it's about trying to talk about birth – about giving life and what choices and responsibilities are involved.'[82]

The play was commissioned by Castledine, then artistic director of Derby Playhouse, while Luckham was an Arts Council-funded Writer in Residence. Luckham explained that she had taken inspiration from her own experiences, though she also highlighted that the importance of personal experience sublimated into writing should not be over-privileged: 'I would hate to suggest that men couldn't write about childbirth, because they haven't experienced it.'[83] Nevertheless, the play's development reflected and successively put in focus its disparate elements: the personal, the feminist and the issue-based drama. Originally, *The Choice* was entitled *Dear Embryo*, and it centred on Luckham's own pregnancy in later life. Like the play's Sal, she was subjected to the amniocentesis test and the all-clear was given only in the fourth month. Luckham grew increasingly preoccupied with the idea of potential health hazards and with the ways in which vital medical information is withheld from or overdosed to patients. A later version – already planned for the Salisbury Playhouse where the play was eventually premièred after Castledine's departure from Derby – was called *I, Barrie,* and relocated the figure with Down's Syndrome to the core of the play. Castledine, however, felt that this emphasis on Barrie meant that 'audiences would be influenced emotionally, so the play would become just another play about an underprivileged person'.[84] Following Castledine's advice, Luckham eventually rewrote the play in its present form – polemical rather than emotional – acknowledging the director's creative input.

Luckham intended the play for a studio venue, with Sal and Ray at the centre of attention, the Consultant and the Midwife 'forming a circle round them, and the Writer encircling them both'.[85] Sal, a journalist, has not considered pregnancy so far, and it was her partner Ray, an illustrator, who initiated this attempt. Sal's age (she is in her mid-thirties), however, is instantly turned into a major problem, as, according to medical evidence, there is a higher incidence of malformations among babies of older mothers. Luckham offers generous space to the medical profession. The Consultant, fully aware of his crucial role in his patients' quest for a baby, projects himself into a role of god-like control. He urges the supremacy of science ('Science can work miracles') and connects medicine with power: 'They see me in control of knowledge and therefore powerful.'[86] Though insisting that she had no intention of stating 'what is right and what is wrong', Luckham is clearly offering a critique of the medical system and its patronizing power: 'You know what obstetrics is?'; 'I hope you, at least, found out about Down's Syndrome.'[87]

She presents medicine as an exclusively male sphere, in which women's voices are considered irrelevant. The Consultant focuses on the mechanistic aspects inherent in giving birth, using such images as 'steel womb' or 'robot birth';[88] paralleling Emily Martin's scientific metaphor of the body as a production factory. According to this metaphor, consultants act as the technicians who run the body efficiently and profitably, as in conditions of capitalism and the free market – which, in their turn, have provided economic support for the medicalization of birth.[89] Sal does not find the resources to oppose medical intrusion directly, in spite of real-life petitions by thousands of women and midwives against control over pregnancy and birth. Despite her instinctive disagreement with medical recommendations, Sal is unable to contest and de-centre the privilege of the 'scientific approach' – a phenomenon deeply embedded in twentieth-century Western culture. In Martin's words, 'Medical culture has a powerful system of socialisation which exacts conformity as the price of participation. It is also a cultural system whose ideas and practices pervade popular culture and in which, therefore we all participate to some degree.'[90]

Sal's attitude illustrates, in fact, another claim made by Martin, according to which women 'represent themselves as lacking a sense of autonomy and feeling carried along by forces beyond their control'.[91] Nevertheless, Sal's case is also a reflection of feminism's failure to deal in a satisfactory manner with the negotiation of power in pregnancy and childbirth. While women's rights to contraception and safe abortions have been 'won' in most areas of the non-Catholic Western world, comparable rights with regard to childbirth – especially concerning autonomy and access to control – are still needed. According to Ann Oakley and Hilary Graham, the entire concept of 'normality' in matters of birth is a source of controversy in itself. For women, 'normal' conveys 'the sense of their individual bodies having the capacity to take on pregnancy and labour, physically and emotionally', as a 'process rooted in their bodies [...] not in a medical textbook'.[92] For doctors, on the other hand, it is connected to the medicalization of the body and success is quantified by the emergence of a healthy baby.

Luckham's Consultant repeatedly calls Sal 'Mrs. Winger', despite the fact that she and Ray are not married. As it happens, marriage constitutes an obsession for Ray as well, mainly linked with the assertion of his paternal rights. Immediately after Sal confirms her pregnancy, he proposes. He sees making her pregnant as a victory, but also as the start of redundancy for him. To compensate, he stakes out his claim to the child, perceiving the baby as personal property. He will be the one less open to arguments for termination and will manifest hardly any anxiety regarding the baby's potential disability. He spends minimal time with Sal in the early stages of her pregnancy as he is always at work, keeping a record of foetal development. This exclusion of Sal's perception on the evolution of the foetus is reminiscent of the misogynist idea that women are only vessels for the male seed and temporary shelters for the foetus to develop, as children are first and foremost the offspring of their fathers.

From a medical perspective, however, the baby's future continues to be insecure. The Consultant offers Sal the latest developments in screening technology, obsessed with the idea of the body beautiful in a climate of perfection. His understanding of the functions of the human body is utterly mechanistic, and for him medical practice and healing are solutions of problems posed in some kind of riddle:

> I want to get that foetus and have a jolly good look at it. I don't want there to be any possibility that there might be something wrong with it. Something I haven't detected. [...] If there is anything wrong I can either attempt to correct it, or I can tell them to forget it and start again.[93]

This stance establishes a direct link to Kitzinger's observation on male medical control and the rise of obstetrics: 'The history of obstetrics is a record of men's struggle to construct a system of scientific certainties on which the management of labour can be based, and to eliminate women's inconvenient emotions, their "old wives' tales", and the passion of giving birth.'[94] In the opinion of an advocate of non-medically supervised births, such an obsession with technology is also located in the medical belief that in the late twentieth century – 'given the information and technology' – almost anything can be done: 'It is this belief which drives hospitals to greater and greater lengths to make birth more predictable, more controlled, more assured of outcome.'[95]

This is the stage in the play that articulates most clearly the medical tendency to split the pregnant woman–foetus unit and concentrate on the foetus alone. According to Rosalind Petchesky, this move was made possible by the development of imaging technologies such as ultrasound, capable of producing a picture of the foetus without emphasizing its location in the womb.[96] Aided by such visuals, obstetrics has created the illusion of being able to interact with the foetus directly – without the mediation of the pregnant mother – women finding themselves, therefore, in yet another instance of marginalization. This idea of the free-floating, independent foetus has been taken up subsequently in both the visual arts and advertising. Rosemary Betterton explored in detail 'the emergence of foetal personhood as a cultural category', and provided analyses of such controversial images as Wrangler (1986) and Benetton (1991) advertisements that showed foetuses wearing jeans and passing not only as self-sufficient miniature adults but also as aspiring fashion icons.[97]

In spite of Ray's strong opposition, Sal does opt for the ultimate clarification, the amniocentesis test. The positive test result, however, redirects the focus onto the Consultant's earlier claims and leads to termination: 'One doesn't expect to have to settle for second best.'[98] In an age aspiring to political correctness, the protagonist's refusal to come to terms with disability might seem anachronistic. The playwright claimed, however, that her target was 'to start talking' publicly about such issues, 'along with childbirth and sex education'; and to facilitate such a discussion she supplied factual reference: 'If you don't know the facts you can't get involved.'[99] As the play's Writer contends, there is an urgent need for more information on disability in order to negotiate relationships between the able bodied and the impaired. Thus, the possibility of choice – at least on a medical level – is shown to function on an inadequate basis, and decision-taking is located with those in authority and power. Sal requests the abortion, but she might have acted differently had she been so advised. Her final reassurance to Ray that she still wants a family, however, has the intensity of defiance and suggests determination: to genuinely exercise her own choices from then on.

The Break of Day

Timberlake Wertenbaker has made a strong point of not embracing any particular feminist direction. She has acknowledged the importance of feminism as a cultural and political intervention; however, she regretted that feminism has been 'a rather class-bound, national rather than international movement' that 'has done very little for the position of women all over the world'.[100] She also problematized the terms 'feminist' writer, 'feminist' playwright or even 'women's playwriting', though she stressed the importance of producing plays by women and about women, especially in the context of what she called the 'more reactionary' nineties.[101] Wertenbaker's work, nevertheless, has addressed central questions for feminism, especially the acquisition of a voice versus the silencing of women.

Wertenbaker has also experimented with the rewriting of classics. She wrote *The Break of Day* as a companion play to Chekhov's *Three Sisters*, in conjunction with which it was first performed by Out of Joint, under the direction of Max Stafford-Clark in 1995. Both plays are set in a *fin-de-siècle* environment, a century apart, Chekhov portraying the turn of the nineteenth century towards the twentieth century and Wertenbaker the end of the second millennium. Both dedicate significant space to the interpretation of the past, and Chekhov's sisters as well as Wertenbaker's protagonists are profoundly disillusioned by the present. While, according to Wertenbaker, Chekhov thought that women's paid work would solve problems in the long run, she investigated what happened when 'women had the opportunity to work but suddenly had allowed themselves not to have children'.[102] Besides the Chekhovian parallels, however, she aimed to write a contemporary play on topical issues: 'The fatigue at the end of the century, the breakdown of a lot of ideals, particularly for women, and this notion of the future and what the future is, what sort of future we are providing for others.'[103]

The Break of Day was poorly received by most critics and did not enjoy box office success. Despite her usual equanimity in response to criticism, Wertenbaker insisted that on this occasion she was upset by the critics' unwillingness to relate to the play. She identified its open-ended nature and profusion of ideas as a reason behind its reception. In fact, the way *The Break of Day* engages with the protagonists' past and the present establishes it as a survey of the developments in women's lives from the seventies to the mid-nineties. In this manner, it illustrates the trajectory of this study itself, moving from plays produced during the zenith of the Women's Liberation Movement to works emerging in its aftermath, in times that re-evaluate the contribution of the different feminist standpoints. The play opens with a scene that invokes the past straightaway: the three protagonists speak nostalgically about their youth, which coincided with the heyday of second-wave feminism. Formerly successful in their careers, Tess and Nina have suddenly become overwhelmed by a sense of paralysis; only April believes in her vocation as a source of hope in the future. Having campaigned in the seventies for women's rights to a career and the possibility of bypassing or delaying parenthood, Tess and Nina now find themselves in the position where they would be prepared to have children but experience biological difficulties.

From the revelation of Tess's and Nina's aspirations towards motherhood the play establishes as its focus the desire to become a parent, and how this ambition reconfigures the individual's future. It is this obsession with parenthood and the way it dislocates the protagonists' previous concerns that has hindered critics from relating to *The Break of Day*.

Tess and Nina talk with extreme emotional involvement about their desire to mother, lament their infertility and address their lack of empowerment in opposition to their earlier feminist commitment. Consequently, the play was widely seen as a backlash manifesto against feminism. For instance, Paul Taylor saw the play as a dramatization of 'how the maternal drive can cause women to betray Orthodox feminism'.[104] Although such a reading is legitimized by Wertenbaker's text, it is not the only approach available. In fact, the very opposite is equally valid; whereby it is precisely the discussion of infertility and maternal desire that connotes a feminist dimension. Elaine Aston, for example, rightly argues that the play 'indexes a need to re-conceive the politics of motherhood' and contends that 'if formerly feminism was concerned with contraceptive technology, it now has to address the issue of how, or indeed whether, women can take advantage of the new reproductive technology, without themselves being taken advantage of (emotionally, economically and medically)'.[105] In other words, instead of betraying the values of second-wave feminism, Wertenbaker invites both her characters and audience to a meditation on topical late twentieth-century issues, such as the right to parenthood and the state of the family.

In opposition to the yearning of Tess and Nina, it is the much younger Marisa who embodies actual motherhood. Marisa stirs their envy through her ability to become a mother, and the two women question her capacity to care financially for the child, advising her to abort and start a career first. Only April places herself on Marisa's side, and is prepared to admit that their feminist circle of friends made a mistake by postponing motherhood for the sake of professional fulfilment. Unlike Chekhov's play, where, as Cousin argues, motherhood is associated with a certain sense of banality via Natasha, Wertenbaker depicts it as something desirable; thus, craving for a baby replaces the longing for Moscow by the three sisters.[106] Despite the optimism associated with the desire for children, Wertenbaker links her protagonist's quest for a baby through the theme of barrenness. Tess needs to appeal to medical assistance in order to conceive, while Nina cannot get pregnant because of a past back-street abortion. Via these cases, the play also discusses the spiritual barrenness of Britain in the mid-nineties; 'no ideology, no thought ha[d] worked', according to Wertenbaker, everything being 'bleak [and] extremely uncertain'.[107]

According to Clare Bayley's 1995 review, the major paradox in *The Break of Day* was that the same women who participated in changing history in their youth suddenly found themselves caught unawares by time.[108] In fact, to quote Wertenbaker, 'They are [also] caught unawares by their own longing.'[109] Their battle for more choices for women did come true for the next generation (like Marisa, who ironically does not want to take advantage of them), but this very involvement led to the closing down of other options. All three friends are caught up in this process but it is Tess who comes out most affected, losing not only her job and husband during the infertility treatment but also ending up perceiving every other woman as a potential rival in her quest for a baby. While Nina is prepared to accept her biological limits and go for adoption, Tess refuses to even consider bringing up someone else's child. Tess cannot avoid positioning herself in relation to Marisa's spontaneous ability to mother. She claims that 'She has what I want',[110] eventually denying both the sisterhood and anti-essentialism of her feminist commitment. The playwright claimed that she wanted to write a play 'about women who seek a solution to [their] unhappiness', and in the case of Tess she was interested in showing 'how somebody very intelligent could be destroyed and turned into a victim'.[111]

Wertenbaker also addressed younger women's attitudes towards women's place in society. She wanted to draw attention to what she called 'one of the dangers of feminism': 'The next generation, feeling that the choices are there, chooses to throw these choices away assuming that they are going to stay. If each generation does not keep fighting, in another twenty years' time one will be back at the fifties, and that *is* a danger.'[112] This next generation, represented by Marisa, do not feel that they owe their forerunners any acknowledgement. They plan their lives according to different patterns, removed from the public sphere that Tess, April and Nina – like Churchill's Marlene – have been so keen to gain access to. Marisa's outburst when she is advised to abort ('So I can end up like you, married to ambition, bitter and childless')[113] echoes the warning addressed to Marlene by the traditional wife in *Top Girls*. In fact, Marisa's reinforcement of heterosexuality, marriage and family, alongside the rejection of feminists as man-hating and embittered women, sounds like a dramatized version of backlash manifestos. Although Wertenbaker was reluctant to classify Marisa in ideological terms, she claimed that Marisa was 'a victim of the failure of feminism [as a middle-class and intellectual movement] to work through the classes'.[114]

Instead of recommending one single alternative, therefore, each of Wertenbaker's women advocates a different option. Marisa gives birth to a baby, fulfilling what might seem to be her biological destiny; Nina bypasses biology by using her financial privilege and adopting someone else's baby; while Tess subjects herself to the emotional and physical exploitation of the infertility treatment. She also ends up relating to other women as potential egg-donors, and reduces Robert to a mere supplier of sperm: 'If it weren't for your sperm, I'd leave you.'[115] The scenes featuring the fertility clinic where Tess is a patient concentrate on the ironically named Dr Glad. He appears as an uncanny reminder of Luckham's Consultant, both in his patronizing attitude and the way he associates himself with the divine: 'We've performed another miracle.'[116] Although Tess has opted for the treatment herself, like Sal, she is not given a voice as it is her body that concerns medical science: 'Throughout history, the woman's body is the terrain on which patriarchy is erected.'[117]

While Tess is reminded of her biological clock, Nina is asked for patience awaiting her baby in an unidentified Eastern European location. Via Nina and Hugh's quest Wertenbaker is alluding to the highly publicized case of a British couple that attempted to smuggle a baby from Romania in 1994, and, probably, to her own personal experience. Wertenbaker portrays the prospective adoptive parents as selfless rescuers of an abandoned child, whose benevolence to extend their comfortable life to another human being is an act of social justice. Nina and Hugh, however, are also exploiters of the fertility of financially underprivileged women and men, as well as of their adopted child whom they perceive as a trophy. A major flaw of the play in this respect is that it only presents the Western perspective, and there is an 'imbalance between the specificity of England's political and social problems [...] and the vague difficulties caused by the end of communism for former Soviet bloc nations'.[118] Another problematic issue is the absence of the East European mother, thus indicating on yet another level the unequal positions of those in the East and West. Wertenbaker presents Eastern Europe as devoid of agency, although she includes alternative parental figures, most notably the adoption fixer, Mihail, who epitomizes the in-between status and argues for cross-border citizenship. In this sense, Wertenbaker indirectly references central issues in postcolonial theory, and perpetuates Gayatri Chakravorty's Spivak's view that 'the subaltern cannot speak', as 'even when the subaltern makes an effort to the death to speak, she is not able to be heard'.[119]

Wertenbaker makes it obvious that Nina and Hugh could not manage without local insider knowledge, or that parentless children would have less of a chance for a decent life in the conditions available in the East. Mihail contends that the future 'will be in the hands of [...] these cross-border children', who will manage to avoid 'narrow ethnic identification'.[120] Thus, hope for the future becomes synonymous with a desire for the 'other': a somewhat naïve urge to move to the West for those in the East, and a symbolic re-enactment of a colonial past for those in the West.

Focusing on Nina's and Hugh's entanglements with local bureaucracy, Wertenbaker presents a climate in contrast with the procedures operating in the West, and locates Eastern Europe as the 'other' of the Western world. She shows an environment governed by corruption caused by poverty, itself connected to a profound sense of disappointment in both communism and post-1990 regimes. Wertenbaker also situates Orthodox religion as the spiritual background to the region's political and economic stagnation and ultimate cultural difference in relation to the West. Despite the fact that some of the above details are accurate and child abandonment constitutes a reality in some countries in Eastern Europe, Wertenbaker's position is highly selective of the *couleur locale*. It reveals an outsider's perspective, captured primarily by the sensational and the exotic, preoccupied with difference to the detriment of the 'same'.[121]

In the concluding act, taking place six months later, Nina and Hugh have succeeded in their quest, but we do not yet have the daughter's version of the story: 'When these children are twenty-five or thirty there will probably be a playwright and you'll get a story. [...] I think it will probably be a very different story of belonging to two cultures.'[122] Tess and Robert, on the other hand, have split up as a result of Tess's extended infertility treatment. Despite the details that Wertenbaker brings to render the emotional and physical traumas suffered by both women, as well as her criticism of the privileges of white, middle-class women – in a position to buy motherhood at almost any cost – she avoids being judgmental: 'Don't judge me!'[123] Tess urges. Wertenbaker is aware of the intricacies of taking a stance about the desire for parenthood in a neutral, ideologically non-engaged way. Although she maps out both the backlash argument on women's biological urges and the individualist discourse that privileges reproductive technologies, for Wertenbaker, motherhood is not merely 'a biological issue, but an economic, cultural and political one', emphasizing that 'any rethinking about female identity must accommodate women's options for motherhood'.[124]

Like Chekhov's sisters who never make it to Moscow, Tess fails to obtain the baby she longs for, but unlike the sisters, Tess considers that she has the right to intervene in the shaping of her destiny. She even contacts Marisa, whom she previously despised, asking her to act as a surrogate mother, and only after being ignored does she take the decision to move on and try to understand what has happened. It is this transferred quest – from obsessive desire to understanding – that reinvents Tess as an agent. Thus, hope ends up associated with preoccupations of the mind and 'the break of day' constitutes the dawning of personal reassessment. In fact, it is this idea of self-awareness – characteristic of the late nineties – that Wertenbaker aims to convey. The ending is ambiguous in many ways: it is a moment of failure, a loss of illusions, but also an occasion for rebirth. Unlike Nina, who has achieved her quest yet somewhat lost interest in its outcome, Tess continues to lay claim to agency as before.

Writing in and about a time generally labelled as post-modern, Wertenbaker voices attitudes ascribed to a new stage in feminism. Her claim to see feminism 'as humanism, and the questioning of authority', and as an ideology from which men have at least as much to 'get as women do',[125] removes her from accusations of essentialism, but instead of allowing for universal scrutiny it mainly generates ideological confusion. By aiming to be all things to all people, Wertenbaker's sense of feminism runs the risk of not representing anyone to an adequate degree, which can lead – as in the case of her characters – to noncommitment instead of engagement.

Addressing the end of the twentieth century, Wertenbaker acknowledges the difficulty of sustaining one's belief in ideologies. Though originally she places all three protagonists in heterosexual partnerships, Wertenbaker shows two of these splitting up. Triggered by various facts, singlehood in *The Break of Day* reflects the trend for atomization in nineties society. Deciding to try for a baby without the support of a partner, Tess is prepared to join the increasing community of independent women, but also to assume the financial difficulties of single parenthood. Both Tess's intended approach to motherhood via IVF and Nina's and Hugh's adoption constitute forms of surrogate parenting, involving such post-modern concepts as substitution and fluidity of boundaries. Ultimately, it is flexibility and the irrelevance of boundaries that Wertenbaker is arguing for, not just when talking about politics and geography, but above all when addressing women's options at the end of the second millennium. Regrettably, she only writes from a Western perspective; however, she allows women to participate in the backlash against feminism or to pursue their rights to understand motives behind events, in an attempt at accepting diversity and critical detachment.

Conclusion

This chapter offers an insight into preoccupations with alternative forms of parenthood in British women's theatre across a politically heterogeneous period between the seventies and mid-nineties, arguing that while dramatic style has altered according to the respective conventions of the time, the intensity with which the playwrights explore their subjects has not diminished. In fact, the chapter contends that the issues raised continue to be topical, yet it also claims that most of this work constitutes some of the most accurate documents of their time. Ranging from seventies agitprop to a meditation on the end of the second millennium, the plays argue for women's right to take a decision on their destiny as mothers, irrespective of sexual orientation and fertility. Thus, Wandor becomes one of the first voices in British theatre to offer her support for lesbian parenthood, investigating both the medical and legal route. Wandor writes as a highly accurate observer, whereas a decade later Daniels voices similar concerns from within the lesbian community itself. Crucially, both playwrights connect the issues on the private terrain with the public lives of their protagonists, professional women in both cases, as does Wertenbaker in her meditation on ageing and addiction to an obsession.

In this case, however, women's options are examined only from a heterosexual point of view, and include the intervention of technology and adoption. Emblematic for the nineties, the latter is a cross-cultural adoption, predicated on financial exchange between East and West. According to Wertenbaker, writing about the adopted children requires another generation to describe their own perspective. For her, adoption is about fulfilling a need for a family in conditions of infertility, and her concerns involve finding a healthy baby who has the potential to integrate into British life. In contrast, Kay opposes the birth mother and the adoptive mother, both irreversibly connected to the daughter, deals with the aftermath of adoption and examines the psychological aspects of growing up in a different racial and cultural context. Unlike the cases above where maternal desire is successful, Luckham dramatizes the failure of this ambition due to biological obstacles, utilizing the case study of a white middle-class professional couple.

Emerging as a writer in parallel with the establishment of second-wave feminism, Wandor came across as a self-consciously political writer. In both *Care and Control* and *AID Thy Neighbour* she interrogates the values according to which mothering and motherhood are negotiated, and demonstrates what she considers the morally right outcome. By locating her lesbian protagonists in a position of success, Wandor also reinforces and challenges women's integration into male-identified linear time – associated with the first, equality-seeking strand of second-wave feminism. On the one hand, her lesbians replicate heterosexual practice via their hierarchical partnership and parenthood in *AID*

Thy Neighbour, in this sense appropriating mainstream societal norms and symbolically reinserting themselves into a quest for equality with men. On the other hand, Wandor dissociates the desire for parenthood from sexual orientation; thus she makes a human rights claim and situates her lesbians outside the patriarchal system, in a radical subversion of its principles.

Sarah Daniels constituted, for many, the embodiment of radical feminism in eighties British theatre and, in fact, found herself vilified in the press for producing dramatized versions of feminist theoretical texts. She examines lesbian motherhood in *Neaptide* and the impact of reproductive technologies in *Byrthrite*, undermining male authority and championing a separate female way of living in both. This approach, of course, tallies with the radical separatist agenda; however, Daniels has since indicated that her primary aim was not a feminist intervention. Jackie Kay also contends that feminism has evolved, and according to her, in order to define feminism one needs to return to its origins, which in Kay's case connotes a quest for equality. Instead of affiliating with a liberal feminist agenda, however, Kay invokes her socialism and identifies as a 'present day, up and running, current feminist'.[126] In fact, she formulates her bewilderment at post-feminism, her problem with the concept being rooted in the fact that the aims of feminism (equal right to pay, work and choice) have not yet been achieved. *The Adoption Papers* as a document of the early nineties confirms Kay as a writer concerned with fairness in a broader context, investigating race, gender and sexuality, and utilizing cross-cultural adoption for an exploration of the flexibility of boundaries.

Luckham and Wertenbaker displayed, throughout the nineties, considerable caution concerning their feminist allegiances. Luckham tones down her militant feminist engagement, while Wertenbaker emphasizes the periodic need to redefine feminism. Both plays discussed feature professional women in their thirties who exhibit character traits of nineties women: they govern their lives independently and aim at a combination of career and family. In both cases, however, the individual protagonists are juxtaposed with representatives of the medical and legal system, in a domestic and foreign framework, and thus the playwrights address broader contexts that integrate family, class, reproductive science and globalization. As Wertenbaker interprets feminism as humanism, she universalizes women's dilemmas and makes an effort at relating them, after two decades of women-centred theatre, to male experience. The protagonists' pursuit of parenthood is inscribed, therefore, into a quest for identity – in changing historical, political and cultural conditions.

6
Alternative Dramaturgies: Rewriting the Maternal Body

Drawing on themes and preoccupations launched at the end of the twentieth century, the voices cited in this chapter amplify the diversity of the debate on motherhood, in terms of both subject matter and theatre aesthetics. The playwrights discussed approach, on the one hand, aspects of the reality of parenthood (Sarah Woods: *Cake*, 2003) and, on the other hand, investigate the desire for parenting in conditions of disability (Kaite O'Reilly: *Peeling*, 2002), ageing or reduced fertility (Anna Furse: *Yerma's Eggs*, 2003). In all cases the work discussed is the result of partnerships between writers and performance companies, and range from devising processes (Furse and Athletes of the Heart) to instances of collaboration (O'Reilly and Jenny Sealey of Graeae, Woods and Jade Theatre Company) and special commission (O'Reilly for Graeae, Woods for Battersea Arts Centre (BAC) in association with Birmingham Repertory Theatre). Furse has also been funded by an Impact Award from Medicine in Society at the Wellcome Trust, and in this way not only establishes a link with science but also contributes to a new genre of performance-making that incorporates cutting-edge technology and raises awareness about the heightened medicalization of the body in recent decades.

In all three cases, as opposed to work discussed in the earlier chapters, the label 'play' only covers some aspects of the work produced, and is hence inadequate as a term to encompass the overall experience. The textual component of this work is, nevertheless, important, and, as a result, both O'Reilly's *Peeling* and Woods's *Cake* were published. All productions have toured a number of venues in the United Kingdom and, to date, one of them has been revived (*Cake*). In terms of scale, all are relatively studio ventures, involving a handful of characters: six performers in *Yerma's Eggs*, and a cast of three in *Cake* and *Peeling*.

Despite their similarities as far as scale is concerned, however, the productions have attracted different audiences. *Cake* started off as a project backed by an organization with a remit for supporting innovative work (BAC), but crucially premièred regionally (Birmingham) and not in London; *Peeling* was staged by a company synonymous with disability theatre (Graeae); and *Yerma's Eggs* introduced a production company created by Furse as an outlet for her own creative endeavours (Athletes of the Heart).

Another feature uniting the writers is their affiliation with academia. Furse teaches on the MA in Performance at the Drama Department at Goldsmiths College, O'Reilly has been the recipient of an AHRC Creative Fellowship in the Drama Department at Exeter University and contributes to practical classes, while Woods runs the MA in Playwriting, initially set up by David Edgar, at Birmingham University. These academic duties vary considerably in time commitment and nature of responsibilities; however, they mark the playwrights' desire to integrate reflection on their own practices with the writing process, alongside involvement with teaching and hence communicating firsthand with a new generation. This phenomenon also reflects the consolidation of practice-as-research in recent years, and suggests a potential rapprochement between the scholarly study of theatre and performance, and the profession.

Peeling

Peeling was commissioned by Graeae Theatre Company and premièred at The Door, Birmingham Repertory Theatre, on 14 February 2002. It subsequently toured nationally and was performed at the Soho Theatre in London and the Edinburgh Festival in 2003. It was also dramatized for BBC Radio 3 and aired on 5 October 2003. These details sum up the parameters in which the work circulated and was received: hailed as a major intervention in disability theatre and as a piece underpinned by innovative dramaturgy. It was *Peeling* that pioneered the trend in juxtaposing sign-language interpretation and audio description with verbal dialogue subsequently seen in Graeae productions such as *On Blindness* (2004) and *Bent* (2004). This dramaturgical interest resulted from writer Kaite O'Reilly's desire to intertwine her expertise as a mainstream playwright with her exploration of a new theatrical language rooted in her personal experience of impairment. Director Jenny Sealey also claims that an integrated approach informs her work as the person responsible for the artistic platform of Graeae, including the writers commissioned and her directorial style that she locates closer to the European tradition than the more traditional paths of some UK companies. She emphasizes Graeae's 'desire to seek what is a fully accessible theatre' and to interrogate whether it is possible 'to create something wholly accessible to a diverse audience'.[1] In other words, *Peeling* brings together theoretical, dramaturgical and political concerns, and aims to involve an integrated audience and a deaf and hearing cast.

O'Reilly contends that she incorporated audio description into her script, rather than simply appending it to the text, because as a visually impaired person, she felt that previous attempts in the area were not satisfactory.[2] Following this initial decision that shaped the entire configuration of the work, in rehearsals Sealey opted to have the whole of the script projected on the back wall. In the director's view this approach is helpful because people do not utilize the same sign language, besides it offering a backbone to the performance in situations where, as requested by the playwright, sections are signed but not spoken on stage. This idea generated controversy in the company, as it was not seen as politically correct to deny access to some members of the audience. For O'Reilly, however, this choice was not about political correctness but about experimenting with dramaturgical devices: 'You can shift the politics and the focus from the stage to the audience, because you have part of the audience having information. People with access to sign language (usually deaf people) will see the signing of this invisible history, to which the predominantly hearing audience will be oblivious.'[3]

Thus, a speech was signed on a generally unheard history of deaf people's experience during the Holocaust and only some of the audience understood it, which, for O'Reilly, was a metaphor of what has happened in fact to many histories. Privileging deaf participants and those who sign created a new dynamic in the audience, and many deaf people felt that 'it was a political act to have this aspect of deaf history told first to the deaf or signing community'.[4] At the end of the performance the story was retold, but not in standard spoken English, rather in a direct translation from British Sign Language (BSL). In this way, the non-disabled audience was put in a position to experience a form of temporary disability and, through the medium of BSL, encounter a very different syntax, normally unavailable to a hearing ear: 'What's most fascinating [...] is the use of the linguistic diversity that people with disabilities often have to master [...]. The fecundity and inventiveness of its many languages counterbalance the stark, sometimes horrific imagery, giving us a depiction of death and sterility that is vivid and abundant.'[5]

Peeling started as a project aiming to explore O'Reilly's and Sealey's respective impairments (visual and aural) and approaches (physical theatre influenced by Grotowski for O'Reilly, and a visual perspective for Sealey). The initial image they agreed on captured three women tied to very high chairs against their will, wearing elaborate gowns and their signing hands appearing through the skirts. The women were on stage but mainly unseen by the audience, located at the very back. O'Reilly then wrote a script, a version she later altered in the light of her inter- action with the performers and then once again, following a cast change. In the production I witnessed, the eccentric and slightly puri- tanical Alpha, deaf and user of British Sign Language and Sign- Supported English, was played by Caroline Parker; the sexy and feisty Beaty, blind and four feet tall, by Lisa Hammond; and the inquisitive Coral, in a wheelchair, by Sophie Partridge.

The factual framework for the piece included details of the Nazi Final Solution regarding people with invisible sensory disabilities alongside current attitudes regarding eugenics. Aware of the taboos for disabled women who consider motherhood, from the perspective of mainstream and disabled communities alike, O'Reilly's aim was to point out the pres- sure coming from both directions. On the one hand, the medical pro- fession insists on not bringing another 'burden' into this world, while, on the other hand, in the view of the disabled community, if the moth- er is disabled and the child is likely to have an impairment, she has a moral obligation to have that child. Termination in this latter view is participation in eugenics and, consequently, is a betrayal. Alpha's story of termination, following the confirmation via amniocentesis that her child is also disabled, responds to this dilemma, and it became a contro- versial issue, Graeae even noting publicly that the views in the play did not represent the views of the company. Nevertheless, there was a sub- stantial response to this storyline from both within and outside the dis- abled community; though for O'Reilly the crucial factor was that people with disabilities appreciated her exploring uncomfortable stories:

> With Kaite O'Reilly's *Peeling*, Graeae has finally produced challenging, accessible theatre rooted in disabled peoples' experience. [...] Disability issues are aired [...] through the characters as they talk from experience, rather than using politically prepared lines. It leads to some pretty chal- lenging viewpoints, if judged against the disability movement's ortho- doxy. But I for one think the play was better for that.[6]

Beaty's story also stems from experience: as a result of medical advice (she has a rare disease, with a low life expectancy) she put her child up for adoption and was sterilized: 'When my apparently normal not-at-all

special baby was delivered, this special mum received a special operation, without consent or knowledge, to ensure no further specials were
conceived.'[7] On looking back, she differentiates between biological and
practising motherhood, and opposes giving birth to long-term caring
for children: 'I've had a child. But I've not been a mother.'[8] In the case
of both Alpha and Beaty, therefore, O'Reilly seemingly looks at women
coerced out of their agency and control over their own body. Refusing
to portray women as victims, however, she balances these stories with
that of a woman (Coral) who decides independently on the future of
her pregnancy. Coral is in the process of making her mind up while
hearing the others' stories, and she is still in control until she starts
bleeding spontaneously. In fact, this build-up towards Coral's decision
constitutes the emotional core of the play, a process during which the
women experience an entire scale of nuances in human relationships.
Initially, Alpha and Beaty appear indifferent to Coral's pregnancy, trying to prevent their own re-living of their past: 'It's not a baby. It's a collection of cells. A blood clot. Little more than a minor thrombosis.'[9]
This lack of solidarity between women is underpinned by constant allu-
sions to diversity (as well as to promiscuity), but in fact, despite pre-
tending that individual routes are different, Alpha and Beaty urge Coral
to follow their path and terminate the baby.

In parallel with the three women's individual stories runs a strand
exploring the fate of women in various historically specific environments, including the Holocaust, in a universal framework of suffering,
sacrifice and eugenics. The two strands are linked by the same women
being members of the chorus in a performance of *The Trojan Women* and
as individuals sharing their personal stories when they are not in character. The women do not move in space to mark the shift from chorus
to individuals, but they are lit differently depending on the situation.
Developments in the 'play within the play', however, deeply impact the
three women's own selves, and it is their confrontation with the meta-
theatrical infanticides that triggers Alpha's and Beaty's private confessions of termination and adoption. The chorus addresses the horrible
responsibility of killing one's own offspring in kindness rather than let
somebody else do it: 'Mamma's precious/Future joy/now rank/sullied/
gone forever/Child. Child.'[10] In a different image, influenced by Sylvia
Plath's poetry as well as O'Reilly's own witnessing of war crimes in the
former Yugoslavia, a child is folded back inside the womb rather than
allowed to 'die by suicide bomb in a crowded discotheque'.[11] In another reference, rooted in the Rwandan genocide, a surviving girl finds her
massacred mother's body curled around her infant son.

These images contribute as much as Alpha's and Beaty's personal advice to Coral's decision. She is concerned with lineage and the transmission of values from mothers to daughters: 'Do you think we all end up just like our mothers?'[12] Fully aware of the responsibility of parenthood, Coral emphasizes the unorthodox circumstances in which her baby would grow up: not in a nuclear family but in an extended unit comprising a carer as well, by definition required to patronize her and potentially undermine her authority as a parent. Ultimately she is inclined to give life a chance, supported by both Alpha and Beaty who, by this stage, have not only put their feud aside but also revisited their own mothers' inadequate parenting and inability to handle with tact their daughters' disabilities. The earlier sequences emphasized the constant tension between Beaty and her mother and there is an image where Beaty is, jokingly, stamping on her mother's grave, so she cannot rise again. This episode re-enacts the psychological mutilation Beaty underwent as a child, but also encapsulates her ability to move on to an unsentimental reassessment of her relationship with her mother. In the final scene, Beaty empties Alpha's knitting bag and takes its contents of baby clothes to Coral's wheelchair, hanging the clothes on the fairy lights set up, as an emblem of their new-found bond, between the three crinolines. As further images of sacrifice and death appear on the screen, Alpha and Beaty formulate their plea to Coral: 'Have the bloody baby. [...] To make up for those we've lost.'[13]

'Graeae has found a bold, engaging way of addressing issues many people would prefer not to be confronted with in a play,'[14] claimed a reviewer, and indeed some members of the disabled community felt betrayed by such public revelations (though others identified with the abortion and adoption stories), while some non-disabled audience members felt uncomfortable about being invited to look at disabled bodies. The performers start the play in elaborate clothing (including their cage-like crinolines) but gradually remove their layers, finishing the play in their underwear. O'Reilly's motivation at stripping her women, apart from the parallel with peeling away the emotional veneer, was the desire to present women's bodies in ways different from currently fashionable trends. This confrontation was meant to be uncomfortable and provocative, but for some audiences the impact remained only at a superficial level, including several reviewers who were unable to get beyond the physical description of the protagonists and missed out on the play's strong disability politics. One of the aims of the production was to call attention to the inadequacies of media representation, and there is a section where the performers complain about being objectified and described as freaks. As it happens, O'Reilly contends, 'the real-life reviewers, who saw this in the play, went away and continued doing it!'[15]

By coining phrases such as 'Cripping up. The twenty-first century's answer to blacking up' and '"Disabled people are the heroes of our time." Peter Brook said that. Heroes for whom?' O'Reilly attacks the lip service associated with disability and with excessive political correctness, and hopes to challenge the play's audience to rethink their preconceptions regarding performers' bodies and the representation of disability in the media.[16] Graeae, as a company composed of disabled artists, has also been endeavouring to contribute to this campaign since their inception, lobbying the mainstream world 'to stop being so frightened of seeing disabled people on stage'.[17] Ironically, O'Reilly has been approached by several theatre companies in order to stage *Peeling*, but invariably with an able-bodied cast. For O'Reilly, allowing the play to be produced with non-disabled performers would undermine its entire politics and is, consequently, unacceptable. In her view, people are simply terrified of using disabled practitioners and it will take time until this state of affairs changes. Sealey also states that there is much to be done and not enough people are involved, but gives due credit to the Arts Council for funding disabled artists. O'Reilly likens the disability movement to the earlier movement in black theatre, noting that as cross-racial casting has become more common, hopefully disabled actors will not just play Richard III either: 'Disabled theatre as such might not be necessary one day, just as women's theatre or black theatre might not be a necessity any more, all entering the mainstream.'[18]

The idea of lip service paid by mainstream society to disability issues was highlighted in relation to the radio version of *Peeling* as well. O'Reilly adapted the script herself and included a section whereby the stage manager made an announcement along the lines of 'in the European Year of the Disabled Person we give lip service to disability politics'.[19] In this way O'Reilly adopted a more provocative tone than she did on stage, and also acknowledged the motivation of the BBC in programming a Graeae show to boost their equal opportunities profile. Another alteration, with an impact on the psychological make-up of the play, was the relocation of Coral from a confrontational character to the audience's confidante. This decision made Coral more likeable for the listener, as onstage she is a fierce arbiter who interrogates her co-performers and, crucially, the audience: 'I watch them – the audience – their heads sleek in the dark [...] I watch them – but it's transgressive – I'm to be stared at, not them.'[20] Referencing Laura Mulvey's dichotomy of the 'active male' and 'passive female', O'Reilly subverts the concept of the male gaze projecting its fantasy onto the female figure. As Mulvey argues,

> In their traditional exhibitionist role women are simultaneously looked at and displayed, with their appearance coded for strong visual and erotic impact so that they can be said to connote *to-be-looked-at-ness*. [...] Traditionally, the woman displayed has functioned on two levels: as erotic object for the characters within the screen story, and as erotic object for the spectator within the auditorium.[21]

Fully aware of the empowerment associated with the bearer of the gaze, Coral gradually overturns the lack of control versus control binary set out both in the female versus male, and disabled versus able-bodied equations, by transforming into a gazer in lieu of the previous gazed at. As she recognizes the potential of female spectatorship, she returns the gaze of the audience – making the latter uncomfortable, not unlike the way Coral herself feels when scrutinized on account of her disability, sexuality and impending motherhood.[22] While the most vulnerable figure transforms into the most powerful one, established hierarchies of gender and corporeal ability are undermined; *Peeling* makes its mark as a radical and 'quietly ground-breaking show for a whole generation of women'.[23]

Cake

Cake, written by Sarah Woods and directed by Emma Bernard, constitutes the latest phase in the long-standing collaboration between Jade Theatre Company and the playwright, to be continued into the future with their forthcoming production *How to Live Well*. Their earlier comedy *Grace* (1997) looked at the world of a woman turning 30, while *Cake* examines aspects of practising motherhood in a surreal comic format. *Cake* was first performed at the Door, Birmingham Repertory Theatre, on 25 September 2003, and played to sell-out audiences at BAC in December 2003. It was revived for a national tour in 2005 (including a week at the Riverside Studios) prior to appearing at the British Council Showcase in Edinburgh.

In a kitchen-cum-television cookery show environment, the protagonist (Mum played by Victoria Worsley) embarks on a quest for the perfect cake, demonstrating the various steps undertaken and assisted by two animators (Rebekah Wild and James Marson) and an arsenal of kitchen utensils. While making a variety of cakes, Mum is exposed to constant distractions from her offspring: a large female doll called John and a number of spoons, ladles and spatulas, all animated by the puppeteers (John was also voiced by Marson).[24] In the process, major philosophical questions, such as love, hate and happiness, are explored in juxtaposition to technical details of cake-making, bringing into focus not only the mother's perspective on her relationship with her children, but also the children's view of their mother and their need for constant parental attention and affection. As Woods clarifies, John is a toddler while the utensils are babies, and 'John is a philosopher – discussing and analysing his actions, whereas the utensils just are – they are simply concerned with being in the present moment'.[25]

Jade was founded by Victoria Worsley in 1992 with the aim of bringing together the structural rigour of new writing with the dynamism and experimental potential of visual and physical theatre. The starting point for a Jade show needs to be a recognizable story, with content as its driving force. The company locates the writer at the core of the creative process and workshops with the full team including designers, choreographers and other specialists so that all relevant theatrical elements are fully integrated. In the case of *Cake*, these ambitions translate into a tightly written script and remarkable puppeteering skills juxtaposed with Worsley's acting, all resulting in a credible chemistry between the animate and non-animate cast. Crossing boundaries in terms of genre and audience expectations, *Cake* emerges as a highly original piece of theatre that gives audiences an enjoyable night out while challenging them to relate in a new way to both dramaturgical possibilities and relationships across the generations.

Cake's connection with animation and puppeteering came from Woods's dislike of work that claims to be about people who have children and then uses an offstage family. In other words, she had to find a way of dramatizing the children without having them present. The initial idea was to animate children's toys, but then they moved on to kitchen implements – 'as a way of authentically presenting that relationship on stage, doing it and not just talking about it'.[26] Woods and Worsley discovered the potential of spoons by working with Steve Tiplady, and then, through a series of development workshops, put them to the test. Woods was interested to look at the functionality of the objects in relation to the story, and to examine John's role in it.

According to the playwright, the piece is about recognition: both of ourselves as mothers, and how we were as children. Woods notes that she could only have written the script having had children herself, because it is very much about that particular perspective. Theatre works best for Woods when 'the personal is also discovered to be universal: so that the particular experience we journey through connects with motherhood as we understand it now'.[27] Woods relates her work to recent trends that combine various art forms, and is interested in theatricality rather than naturalism. She is preoccupied with issues of identity and modern existence, and acknowledges being influenced by feminist theory. She feels that women today face a complex situation, where they seem to have access to an abundance of choices but in reality that can signify very busy lives which juxtapose the identities of fifties housewife and career woman. Worsley continues to see feminism 'as working towards the liberation of women' as, on the one hand, many old beliefs have remained unchallenged and, on the other hand, 'constraining pressures [were] left over from early forms of feminism'.[28] She stresses the need for collaboration with men, together with revisiting women's role in theatre in a variety of capacities. She laments that women's chances for entering management posts arises only in moments of financial crisis, but celebrates the contribution of women as far as the gender representation on stage is concerned. Worsley adds:

> Feminism has also played a part in challenging the idea of what a play is in terms of its form, where it is performed and how it is made, in providing the impetus for some of the agit prop, collective devising, performance art, and other innovations in writing and performing since the late 1960s.[29]

Woods contends that the idea for *Cake* has come from the feeling that 'women are juggling so many things that it has become almost impossible to achieve any one thing without great trial and complexity'.[30] Her initial aim was 'to put the distracted parent's state of mind centre stage',[31] an idea subsequently developed in partnership with the animators. Thus, the final script – not unlike O'Reilly's earlier integration of sign language – incorporated specific details with regard to animations, alongside mirroring some of the personal experiences of the collaborators. Director Emma Bernard notes in this sense how *Cake* 'connects' with her 'experience of parenthood' and emphasizes the importance of recognizing herself – 'trying to sound like a serious, mature professional while my children destroy the house in the pursuit of fun, and can't understand why I'm not playing'.[32] Research for the production was also informed by Woods's encounter with cake artist Janet Morgan and discussions with Dr Iain Law at Birmingham University on the definition of well-being. Inspired by Law's comment that philosophers 'take seriously the childish questions that other people have grown out of',[33] Woods delves into precisely such a universe of constant inquiry in order to pin down what is a good life from the twin perspectives of parents and children.

In the process, priorities are established and discarded and love is intertwined with instances of hate and violence. As David Edgar notes in his preface to the published text, Woods is 'adept at expressing the mounting panic of women feeling their life slipping out of control'.[34] The playwright emphasizes the enormous pressure that the practice of motherhood entails, and centres on the ways in which Mum addresses this issue. Following Mum's perspective, *Cake* renders the fluctuation between varying degrees of patience in response to the attention-seeking and awkward questioning – especially John's emotional blackmail. Mum constantly interrupts her work with revelations, addressed to the audience, on how little of her life is under her own control; however, she also reiterates her unconditional love for her children. In fact, Mum's confession, that she adores her children yet still dislikes certain things that they do, constitutes a simultaneously transgressive and highly plausible aspect of the piece:

> MUM: When cake doesn't stop your children hitting each other and wanting to kill each other, and you sometimes doubt your own ability to stop yourself hitting your own children. When even though you don't have enough eggs to make cake for all the children, you know that you are not a bad person and nor are your children or any of the other children and cake is such a good thing.[35]

Concurrently, the audience is also invited to note that making cakes is Mum's way of integrating a personalized routine for herself into the domestic chores, while, as she claims, she is working for the benefit of the family:

> MUM: I don't make cake for my own amusement.
> JOHN: I think you'll find you do.
> MUM: I'm doing this for you. We're making cake together.
> JOHN: We're not. You're making cake. [...]
> MUM: The whole point of the cake is that it's for all of us.
> JOHN: I think it's for your personal satisfaction.[36]

Mum talks about the 'cake event' as opposed to John's perception of 'the prison made of cake' and his open confrontation of the entire endeavour: 'If this cake is making none of us happy, why are we here?'[37]

Visually the production verges on the exuberant as water, flour and eggs fly around in abundance on the set, and Worsley dives into the sink to rescue and resuscitate a wooden spoon and then lay it to rest in a bed of tea-towels, or the uncanny as the entire bunch of utensils appear to breastfeed on her. The utensils belong to a group or are individualized, as their animators change body language and facial expression. Referring to the utensils disrupting the relative order of Mum's world, Edgar points out their innovative nature as 'theatrical images', which make 'Mum's inner life visible and as such do the same job as the Greek chorus, the Shakespearean soliloquy and the Restoration aside'.[38] It is in her interactions with the utensils that Mum grows to understand not only her own unconditional love but also the emotions she is the recipient of; and as the play climaxes, Mum and all the utensils try a piece of the cake made together, even John admitting that he would join in if he could:

MUM: I love you.
(TEA SPOON brings her a mouthful of cake. She leans down and takes it with her mouth – chews and swallows, although it sticks in her throat.)
JOHN: I love you very much.
MUM: I would die for you, John.
JOHN: And I would eat cake for you, Mummy, if I could.[39]

Yerma's Eggs

Unlike most case studies in this volume, *Yerma's Eggs* constitutes only a phase in Anna Furse's long-term project to deal with the biological and psychological challenges of becoming a parent. Furse overtly acknowledges drawing on personal experience, and wishes to provide an artistic interpretation of her own traumatic journey through reduced fertility and medically assisted reproduction. Furse's response to the topic includes various manifestations in different media, starting from her *Infertility Companion* (published soon after the birth of her child via IVF at the age of 42); *The Peach Child* (a play written for children); *Yerma's Eggs*; an academic research project and various affiliated articles addressing barrenness and infertility; and an interactive installation exploring our relationship to our bodies as it is presented through imaging technologies, entitled *Glass Body: Reflecting on Becoming Transparent*.[40] Talking in 2005 about her work as an artist negotiating the domestic, Furse indicated her method of intertwining poetry and technology, and the importance of acknowledging the psychological trauma of reduced fertility (she calls it 'sub-fertility') and of pinpointing the availability of medical procedures: 'Because that's how I experienced it – an odd cyborgian synthesis in which my heart ruled my head but my political self somehow kept my eye on the what-is-going-on-here angle.'[41]

The idea of developing an idea over time and in its different hypostases is, therefore, significant to Furse's approach, as well as reaching out to diverse audiences. Furse conducts workshops in schools to this end and collaborates with science and religious education as well as drama teachers, also offering material to be used in class. The teachers' resource packs to accompany *Yerma's Eggs*, written and compiled by Furse and Emma Rosenberg, bring together biological facts with questions on religion and bioethics, drama and creative writing exercises, artistic images and poems about being infertile. Continuing the idea of intellectual and artistic process and of reaching multiple audiences, the London performances of *Yerma's Eggs* were presented in conjunction with a series of bioethical discussions. Chaired by Julie Tizzard, the discussions focused on topics such as designer babies and embryo selection, IVF and the non-traditional family, and human cloning (Figure 4).

Yerma's Eggs premièred at the Riverside Studios in London on 28 May 2003, and subsequently toured to the Harbourside in Bristol. It was presented by Athletes of the Heart, a company founded by Furse as artistic director and launched with this production. Aiming to create productions in various media about the changing world in the early third millennium, the company operates as a framework for collaborations between Furse and other artists, such as deviser–performers Joy Elias-Rilwan, Shobu Kapoor, Anthony Newell, Giovanna Rogante, Helen Spackman, Carlos Vesga, the composer Sylvia Hallett and the designer Agnes Treplin. In *Yerma's Eggs* excerpts from the translation by Peter Luke of Frederico Garcia Lorca's *Yerma* constituted the backbone of the spoken text,[42] interspersed with sections written by Furse herself and devised by the company. Crucially, however, the spoken text amounted to only one aspect of the production, as Furse noted:

> I didn't want to write a play, impose my authority on a single-track narrative, as this would imply working on but one of so many possible medical infertility factors. I wanted to get under the skin of the subject via the body in performance – expressionistically, viscerally, and reflect complexity and contradiction via a layering of elements.[43]

Throughout, film material shot by Steve Hopkins, Ajaykumar, Robin Scobey, Steve Rafter and Anna Furse was projected on the walls and floor of the performance space and on the bodies of the performers, together with the projection of medical images, such as 4D ultrasound

Figure 4 Image from *Yerma's Eggs* by Anna Furse, Athletes of the Heart at the Riverside Studios, 2003 (photo: Hugo Glendinning, reproduced by photographer's permission).

of a baby *in utero*, the egg cell, sperm fertilizing the egg and ICSI (intra cytoplasmic sperm injection – a single non-motile sperm injected directly into the egg cell in cases of male infertility). The sources of these images reveal the company's ambitions to connect with experts and the latest technologies in the field, Professor Stuart Campbell, the laboratories of Simon Fishel of CARE, Nottingham and the Wellcome Trust medical photographic library. In order to offer an alternative to scientific rigour and to counterbalance the timelessness and expressionistic framework of the production, as well as to create a sense of actual public awareness of the issues raised, the production opened with five minutes of *vox pop* interviews (conducted in schools and on the street) projected in the auditorium before the start of the performance. Questions included the likes of: 'How many eggs is a woman born with?' 'How many eggs and sperm are needed to make an embryo?' or 'What does IVF stand for?' Most respondents were unsure of the correct answers, thus not only framing but also reinforcing Furse's claim for the necessity of addressing such issues in any manner possible.

The production aimed to explore the current status quo regarding the public perception of biomedical technology, via the opposition between human and microscopic scale, and confronting medical imagery in a fresh environment. Projected throughout the performance space, these images redefined both the audience's and the performers' sense of boundaries, and challenged them to reassess not only their understanding of private versus public but also of spectacle and spectatorship. Like Furse, all the performers had some previous involvement with infertility and/or alternative forms of reproduction, and all brought their respective cultural heritage to the production. Aiming at universalizing the Spanish source text, the performance celebrated multiculturalism as Joy Elias-Rilwan integrated Nigerian, Shobu Kapoor Indian, Giovanna Rogante Italian and Carlos Vesga Colombian references to Anthony Newell's and Helen Spackman's British experiences. All performers brought a song handed down from their grandmother to their mother (some explicitly about the inability to have children), and all devised some elements of the production.

Yerma's Eggs opens with a six-minute scene re-enacting birth, in which the company and the audience watch as a performer emerges, toe by toe from under a pile of flesh-coloured textile. She is Yerma, envisaging herself into a baby. In the course of the show all the performers assume the role of Yerma, irrespective of gender, race or age, and take their turns to comment, like Lorca's washerwomen, on the trope of the childless woman. Utilizing sections verbatim from Lorca, barrenness is opposed to fertility, and the social stigmatization of the ageing childless woman is highlighted. Juxtaposing the individual versus the group, the play reflects on envy and lack of solidarity between women when it comes to motherhood. Neither Maria, pregnant after just five months of marriage, nor Yerma, unable to conceive, can rely on the genuine support of their community. As the performers engage in overlapping dialogue, speeches end up superimposed on one another and individual voices are left unheard. Roles get constantly changed and lines are repeated and passed on from performer to performer:

> MARIA: Well, it's happened!
> YERMA: After only five months? [...] Are you sure? [...] What does it feel like?
> MARIA Oh, I don't know. Have you ever held a live bird in your hands? [...] well, it feels the same – but more inside your blood, somehow. [...]
> YERMA: [...] You're so lucky![44]

Underpinning the Lorca references, a key staple of the production is the constant integration of two elements: water and sand. The play begins with the sound of water and finishes with images of a playground, settling on a lone daffodil in the sand. The playground as a site of longing for a child is suggested by images projected on the walls in the latter part of the piece, and constitutes a personal memento to Furse's own experience while under infertility treatment.[45] Sand is also connected to the frustration of the woman unable to conceive, throwing sand about in one scene, and to the contemporary technological scenes, for instance, when a couple is shown being offered a consultation by a fertility expert, where hands and fingers are held in a Michelangelo-style creation manner, sand being sieved through them. Water is often introduced as an antidote for heat, aridity and thirst, and waiting for the rain, waiting for something to happen, parallels the longing for fertility. For instance, in one scene a woman with a child tries to sneak past the set, trying not to make the current reincarnation of the barren Yerma, situated centre stage, resentful:

YERMA: It isn't envy, it's despair! How can I help it when I see you and all the others in full bloom, while I am withering away.[46]

In the scene above, Yerma is transposed into an African context featuring a female protagonist; however, the role is later offered to a male performer wearing a colourful peasant shirt and thus connoting a timeless Southern Europe or South America. This time Lorca is invoked in the Spanish original as well, and attention is being focused on some of the causes behind infertility. Unlike other scenes where barrenness is exposed as a fact, or hope in a turn towards fertility is fantasized about, this instance attempts to unveil the secret about something left unspoken and to inquire into destiny itself: 'Why am I childless? Must I spend the rest of my life like this?'[47] In another re-enactment of Yerma, we see a frail, older woman with a twig in her mouth, arms stretched towards the audience. Like in an earlier sequence, all others watch her and laugh, starting to gossip as children's voices are heard in the background. As they recreate elements of the Yerma–Maria dialogue, scientific images are projected on the walls, accompanied by the sound of rain. All actors cross the stage before the images of babies *in utero*. Yet another Yerma, in a slow-moving dream-like setting, addresses her imaginary baby rather than look for causes for barrenness or seek social approval: 'You must come, my love, my child. Because the sea gives salt and the earth fruit.'[48]

The pressures of time and ageing are foregrounded throughout, on the one hand by sharing the role of Yerma between a range of performers, and on the other hand by sound effects, including the repetitive toll of bells and chimes in an attempt to recreate the ticking of the biological clock. Time, however, is also a fluid phenomenon and the performance acknowledges the varying perceptions of it depending on cultural location. Apart from the pace of the respective scenes and casting itself, it is music that emphasizes this difference, for instance, by conjuring up a fast-paced psychedelic atmosphere in the contemporary European/Western scenes, and featuring soothing lullabies in the scenes invoking India or Africa. Colour symbolism also sets up a sense of dichotomy, mainly opposing the blue and bright yellow of the contemporary scenes in which technology is being referred to, and the warm hue of oranges and reds in the scenes recreating a traditional, timeless world.

In other scenes based directly on Lorca, the performance explores the opposition between the varying desires for a child of men and women. The blue light and fast pace suggest a contemporary environment, though the issue stems directly from the Yerma–Juan opposition:

> WOMAN: I thought I heard a child crying. [...]
> MAN: I can't hear anything.
> WOMAN: I must have imagined it.[49]

Introduced by a Spanish song, a young woman, another Yerma, is captured in front of a magnified projection of a five-week-old embryo, superimposed on her body. As above, her desire for a child is not reciprocated by her husband. Using a verbatim dialogue from Lorca, he is unable to understand his wife's need for having her own offspring, and can only highlight the destructive aspect of such an obsessive desire. In Lorca's play it is this scene that leads Yerma to strangle her husband, Juan, in *Yerma's Eggs* it is one of the several debates taking place between couples on the subject.

Two gay characters, for instance, offer a different picture as far as the desire for parenthood across the gender divide is concerned. They connect giving birth to both the male and female realm, and acknowledge the question of immortality achievable via reproduction:

> I'd like to know what it feels like to give birth. It's such an amazing thing.
> Would you like to see yourself reborn through your kids?
> - No, I wouldn't wish myself on anyone.

- You're beautiful.
- We won't reproduce ourselves. They think it's selfish.
- We are mortal beings, you and I, getting older every day. The breeders of this world have access to a sense of immortality.
- Do *you* want children?[50]

A crucial theme of *Yerma's Eggs* is the issue of privacy and integrity versus the medical invasion of the body. In a confessional scene recalling childhood memories, medical intervention in general is presented as intrusive. Unlike the physicality of most scenes, this is a static sequence where the performer talks to the audience direct. She claims that getting inside the body, for instance via video equipment, equals going 'too much near the future', which should be left mysterious.

In contrast, one of the longest and best accomplished scenes looks at the current medical obsession with the inside of the body. It is interspersed with scientific terminology regarding IVF, yet it does not deviate from the poetic mode of the rest of the piece. Integrating solemn music and the projection of images on various procedures associated with IVF on the walls and the body of the female performer, the scene succeeds in intertwining the scientific and the human, the public and the private. It also makes pertinent points about the motivations of those seeking such treatment: 'I measure time in menstrual cycles. [...] Doctor declared me infertile. [...] I don't recognize myself. I'm engulfed in my own emptiness.'[51] Crucially, the passage refrains from celebrating medical expertise – in fact it calls attention to its invasiveness and voyeurism as sharply as the previous memory scene – seeking instead to examine its psychological as well as biological impact on those involved in the treatment. In yet another layer of explorations, an article addressing her own experience of infertility treatment and the making of *Yerma's Eggs*, Furse emphasizes the emergence of a new relationship with her body and her desire to remain in control of her 'project and all its science (knowledge) and technology (art)'.[52] For Furse it is crucial to voice the sub-fertile woman's perspective, which often tends to get marginalized in media coverage. She is adamant on revisiting the context in which such a topic is discussed, and points out the damaging effect of presenting the fertility experts as 'playing God' and the sub-fertile as selfish or pathetic victims: 'We have to be in charge here. Doctor is not god, nor father for the baby.'[53]

Another major concern for Furse, in relation to the aftermath of IVF, is the idea of the intra-uterine development becoming a spectacle. In standard cases of pregnancy the embryo is unseen till a relatively late stage, but for IVF patients the visual encounter with their unborn babies commences almost immediately after conception. This visualization is carried out in order to monitor the evolution of the new life, but it deeply impacts on the way the pregnant woman experiences her relationship with her child. Moreover, since scientific attention in such cases is almost exclusively geared towards the foetus, the outcome is a literal as well as symbolic writing out of the mother: 'Fetal interpellation manifests a new form of the old desire to absent (or deny) the mother.'[54] With the latest advances in 4D ultrasound it is possible to spectate the foetus in the womb almost straightaway, locating women in the twin position of the gazer and the gazed at. Thus, women find themselves – as also formulated by O'Reilly's Coral – simultaneously experiencing the vulnerability of objectification, replicating the traditional male perspective of voyeuristic pleasure, and also experimenting with the feminist appropriation of spectatorship. With Donna Haraway's theoretical support, however, Furse also calls attention to the potentially damaging effect of overexposure: 'The technologies of visualization recall the important cultural practice of hunting with the camera and the deeply predatory nature of a photographic consciousness. Sex, sexuality and reproduction are central actors in the high-tech myth systems structuring our imaginations of personal and social possibility.'[55]

Furse notes, dwelling on the work of medical historians, that contemporary imaging tools offer not only an overall picture of the inside of the body as in an X-ray, but snapshots of isolated sections:

> Human eggs, sperm and embryos can now be moved from body to body or out of and back into the same female body. The organic unity of fetus and mother can no longer be assumed, and all these newly fragmented parts can now be subjected to market forces, ordered, produced, bought and sold.[56]

Haraway famously stated that 'Cyborg replication is uncoupled from organic reproduction',[57] which in Furse's interpretation translates into the following observation, 'Our reproductive bits have a potential all of their own, even without us. Our private parts become moveable parts. We paradoxically dis-integrate our organic selves, even if temporarily, in our quest to experience integrity, the fulfilment of our reproductive desires.'[58] As a result of medical expertise it is now possible to dissociate heterosexual sex altogether from reproduction; a landmark stage in terms of sexual politics, making parenthood potentially available to everyone, irrespective of sexual orientation or partner support.

Through this technology it is equally possible to delay pregnancy until beyond the time when a woman's body produces viable eggs, thus dislocating age boundaries and expectations with regard to an adequate timing of motherhood. By highlighting these aspects, Furse also connects to Sadie Plant's brand of cyberfeminism, according to which technology is not necessarily a patriarchal instrument. For Plant, it is men – rather than women – who have lost out more significantly by surrendering their traditional powers to the likes of computers and reproductive technologies, and hence find themselves on the brink of redundancy.[59]

Despite such advances in technology, the public perception of childlessness has traditionally been gendered and associated with a language of failure and incompetence oriented at women. Emily Martin charts a picture of menstruation as a pathological phenomenon, and addresses the long-term association between women's periods and unsuccessful processes of production. She quotes medical journals published as recently as in the mid-eighties that perceive menstruation as 'the uterus crying out for a baby', and she establishes parallels between the menopause – seen as a 'kind of failure of the authority structure in the [female] body' – and menstruation: 'a failed production', 'a production gone awry, making products of no use, not to specification, unsaleable, wasted, scrap'.[60]

Responding to this idea, Furse's Yerma repeatedly picks up verbatim on Lorca's words: 'I'm sick and weary. Weary of being a woman not put to proper use. [...] And here I am with two hammers beating at my breasts where my baby's mouth should be [...].'[61] Yerma is the barren woman *par excellence*, and both Lorca and Furse explore the dry landscape and heat to oppose her to the orchards and water linked to fertility. Thus, Yerma is associated with both nature and deviation from nature at the same time, an opposition Furse embraces when addressing medically assisted reproduction. She points out how IVF users end up stigmatized by public opinion for interfering with nature, yet find themselves encouraged by medical technology to extend the boundaries of 'natural' conception.[62]

Joining the debate on the legal status of the unborn child and exploring issues of personhood and bioethics are among the major goals of the production and its accompanying workshop series. Several scenes call attention to the responsibility of those involved, in any capacity, in the process of artificial reproduction, and formulate questions as to reproductive rights and the ownership of the yet unborn, such as 'When does the embryo become human?' 'Who owns frozen embryos?' 'Are embryos a commodity?' 'Who has the right to reproduce?'[63] The play also touches on the relationship between assisted conception and eugenics, and signals the existence of an ongoing controversy.

Rather than merely setting out an opposition, however, the focus is on versatility. Utilizing the simile of the knife, simultaneously a murderous weapon, a tool instrumental in feeding the starving and a life-saving device through its role in surgery, *Yerma's Eggs* explores the importance of taking a broader view on the potential of technology and on assessing its suitability to every individual case in part.

This focus on the individual is continued in one of the most moving sections of the play, in which the performers approach the audience on a personal level and share their own stories. As Jane Edwardes rightly argues, despite being 'funded by the Wellcome Trust, the production [...] concentrates on the emotions of the desperate would-be mothers, rather than the science';[64] and these stories hark back to different childhood experiences, and bring together a multitude of approaches with regard to conceiving and raising children. Thus, coming to terms with being given up for adoption and not knowing one's biological parents is juxtaposed to addressing cloning, by a parent for the benefit of a child, and thereby reducing the essence of what is human to the level of perception available to a three-year-old. The impact of a child's death on the mother, witnessed from the perspective of a medical practitioner, focuses on the parent's trauma and ritualistic self-destruction, while imagining a time before one's birth and connecting to a moment when one's parents were of the same age, investigates the problem of lineage from the point of view of a young girl. Last but not least, one performer claims to have been born naturally, thus paving the way for the investigation of what is regarded as natural in contemporary society.

Uttered by a male performer and addressed directly to the audience, a selection of items are suggested for further consideration. Compiled by Furse, the list offers a snapshot of goods and experiences a person living in the Western world at the turn of the third millennium is likely to encounter on a more or less regular basis.[65] During the slow pace of a lyrical enunciation the cast re-enact via body language earlier stages from the play. Throughout this process, music continued to be played and enormous images of playgrounds were projected on the performers' bodies and the stage. Subsequently, a version of this list has been used in workshops in schools and Furse claims that the items provoke debates that reveal how illogical and sentimental our feelings about nature are. Prompted by these terms, the conversation can move onto the terrain of bioethics and examine factors such as religious or cultural conditioning, and Furse indicates that talking about her own experience of successful IVF and raising her child in the knowledge of her history can help others to relate to the subject.[66] This is why she chose to end the performance with a contribution from her daughter: 'There was a block, you had to go to hospital, the doctor took some of your eggs [...], then put into it daddy's sperm [...], and then I was made.'[67]

This matter-of-fact analysis of origins truly concludes the play's multiple preoccupations, suggesting a new generation's coming to terms with reproductive technology and their ability not to get entangled in reservations with regard to such an intervention. As the list is completed and the colours projected onto the performance space turn into black and white, a yellow daffodil emerges in the playground sand. The image of hope introduced earlier comes full circle, underpinned by the promise of vitality and fulfilment. The piece ends, therefore, with the voice of a child, reinforcing the personal note of Furse and her collaborators. The performance, however, goes beyond the confines of the autobiographical as it successfully intertwines medical and technological processes with visual and physical theatre. The performance can be perhaps, at times, an unsettling experience for the audience, as, in Furse's words,

> Making babies should be a private affair. With IVF it can't be. As a woman, a writer and theatre maker I have embraced this lack of privacy and tried to make it work for me, by taking possession of it, articulating it, refusing to be silenced by the pain and humiliation of it all.[68]

Conclusion

As the works discussed in this chapter illustrate, the debate on parenthood has further diversified in the twenty-first century, also elaborating on issues articulated at the close of the previous millennium. Thus, the desire for motherhood has been discussed from a disability perspective by Kaite O'Reilly, who also juxtaposes parenthood with renunciation, via termination and adoption; the interrogation of fertility and reproductive technologies have been examined involving both dramatic intertextuality and contemporary science by Anna Furse; whereas practising motherhood has appeared as the topic utilized by Sarah Woods. Unlike earlier playwrights, none of the authors included here looks at mother and (adult) daughter relationships; however, Woods examines a young mother in relation to her toddler and babies, and she features a domestic environment in opposition to O'Reilly's and Furse's public settings.

Feminist ideas have continued to inform the politics of playwrights, practitioners and theatre companies, more overtly in the case of those who started their careers in the latter part of the twentieth century, and more covertly for the younger generation. Anna Furse talks in 2005 about the imminence of 'unfinished sexual political business',[69] in relation to women still doing the majority of domestic work often in addition to full-time employment, and the lack of adequate male involvement in child-care. This perspective ties in with Victoria Worsley's observation that although there have been feminist advances, there is 'still a long way to go'.[70] For others, feminist concerns appear in conjunction with major civil rights issues, such as disability politics for Kaite O'Reilly and Graeae. In fact, O'Reilly draws a parallel between developments in women's liberation – as well as the black movement – and the disability move-ment, and hopes to see similar advances and a general sense of awareness of current issues in due course.

In terms of dramaturgy, most of the work examined investigates new pathways. Writers collaborate intensely with theatre and production companies, and incorporate references to the full performance apparatus into their scripts. Thus, O'Reilly pioneers the integration of audio descrip-tion and sign language with verbal dialogue, Sarah Woods scripts puppeteering into her play, and Anna Furse layers her piece, also inter-textual with Lorca, with multimedia elements and projections of medical and scientific imagery. In other words, addressing ardent issues – such as the desire for a child in conditions of reduced fertility or disability, as well as the practical challenges of being a parent – appears in tandem with a search for a new dramatic language, stemming from the playwrights' desire to expand the boundaries of dramaturgy and experimentation in performance. Thus, Graeae, Jade and Athletes of the Heart make their mark as companies at the avant-garde of innovation in British theatre, also setting new standards as far as the composition of their cast is con-cerned: from inanimate objects appearing alongside an actor in *Cake,* to disabled performers taking centre stage in *Peeling* and a multinational cast in *Yerma's Eggs.*

Conclusions

This study has been concerned with multiplicity and diversity regarding the work of British women playwrights, in relation to successive configurations of motherhood between the mid-fifties and the present. Making use of feminist theory in particular, and referencing transformations in cultural, social, historical, political and medical contexts, it has reflected on dramatic representation and aspects of stage performance via a broad range of case studies, covering established and emerging playwrights, single-authored and collaborative work, text-based and devised material. The study has aimed at offering a representative sample of relevant work staged in Britain, and made an attempt at bringing together plays and productions by authors and practitioners from a variety of racial, sexual and class backgrounds and artistic and political platforms, presented at mainstream as well as fringe venues, and at highlighting aspects of audience and critical reception. The study has equally examined the circumstances in which women's work gets produced, and pinpointed the importance of nurturing new talent.

Women's playwriting in the fifties was marked by an aesthetic diversity, and constituted a turning point in British theatre. Rejecting biological determinism, dissociating parenting from the feminine and opening it up for both genders – while also locating the maternal as sensual and as a source of power – Enid Bagnold, Shelagh Delaney, Doris Lessing and Ann Jellicoe identified *avant la lettre* feminist concerns. Informed by bourgeois liberal as well as socialist feminism, Pam Gems's and Caryl Churchill's seventies and early eighties plays focused on the mutual exclusion between maternity and professional success. But while for Churchill's protagonists this choice was voluntary, Gems's Queen Christina was deprived of agency in this sense. Churchill considered and rejected surrogacy as an option in *Owners* and located it as a temporarily viable yet ultimately unsatisfactory arrangement in *Top Girls*. Thus, Churchill problematized both biological and surrogate parenthood, while Gems pinpointed the latter's failures, endorsing the supremacy of biological bonds.

When discussing mother–daughter relationships British women playwrights have covered a wide range of dynamics, whether the examination includes the wider community, the female line across several generations or mothers and daughters in a nuclear family. The theme was particularly prominent in eighties and nineties work, and included the discussion of difficulties in communication leading to inadequate or intrusive mothering (Louise Page, Shelagh Stephenson, Winsome Pinnock, Charlotte Keatley, Diane Samuels), as well as the reversal of the caring role, whereby the daughter assumed temporary responsibility and control (Page, Phyllis Nagy, Sarah Kane). Playwrights have also discussed the desire for motherhood as a route for self-affirmation and agency, especially on behalf of the teenage subject. Grace Dayley, Sharman MacDonald and Trish Cooke featured adolescents considering pregnancy and facing the adult world's reticence, while the Women's Theatre Group utilized such a situation to raise awareness about responsible sexual behaviour.

Whereas work produced between the fifties and mid-seventies took the possibility of motherhood for granted, being concerned with its inherent problems or with ways of circumventing or delaying it, starting from the late seventies preoccupation with maternal desire has also arisen. Michelene Wandor and Gay Sweatshop celebrated lesbian parenting, aiming to legitimize parental desire irrespective of sexuality, while Sarah Daniels raised the issue of child custody in non-heterosexual partnerships. The majority of post-nineties work has been looking at the relationship between biology and technology, or at non-biological forms of parenting. Jackie Kay and Timberlake Wertenbaker considered cross-cultural adoption, and both highlighted the intricacies of the process involved; but while Kay integrated a three-fold view (birth and adoptive mothers, and the daughter), Wertenbaker focused on the prospective adoptive parents only. She thus marginalized the experiences of the birth mother and the child, and reiterated the significant power and financial division involved in the adoption process.

Examining transformations in women's commitment to family, parenting and work throughout the late eighties and nineties, Trish Cooke, Claire Luckham and Timberlake Wertenbaker centred on career women wishing to start a family. For all these women conception or gestation was made problematic by age-related physiological difficulties, and was connected to a loss of agency. Despite the protagonists' genuine longing for motherhood, the playwrights mainly concentrated on their failure to achieve this goal, although in some cases they also indicated the reclamation of agency as a source of hope and compensation. Case studies from the early twenty-first century, on the other hand, have returned the focus on more positive ways of addressing the maternal: juxtaposed to the examination of disability and human rights agendas (Kaite O'Reilly), via a consideration of practising motherhood and the philosophy of caring (Sarah Woods), and last but not least, in relation to appropriating cutting-edge science (Anna Furse).

Lately, in fact, the very term 'motherhood' has become restrictive, and it has frequently metamorphosed into the more inclusive 'parenthood', alongside a continued interest in generational lines, parental longing, advances in technology and negotiating childcare in the family. The topic is increasingly appealing to authors of both genders, and as the examples below demonstrate, has generated a wide range of dramatic examinations. *Lear's Daughters* (1987), jointly scripted by Elaine Feinstein and the Women's Theatre Group, is a play on father–daughter relationships seen from a multiplicity of female perspectives, not only the daughters' but also that of a female company re-appropriating a canonical male-authored text. (This type of intertextuality has been signalled earlier, for instance, through the references to Chekhov by Wertenbaker.) Equally, *Lear's Daughters* scrutinizes the inability to bear sons (see *Queen Christina*) and the renunciation of biological motherhood for the sake of surrogacy. Drawing on the story of the biblical Abraham and Sarah, Michelene Wandor's *Wanted* (1988) brings together the desire for children, infertility, ageing and surrogate motherhood – prefiguring preoccupations of nineties theatre. *Wanted* emphasizes the pressure the media exercises on society in reinforcing particular models of beauty and behaviour, and references the medical route in operation to this day towards preventing foetal malformations. As Wandor highlights the role of science in both opening up new avenues for experimentation with human life and in exercising immense control, she ties in the discussion of reproductive technologies with surrogate parenthood, and examines the motivations of those involved. Although the question of economics in reproduction deserves more of an analysis, Wandor notably advocates the dissociation of parenthood from sexual orientation or marital status.

Exploring obsessive maternal desire, Ayshe Raif's *Caving In* (1989) investigates the protagonist's inner conflict between her longing for a child and loyalty to her husband. Faced with ageing and the absence of a partner, Maggie contemplates taking a decision on parenthood on her own, before – like Wertenbaker's Tess – she is forced to give up on her quest. Unlike Tess, however, Maggie does not have access to contestation; instead of searching for causes behind events she simply yields to defeat, thus replicating the resignation of Chekhov's sisters. Caryl Churchill's experimental play *The Skriker* (1994) analyses the relationship between vulnerability and motherhood, including the issue of how babies impact their mothers' lives and how they involuntarily determine the latter's actions. Churchill opposes the title character, able to metamorphose into different guises, and two young women, Josie and Lily. The play explores the Skriker's fascination with fertility, connected to the two women (Josie is in a mental institution, as she killed her baby while suffering from post-partum depression, and Lily is pregnant) and the complex power relations and dynamics of caring between the protagonists.

Ruth Carter's *A Yearning* (1995) – adapted from Lorca's *Yerma* – was written for Tamasha, a company aimed at reflecting through theatre the Asian experience. Carter relocates the play to nineties Birmingham, and explores the plight of women married into a society where their worth is measured by the ability to reproduce. For both the Asian community and Carter's Yerma-figure, Amar, having a child is the ultimate legitimization of a woman's destiny. Unlike many traditional communities, however, Amar's husband – like Lorca's Juan – is uninterested in fatherhood. Amar's yearning is further amplified by the contrast with women whose unproblematic ability to mother sets up an unattainable standard, and their lack of genuine sympathy a sense of worthlessness. As in Lorca, Amar's hopes are finally shattered by her husband's revelation of disinterest in fatherhood. It is, however, his dissociation of sexual activity from reproduction that leads to Amar's retaliation, even if this entails an ultimate closure of choices for herself too. Liz Lochhead's *Perfect Days* (1998) centres on Barbs, a Glasgow celebrity hairdresser in her late thirties. She is popular and surrounded by friends and family, but it is a baby that she craves above all else. So when she falls for a man ten years her junior, she instinctively grabs her last chance at unassisted conception. Lochhead presents Barbs's quest for motherhood as a project she pursues with full agency; however, due to the play's subversive comic format, she avoids a sentimental approach. Despite the Traverse production's mixed reviews, Lochhead's treatment of a genuinely contemporary dilemma deserves to be perceived outside individual moral considerations.

Via the dramatic representation of ageing female characters prepared to take decisions on parenthood on their own, without the involvement of male partners, both Carter and Lochhead signal a significant thematic breakthrough. Shelagh Stephenson, on the other hand, juxtaposes new and old concerns: the female body as a site of deviance and spectacle, alongside the examination of cloning and genetic engineering as emerging forms of human reproduction (*An Experiment with an Air Pump*, 1998). Stephenson's parallel historical strands are related via their exploration of the boundaries of the 'natural', whilst also investigating the moral responsibility of those in a position to transgress such boundaries. Ultimately, the present is haunted by the past, not only symbolically – via inner dilemmas and clashing arguments – but more literally by the spectral victims of former abuse by the medical profession. Caryl Churchill's *A Number* (2002) also responds to moral questions arising from current debates on human cloning. The play is set in the near future, involving a father and three of his sons, an original and two clones. Following a routine visit to hospital, son Bernard finds that he has been cloned and is just one of an unspecified number of 'sons'. Churchill focuses on the confrontation between sons and father as they address the consequences of scientific engineering. In the process the gap between the protagonists only widens instead of closing, while Churchill raises questions on the ethics of cloning and on the impact of education and environment on the human condition.

Rona Munro's *Iron* (2002), written for the Traverse, revisits the genre of prison drama. Munro maintains a certain thriller-like quality and doubles it with a feminist perspective, but ultimately, her aim is to address the impact of devastation, and the way human beings deal with the unbearable. The play centres on Josie's visits to her mother Fay's cell, imprisoned for the murder of her husband. Munro examines the development of a mother–daughter relationship after 15 years of absence, trying to transcend the limitations of time, memory and punishment. She also taps into the audience's expectation of motives behind events, while conveying an argument for the psychology of female violence. Kate Wyvill's *Going Potty*, first performed at the Edinburgh Festival in 2004, explores the difficulties of practising parenthood, by centring on a couple and their three children. Overwhelmed by the responsibility of looking after her family, Emma's sole route for rebellion is to hide herself for a day. Without having been warned, her husband finds himself left to deal with the children, and consequently forced to readjust his routine. Wyvill's sharply observed comedy highlights the non-negotiated expectations couples often have of each other; however, it also indicates hope, suggesting a fresh potential for communication and bringing to the fore the timely debate on gender inequalities in parenting.

Having examined a wide range of options in terms of dramatic form and content, recent contributions to British women's theatre return full circle to some of the concerns highlighted at the beginning of the study. Laura Wade revisits the genre of family drama practiced by Bagnold; however, instead of reinforcing the primacy of the nuclear family she signals its fallibility as a viable institution. She also highlights new concerns, such as a lucid attitude towards mortality and the reclamation of dignity and agency at any stage in life. Wade's *Colder Than Here* premièred at the Soho Theatre in February 2005, almost simultaneously with her *Breathing Corpses*, staged at the Royal Court. Launched by these productions, Wade has received further commissions and has been rated one of the most exciting playwrights working in Britain today. *Colder Than Here* explores the theme of emotional repression, by centring on a middle-aged couple and their daughters. Diagnosed with cancer, Myra has around half a year to live, and the play examines the ways in which she and her family come to terms with the imminence of death. Ironically, it is Myra herself who is most open about this fact, and her husband the most reluctant. As the family makes arrangements about the funeral, however, they find themselves in need of more communication with each other than ever before. Initially, the daughters and the husband only interact via Myra's mediation, but gradually, encouraged by Myra, they develop abilities to relate to one another and contemplate a viable future in the absence of the mother, as independent yet interconnected beings.

Although a number of playwrights and companies have stopped operating, mainly due to lack of funding or the difficulties of staging new material (for instance, Grace Dayley, Trish Cooke, the Women's Theatre Group in its initial composition), the above range of work testifies that British women's theatre will maintain its diversity in terms of genre and subject matter, and it will carry on investigating women's stance with regard to maternity, parenthood and the family. One can only hope that in the future social and economic circumstances will enhance rather than obstruct the visibility of women's theatre, in terms of making and producing new material. As Charlotte Keatley argued, dramatizing 'women's and men's lives right now' constitutes a 'responsibility'; and although it is difficult to make sense of some events that occurred at the end of the twentieth century – following 'the failure of all political ideals' – in Timberlake Wertenbaker's words, it is crucial to make an effort, as 'any contribution that can be made *is* a good one'.[1]

What precise manifestations motherhood and parenthood will take is, of course, for the future to reveal. Today, despite the glass ceiling and discriminating gender biases, women have gained educational and economic access as a result of egalitarian feminist efforts, but despite this integration there is never a 'right time' for having a baby. Pregnancy and parenthood interfere with personal independence, require long-term commitment and impact on lifestyle choices. In a society that celebrates consumption and individual options, paradoxically, women find themselves self-limited by pursuing professional and hedonistic goals, often repressing their maternal urges. In situations where women do have children, returning to a job highlights other problems; on the one hand it calls attention to the frustrations of childrearing, as women find themselves relinquishing control over their time and priorities and, on the other hand, it stirs inadequacies in them as mothers, since they barter maternal presence with monetary power. Mothers, however, are also perceived as failing in the labour market, as they are considered to be less productive and ambitious than men and/or childless women. The current status quo in which parents' desire to take care of their own children is undermined by the economic pressure of paid employments, and in which paying for specialized childcare is a major financial investment, doubled by the fact that for many women careers cannot be put on hold for unlimited periods, reiterates the necessity for more government help and initiative.

The 1988 Clause 28 has underwritten discrimination against the gay community, in 1990 Parliament voted to limit abortions to 24 weeks, while in 1993 the Conservative Government attacked single mothers and welfare benefits. Legislation as recent as 1989 (The Children Act) and 1996 (The Family Law Act) have made attempts at reinforcing the primacy of the nuclear family, although statistical data have registered not only the highest ratio of divorces but also of cohabiting couples and of children born out of wedlock, as well as of arrangements based on multiple allegiances ever encountered in the UK.[2] At a time when cross-cultural adoptions are regularly practiced, and spontaneous fertility rates are at an all-time low, yet due to advances in reproductive technology even post-menopausal women can give birth – not to mention that reproduction has been successfully dissociated from sexual activity – it is imperative to grant due legal status to alternative forms of parenting and family structures.³ It is equally crucial to include the perspectives of all parties concerned in the debate, potential parents as well as representatives of the medical and legal profession, and, in the case of adoptions, birth parents, often located in an economically disadvantaged position. Ethical issues are equally relevant in the inadequately regulated globalized infertility business, whereby, due to the commodification of sperm and eggs, the desire to become parents is often fulfilled at the cost of others, thus creating areas for conflict that lead to a new form of colonialism. In conjunction with the alarmist prospects of the decline in human reproductive health, especially in rich countries, paradoxically, there are increasing concerns regarding population pressure and related environmental problems with an imminent global impact.

Since this study has privileged the work of women playwrights, it welcomed the fact that the predominant voice has been that of female protagonists, whose claim to agency is an important achievement of successful feminist interventions. The study has also highlighted, however, that the women playwrights and practitioners surveyed have addressed parenthood and reproduction almost exclusively from a female perspective, only marginally integrating male views. Taking into account the fact that several recent commentators have remarked on the continued inequalities between men and women as far as the responsibility for raising the next generation is concerned, this area would constitute a welcome topic for future artistic debate. In terms of cultural and geographical context, this study has concentrated on Britain, and examined the transformations over five decades on the terrain of motherhood and parenthood. The final years of the twentieth century, however, have increasingly called attention to the impracticality of nation-based investigation, and posited global access and communication as pathways for the future. British women's theatre has notably tapped into this changing territory, especially via plays on cross-continental adoption; however, the interrogation of the broader world as an environment suited for raising children awaits further dramatic treatment.⁴

Another major challenge is the negotiation between the tendency for individualism that has consolidated since the eighties and the innate human impulse for belonging to organized structures. Following the mass appeal of early feminism and the emergence of simultaneous feminist positions in the late seventies and eighties, by the nineties the entire concept and practice of women's association has undergone major transformations. Unlike earlier attempts to erase hierarchies, feminists in the nineties acknowledged the rigidity of categories such as race and sexuality, and embraced multiplicity as a route towards alternative patterns of institutionalization. Thus, rather than providing a universal framework to suit all women, there emerged a multitude of different, non-hierarchical positions to reflect everyone's specific background and politics. As a result, the very term 'feminism' has lost its specificity, and my study has documented precisely this reservation with regard to the 'feminist' label. As Laura Wade, the female playwright generating most attention in 2005-06, indicated: 'I don't think I write from any necessarily feminist impulse. I think being a woman I have an interest in writing good female characters and we are still working against a long, long theatre history that has been very male-dominated.'[5] Besides illustrating the fragmentation within feminism, such tendencies can be seen as an indicator of an increasing sophistication that marks a distantiation from the didacticism practised in the seventies, but also as a symptom of ideological detachment. As Wertenbaker's characters point out, feminism at the turn of the third millennium 'is a peace treaty, not a love feast',[6] rightly urging for the complex network of women-oriented positions to re-evaluate one another, in order to yet again reinvent themselves.

Notes

Introduction

1. Nagy argues that the publication of play texts is unnecessary as it encourages people to simply read plays. Ironically, without allowing work to be published there are fewer chances for having them staged. (P. Nagy, speaking at the University of Hull, 20 November 2002).
2. The preoccupation with motherhood has been dominant in contemporary Irish women's drama as well, where the traditional imagery of Mother Ireland often gave the subject an allegorical and political meaning, which was absent in mainland U K. For an analysis of the work of Marina Carr, Anne Devlin and Christina Reid, see my article 'The Troubles and the Family: Women's Theatre as Political Intervention', in *Representing the Troubles*, eds. Eibhear Walshe and Brian Cliff (Dublin: Four Courts Press, 2004).
3. I utilize the term *proto-feminism* to refer to work produced before the emergence of second-wave feminism, and *post-feminism* to collate the different feminist inquiries emerging in the nineties, predominantly via a generation reaching adulthood after the heyday of the Women's Liberation Movement. I address *liberal feminism* as a quest for gender justice that has required a re-examination of the rules that govern the public world, so that it does not block women's access. Later strands in feminism have critiqued this inclusive approach, pointing out that liberal feminists were uninterested in demanding the alteration of the social system as a whole. Especially in an American context, this strand is also termed *bourgeois feminism* by *Marxist/socialist feminists,* whose interventions have focused on challenging class society, the supremacy of private property and capitalism itself. *Radical feminism,* on the other hand, has provided an argument against the patriarchal system as such, that they perceive as oppressing women and which cannot be reformed. As a development of the latter, *cultural feminism* has located the existence of women's specific culture at the centre of their analyses. Cf. R. Tong, *Feminist Thought: A Comprehensive Introduction* (London: Routledge, 1992), pp. 2–5. Also see S. Andemahr, T. Lovell, C. Wolkowitz, eds. *Feminist Theory: A Glossary* (London: Arnold, 2000).
4. Cf. J. Kristeva, 'Women's Time', in *The Kristeva Reader,* ed. T. Moi (Oxford: Basil Blackwell, 1986b).
5. C. Clément, 'The Guilty One', in Cixous and Clément, *The Newly Born Woman* (Minneapolis: University of Minnesota Press, 1991).
6. It is crucial to stress that, traditionally, individual playwrights have been more likely to acquire canonical status than work produced collaboratively. In parallel with ongoing concerns in Performance Studies and in the light of significant critical attention to experimental companies such as Forced Entertainment, however, this approach is likely to change in the future.

1 Rethinking Motherhood: Instances of Proto-Feminism

1. E. Wilson, *Women and the Welfare State* (London: Tavistock Publications, 1977), p. 66.
2. M. Pugh, *Women and the Women's Movement in Britain, 1914–1959* (Basingstoke: Macmillan, 1992), p. 284.
3. Cf. the work of Melanie Klein, Donald Winnicott and Benjamin Spock on the importance of constant attention and love in the upbringing of children. While it was considered permissible for mothers to leave their babies in the care of fathers or grannies in cases of emergency, 'the exacting job [of motherhood was] scamped at one's peril'. J. Bowlby, quoted in D. Riley, *War in the Nursery: Theories of the Child and Mother* (London: Virago, 1983), p. 101.
4. A. Myrdal and V. Klein, *Women's Two Roles: Home and Work* (London: Routledge and Kegan Paul, 1956), p. 117. H. Gavron, *The Captive Wife: Conflicts of Housebound Mothers* (Harmondsworth: Penguin Books, 1966).
5. B. Friedan, *The Feminine Mystique* (London: Gollancz, 1963), pp. 68, 9.
6. Ibid., pp. 180, 293.
7. A. Sebba, *Enid Bagnold: The Authorized Biography* (London: Weidenfeld and Nicolson, 1986), p. 181.
8. K. Tynan, *Curtains: Selections from the Drama Criticism and Related Writings* (London: Longmans, 1961), p. 127.
9. L. Taylor, 'Early Stages', in *British and Irish Women Dramatists since 1958*, eds. T.R. Griffiths and M. Llewellyn-Jones (Buckingham: Open University Press, 1993), p. 13. Using terms launched independently by Elaine Showalter and Patricia Erens, Taylor distinguishes three phases in women's writing. The first – 'feminist-reflectionist' – refers to works that investigate the female condition yet fail to challenge the status quo in a radical way. The second – 'feminist/revolutionary' – denotes works that succeed in questioning both ideology and dramatic form, such as Caryl Churchill's 1979 *Cloud Nine*. The third category – 'female/ritualistic' – is utilized for experimental works, often centred on visual and non-verbal means of communication, such as Ann Jellicoe's *The Sport of My Mad Mother* discussed later in this chapter.
10. Ibid.
11. E. Bagnold, *The Chalk Garden* (London: Samuel French, 1956), p. 14.
12. *Bagnold*, in Sebba, p. 197.
13. *The Chalk Garden*, p. 22.
14. Ibid., p. 23.
15. Tynan, p. 127.
16. Ibid., p. 128.
17. C. Spencer, 'Review of Enid Bagnold's *The Chalk Garden*', *The Daily Telegraph* (4 April 1992). *The Chalk Garden* was also adapted for the screen in 1964, starring Dame Edith Evans, Deborah Kerr and Hayley Mills.
18. After the initial run starring Frances Cuka as Jo and Avis Bunnage as Helen (27 performances, première on 27 May 1958), the play was revived at the Theatre Royal in 1959 and subsequently transferred to the West End. Following a run of 368 performances, this production continued for over a year in New York, from October 1960. In 1961 *A Taste of Honey* was turned into a successful New Wave film by Tony Richardson, starring Rita Tushingham as Jo.
19. Griffiths and Llewellyn-Jones, p. 4.

20. R. Williams, 'New English Drama', in *Modern British Dramatists: A Collection of Critical Essays*, ed. J.R. Brown (Englewood Cliffs, New Jersey: Prentice Hall, 1968), pp. 32–33.
21. D. Shellard, *British Theatre since the War* (New Haven: Yale University Press, 1999), p. 70.
22. S. Bennett, 'New Plays and Women's Voices in the 1950s', in *The Cambridge Companion to Modern British Women Playwrights*, eds. E. Aston and J. Reinelt (Cambridge: Cambridge University Press, 2000), p. 41.
23. T.C. Worsley, 'The Sweet Smell', *New Statesman* (21 February 1959), p. 251.
24. J. Littlewood, 'Plays for the People', in *The New British Drama*, ed. H. Popkin (New York: Grove Press, 1964), pp. 557–60.
25. S. Delaney, *A Taste of Honey* (London: Methuen, 1988), p. 12.
26. Ibid., p. 35.
27. Ibid., p. 55; S. Lacey, *British Realist Theatre: The New Wave in Its Context, 1956–1965* (London: Routledge, 1995), p. 95.
28. *A Taste of Honey*, pp. 71–72.
29. Ibid., p. 75.
30. N. Chodorow, *The Reproduction of Mothering: Psychoanalysis and the Sociology of Gender* (Berkeley: University of California Press, 1978), pp. 136–37.
31. Ibid., p. 165.
32. *A Taste of Honey*, p. 55.
33. Ibid., p. 56.
34. M. Wandor, *Look Back in Gender: Sexuality and the Family in Post-War British Drama* (London: Methuen, 1987), p. 42.
35. S.-E. Case, 'The Power of Sex: English Plays by Women, 1958–1988', *New Theatre Quarterly*, vol. VII/27. (August 1991), p. 238.
36. L. Taylor, p. 19.
37. D. Lessing, 'Author's Note', *Play With a Tiger* (London: Davis-Poynter Ltd, 1972), p. ii.
38. M. Wandor, *Looking Back in Gender: Post-War British Drama* (London: Routledge, 2001), p. 70.
39. H. Keyssar, *Feminist Theatre* (London: Macmillan, 1984), p. 47.
40. Cf. C. Chawaf, 'Linguistic Flesh', in *New French Feminisms: An Anthology*, eds. E. Marks and I. de Courtivron (Hemel Hempstead: Harvester Wheatsheaf, 1981), pp. 177–78.
41. H. Cixous, 'The Laugh of the Medusa', in *New French Feminisms*, pp. 250–51.
42. A. Jellicoe, The Judith Wilson Lecture, *Some Unconscious Influences in the Theatre*, 10 March 1967 (Cambridge: Cambridge University Press, 1967), p. 17.
43. A. Jellicoe, 'Covering the Ground', in *Women and Theatre: Calling the Shots*, ed. S. Todd (London: Faber, 1984), p. 84.
44. J. R. Taylor, *Anger and After* (London: Methuen, 1962), pp. 74–75.
45. Jellicoe, preface to *The Sport of My Mad Mother* (London: Faber, 1964).
46. K. Tynan, preface in *The Observer Plays* (London: Faber, 1958), p. 12.
47. A. Artaud, 'The Theatre of Cruelty', in *The Theatre and Its Double* (London: Calder Publications, 1993), p. 70.
48. J. R. Taylor, p. 76.
49. A. Jellicoe, 'Ann Jellicoe Talks to Sue Todd', *The Sport of My Mad Mother* (London: Faber, 1985), p. 12.

50. J. R. Taylor, p. 75. Also cf. Artaud, 'Abandoning our Western ideas of speech, it [theatre language] turns into incantation.' p. 70.
51. Wandor, 1987, p. 44.
52. Jellicoe, quoted in Wandor, 1987, p. 43.
53. Hindu hymn, used as a motto of the play.
54. A. Jellicoe, *The Sport of My Mad Mother* (London: Faber, 1985), pp. 111–12.
55. Keyssar, p. 46.
56. *The Sport of My Mad Mother*, p. 157.
57. Ibid., p. 165.
58. Ibid., p. 167.
59. Ibid., p. 168.
60. A. Jellicoe, 'The Rising Generation', in *Playbill Two,* ed. A. Durband (London: Hutchinson, 1969).
61. Jellicoe, in Todd, p. 90.
62. Ibid., p. 96.
63. Cf. J. Arden, *Vagina Rex and the Gas Oven* (London: Calder and Boyars, 1971); M. Duffy, 'Rites'; C. Luckham, 'Trafford Tanzi', in *Plays by Women*, vol. 2., ed. M. Wandor (London: Methuen, 1983).
64. Duffy, endnote to 'Rites', p. 27.
65. *Vagina Rex and the Gas Oven*, pp. 10, 11.
66. Ibid., p. 55.
67. Ibid., p. 63.

2 Irreversible Choice: Female Professional Success

1. S. Rowbotham, *A Century of Women: The History of Women in Britain and the United States* (London: Viking, 1997), p. 399.
2. Helène Cixous, 'The Laugh of the Medusa' (originally published=1976), in *New French Feminisms*, ed. E. Marks and I. de Courtivron (Hemel Hempstead: Harvester Wheatsheaf, 1981).
3. Rowbotham, p. 400.
4. D. Edgar, *The Second Time as Farce* (London: Lawrence and Wishart, 1988), p. 119.
5. S. Hall, 'The Great Moving Right Show', in *The Politics of Thatcherism*, eds. S. Hall and M. Jacques (London: Lawrence and Wishart and Marxism Today, 1983), pp. 19–39.
6. Thatcher, 1984, quoted in I. Gilmour, *Dancing with Dogma: Britain under Thatcherism* (London: Simon and Schuster, 1992), p. 142.
7. M. Thatcher, 'Women in a Changing World', Press Office, July 1982, quoted in L. Segal, 'The Heat in the Kitchen', in *The Politics of Thatcherism*, p. 208.
8. Thatcher, quoted in H. Young, *One of Us: A Biography of Margaret Thatcher* (London: Pan Books, 1993), p. 306; B. Campbell, *The Iron Ladies: Why Do Women Vote Tory?* (London: Virago Press, 1987). Campbell stresses (p. 112), drawing on MORI polls, that women have traditionally been more likely to vote Tory than Labour (by 5–10%).
9. B. Castle, *Fighting All the Way* (London: Pan Books, 1994), p. 458.
10. Campbell, p. 246.

11. K.H. Burkman, 'The Plays of Pam Gems: Personal/Political/Personal', in *British and Irish Drama since 1960*, ed. J. Acheson (London: St. Martin's Press, 1993), p. 190.
12. Gems, interview with A. McFerran, *Time Out* (7 October 1977a).
13. Gems, quoted in L. Goodman, *Contemporary Feminist Theatres: To Each Her Own* (London: Routledge, 1993b), p. 17.
14. S. Bassnett-McGuire, 'Towards a Theory of Women's Theatre', in *Semiotics of Drama and Theatre: New Perspectives in the Theory of Drama*, eds. H. Schmid and A. van Kesteren (Amsterdam and Philadelphia: John Benjamin, 1984), pp. 445–66.
15. Gems, afterword to 'Queen Christina', in *Plays by Women*, vol. 5,, ed. M. Remnant (London: Methuen, 1986).
16. Gems, in H. Stevenson and N. Langridge, *in Rage and Reason: Women Playwrights on Playwriting* (London: Methuen, 1997), pp. 91–92.
17. Gems, in G. Brown, 'Something Out of the Ordinary', *The Independent* (31 January 1996).
18. E. Aston, 'Pam Gems: Body Politics and Biography', in *The Cambridge Companion to Modern British Women Playwrights*, eds. E. Aston and J. Reinelt (Cambridge: Cambridge University Press, 2000), p. 158.
19. 'Queen Christina', p. 17.
20. Ibid.
21. Gems, afterword to 'Queen Christina', p. 47.
22. 'Queen Christina', p. 29; Aston, 2000, p. 160.
23. G. Cousin, *Women in Dramatic Place and Time* (London: Routledge, 1996), p. 153.
24. 'Queen Christina', p. 19.
25. A. Kuhn, *The Power of Image: Essays on Representation and Sexuality* (London: Routledge and Kegan Paul, 1985), p. 50.
26. 'Queen Christina', p. 24.
27. S. Firestone, *The Dialectic of Sex: The Case for Feminist Revolution* (London: The Women's Press Ltd., 1979), p. 193.
28. Ibid., p. 121.
29. Cf. *The Body Politic*, ed. M. Wandor (London: Stage 1, 1972), p. 2.
30. 'Queen Christina', p. 25.
31. Ibid., p. 27.
32. Aston, 2000, p. 160.
33. Cf. A. Fisher, quoted in G. Greer, *The Whole Woman* (London: Doubleday, 1999), p. 237.
34. Sylvie Pierce, chief executive of the London Borough of Tower Hamlets, in N. Walter, *The New Feminism* (London: Little, Brown and Company, 1998), p. 110. A similar idea is explored in a 1983 statement: 'Sometimes the disappointment of discovering that lesbianism, which was and is seen by many feminists as a political solution to the problem of men, could be just as bitter and painful and debilitating as heterosexuality, was devastating.' F. Rickford, 'No More Sleeping Beauties and Frozen Boys', in *The Left and the Erotic*, ed. E. Phillips (London: Lawrence and Wishart, 1983), pp. 139–47.
35. 'Queen Christina', p. 44.
36. Ibid.
37. Ibid., p. 45.

38. Ibid.
39. For further insights into the interpretation of hysteric fits as rebellion and contestation see C. Clément and H. Cixous, *The Newly Born Woman* (Minneapolis: University of Minnesota Press, 1991).
40. Cousin, 1996, p. 158.
41. 'She was like the odd mare steeple-chasing.' Gems, in Stevenson and Langridge, p. 93.
42. C. Churchill, 'Owners', in *Plays: One* (London: Methuen, 1985), p. 66.
43. E. Aston, *Caryl Churchill* (Plymouth: Northcote House in association with the British Council, 1997b), p. 23.
44. 'Owners', p. 67.
45. G. Greer, *The Female Eunuch* (London: MacGibbon and Kee, 1970), p. 235.
46. Ibid., p. 236.
47. Churchill, in C. Itzin, *Stages in the Revolution* (London: Methuen, 1980), p. 282.
48. Cf. Churchill, interviewed by McFerran, 1977b.
49. Aston, 1997b, p. 20.
50. J. Vidal, 'Power and the Woman', *Guardian* (9 April 1987).
51. C. Innes, *Modern British Drama* 1890-1990 (Cambridge: Cambridge University Press, 1992), pp. 460–61.
52. G. Austin, *Feminist Theories for Dramatic Criticism* (Ann Arbor, MI: The University of Michigan Press, 1990), p. 6.
53. *Top Girls* itself came to be seen as a visionary piece. By the time of Max Stafford-Clark's 1991 revival of his original 1982 production, what had initially been interpreted as a provocative play about women's status was reconsidered as a 'prophetic play about the conflicts faced by women in the modern age more generally'. Cf. L. Goodman, 'Overlapping Dialogue in Overlapping Media: Behind the Scenes of *Top Girls*', in *Essays on Caryl Churchill: Contemporary Representations*, ed. S. Rabillard (Winnipeg, Buffalo: Blizzard Publishing, 1998), p. 76.
54. Chicago's installation consists of a triangle-shaped table with 999 references to names and 39 place settings, each including a chalice and a plate and commemorating a woman from myth or history. By staging the encounter of famous women over a meal, Chicago seemingly legitimizes the mainstream tendency to associate women with the domestic, but she also subverts this conventional image, as these women are being honoured and serviced in a manner generally reserved for men. In the British context, the piece gained an extra 'theatrical' and activist–feminist dimension by being brought to London via the mediation of Monstrous Regiment with whom Churchill worked on *Vinegar Tom* in the late seventies.
55. Concept introduced in 1974 by the American feminist activist, Jo Freeman (Joreen) and circulated by the Anarchist Workers' Association. Cf. Freeman, *The Politics of Women's Liberation: A Case Study of an Emerging Social Move* (New York: McKay, 1975).
56. H. Keyssar, *Feminist Theatre* (Basingstoke: Macmillan, 1984), p. 97.
57. J. Brown, 'Caryl Churchill's *Top Girls* Catches the Next Wave', in *Caryl Churchill: A Casebook*, ed. P. Randall (New York, London: Garland Publishing, 1988), p. 117. Brown continues with a prophetic observation prompted by the second section of the play, thus intertwining past, present

and future: 'The child's dream of the future reminds us of what is at stake in the feminist struggle for societal transformation.'

58. Innes, p. 465.
59. J. Brown, p. 128.
60. Churchill, *Top Girls* (London: Methuen, 1991), p. 59.
61. A. Neustatter, *Hyenas in Petticoats: A Look at Twenty Years of Feminism* (London: Harrap, 1989), p. 14.
62. Thatcher welcomed this idea of succession: 'I presided over a very successful economy' and Mr Blair 'inherited the economic boom'. Cf. A. Grice, 'Ten Years after the Fall of Thatcher, Blair Says It's Time Politics Moved On', *The Independent* (23 November 2000).
63. M. White and R. Norton-Taylor, 'Irate Blair Savages Thatcher', *Guardian* (24 November 2000).
64. A. Howe-Kritzer, 'Labour and Capital', in Kritzer, *The Plays of Caryl Churchill: Theatre of Empowerment* (London: Macmillan, 1991), p. 141.
65. Ibid., p. 86.
66. Hall, *The Hard Road to Renewal: Thatcherism and the Crisis of the Left* (London: Verso, 1988), p. 46. 'Families', the second term originally included in Thatcher's statement ('the basic units of society are individuals and families') has been considered less shocking, and was subsequently, a lot less commented upon.
67. Churchill claims: 'Angie says she thinks Marlene is really her mother, I didn't mean her to know it; I meant it to be wishful thinking.' Cf. Churchill in Goodman, 1998, p. 91.
68. Max Stafford-Clark emphasized the prophetic nature of the play in this respect: 'When you see the increased number of people begging in the streets, and you realize that [that sight] would have been shocking in the context of the early eighties, or fifteen or twenty years ago, you see that the play is prophetic.' Stafford-Clark, in Goodman, 1998, p. 90.
69. L. Wakefield, quoted by J. Brown, p. 120.
70. J. Brown, p. 128.
71. E. Aston, *Feminist Views on the English Stage: Women Playwrights, 1990–2000* (Cambridge University Press, 2003), p. 23.

3   Challenging the Bond: Mothers versus Daughters

1. L. Goodman and J. de Gay, eds. 'Introduction to Part II: Feminist Stages of the 1980s', *Feminist Stages* (Amsterdam: Harwood Academic Publishers, 1996), p. 97.
2. H. Stephenson and N. Langridge, *Rage and Reason: Women Playwrights on Playwriting* (London: Methuen, 1997), p. 129.
3. L. Page, in Goodman and de Gay, pp. 73–74.
4. *Salonika* was first performed at the Royal Court Upstairs on 2 August 1982, directed by Danny Boyle and adapted for film in 1988. *Real Estate* premièred at the Tricycle Theatre, London on 3 May 1984, directed by Pip Broughton.
5. Ibid., p. 70. Interview taken in 1988 by Elizabeth Sakellaridou, edited in 1995 by Goodman.
6. Ibid., p. 71.

7. Page, 'Salonika', in *Plays: One* (London: Methuen, 1990), p. 70.
8. Page, in Goodman and de Gay, p. 72.
9. Page, quoted in M. Llewellyn-Jones, 'Claiming a Space', in *British and Irish Dramatists since 1958*, eds. T.R. Griffiths and M. Llewellyn-Jones (Buckingham, Philadelphia: Open University Press, 1993), p. 41.
10. 'Real Estate', in *Plays: One* (London: Methuen, 1990), p. 145.
11. Ibid., p. 195.
12. Page, in Goodman and de Gay, p. 75.
13. S. Stephenson, *The Memory of Water* (London: Methuen, 1997), pp. 50–51.
14. G. Austin, *Feminist Theories for Dramatic Criticism* (Ann Arbor, MI: University of Michigan Press, 1990), p. 1.
15. I am indebted to Elaine Aston's analytical categories utilized in relation to *My Mother Said I Never Should*. Cf. Aston, *Feminist Theatre Practice: A Handbook* (London: Routledge, 1999b), p. 125.
16. L. Irigaray, *Sexes et parentés* (1987), trans. G.C. Gill as *Sexes and Genealogies* (New York: Columbia University Press, 1993).
17. *The Memory of Water*, p. 21.
18. Ibid., p. 92.
19. Keatley, in L. Goodman, 'Art Form or Platform? On Women and Playwriting', *New Theatre Quarterly*, vol. VI/22. (May 1990), p. 132.
20. Keatley, Platform Performance and discussion of *My Mother Said I Never Should*, Royal National Theatre (8 November 1999). Keatley's play – alongside Timberlake Wertenbaker's *Our Country's Good*, Caryl Churchill's *Top Girls* and Shelagh Delaney's *A Taste of Honey* – was one of the handful of plays by women selected for the '100 Plays of the Century'.
21. Keatley, interviewed by J. Komporaly (17 November 1999); Keatley, in Stephenson and Langridge, p. 75.
22. Keatley, in Goodman, 1990, p. 130.
23. Keatley, in Komporaly.
24. The play has also been compared with Churchill's *Top Girls*, since both feature all-female casts, have been produced in main-stage venues and investigate different feminist standpoints. Also, both have generated 'misreadings': *My Mother Said I Never Should* has acquired a radical reputation despite being largely a naturalist piece, whereas *Top Girls* has been labelled as a plea for egalitarian feminism despite its attack on Thatcherism.
25. B. Larmour, Platform performance and discussion of *My Mother Said I Never Should*.
26. Following these two phases, Kristeva heralded the emergence of a third phase to negotiate linearity and cyclicity, in an overall attempt at deconstructing binary oppositions and problematizing the very category of gender. Keatley's use of time predominantly illustrates the second phase in the Kristevan division, although she also maps out – via Rosie – the potential for a third phase.
27. G. Hanna, in interview, *Feminism and Theatre: Theatre Papers*, 2nd series, no. 8, (Dartington: Dartington College, 1978), p. 8.
28. Keatley, in Goodman, 1990, p. 130.
29. Keatley in Komporaly.
30. Ibid.
31. Keatley, *My Mother Said I Never Should* (London: Methuen, 1997), p. 54.
32. Ibid., p. 7.

33. Reference to Margaret's statement (p. 30.): 'I'm not wasting my life.'
34. *My Mother Said I Never Should*, p. 31.
35. Ibid.
36. J. Kristeva, 'Motherhood According to Giovanni Bellini', in *Desire in Language: A Semiotic Approach to Literature and Art*, ed. Leon S. Roudiez (Oxford: Basil Blackwell, 1980), p. 239.
37. *My Mother Said I Never Should*, p. 29.
38. Ibid., p. 26.
39. Keatley, in Komporaly.
40. W. Pinnock, in Stephenson and Langridge, p. 46.
41. Ibid.
42. Ibid., p. 49.
43. Ibid., p. 51.
44. 'Leave Taking', in *First Run: New Plays by New Writers*, ed. Kate Harwood (London: Nick Hern Books, 1989), p. 152. Cf. G. Griffin's analysis of this play in the light of Avtar Brah's concept of 'diaspora' and in-betweenness, in *Contemporary Black and Asian Women Playwrights in Britain* (Cambridge University Press, 2003), pp. 37–63.
45. 'Leave Taking', p. 153.
46. An earlier Jamaican-born author also examined a young mother being trapped between a white doctor and the voodoo cult in Jamaica. Cf. Barry Reckord's *Flesh to a Tiger*, staged at the Royal Court in 1958 with Cleo Laine as Della.
47. D. Samuels, 'Author's Note', *Kinderstransport* (London: Nick Hern Books, 1996), p. vii.
48. Anne Karpf, *The War After: Living with the Holocaust* (London: Heinemann 1996), pp. 244–45. The subject of the Kindertransport has since been scrutinized in different media, including the documentary 'Into the Arms of Strangers' by Mark Jonathan Harris (2000), the sculpture/installation 'Für das Kind' by Flor Kent (2003) – displayed at Liverpool Street Station to mark the refugees' arrival, and an exhibition at the Imperial War Museum North, Manchester (2004).
49. A. Birk and T. Wald, '"Let the Witches and the Magic Back in": Interview with Diane Samuels', *Gender Forum: AnyBody's Concerns* 6(2003), http://www.genderforum.uni-koeln.de/anybody/interview_Samuels.html, accessed 10 January 2006.
50. Ibid.
51. Samuels, *Kindertransport*, p. 2.
52. Ibid., p. 11.
53. Karpf, p. 178.
54. *Kindertransport*, pp. 62–61.
55. B. Neumeier, 'Kindertransport: Childhood Trauma and Diaspora Experience', in *Jewish Women's Writing of the 1990s and beyond in Great Britain and the United States*, eds. U. Behlau and B. Reitz (Trier: Wissenschaftlicher Verlag, 2004), p. 66.
56. *Kindertransport*, p. 87.
57. Neumeier, p. 67.
58. Birk and Wald.
59. E. Aston, *Feminist Views on the English Stage: Women Playwrights, 1990–2000* (Cambridge: Cambridge University Press, 2003), p. 114.

60. P. Nagy, in Stephenson and Langridge, p. 21.
61. A. Sierz, *In-Yer-Face Theatre* (London: Faber, 2001), p. 50.
62. 'Butterfly Kiss', in P. Nagy, *Plays: One* (London: Methuen , 1998), p. 82.
63. Sierz, p. 51.
64. 'Butterfly Kiss', pp. 53, 83.
65. M. Coveney, 'Introduction', P. Nagy, *Plays: One* (London: Methuen, 1998), p. xii.
66. Nagy, in Sierz, p. 51.
67. Nagy, in Stephenson and Langridge, p. 24.
68. Ibid., p. 27.
69. Nagy, speaking at the Drama Department, University of Hull (20 November 2002).
70. Nagy, in Stephenson and Langridge, p. 28.
71. The play was performed more frequently abroad (Deutsche Theater Baracke Berlin, 1997; Paris, 2003) than in the UK, where its so far second professional production, directed by Anne Tipton, was co-produced by Bristol Old Vic, the Barbican and the Young Vic in November 2005.
72. S. Kane, in Sierz, p. 109.
73. G. Saunders, *'Love Me or Kill Me': Sarah Kane and the Theatre of Extremes* (Manchester: Manchester University Press, 2002), p. 76.
74. D. Greig, 'Introduction', S. Kane, *Complete Plays* (London: Methuen, 2001), p. ix.
75. Sierz, p. 107; 'Phaedra's Love', p. 73.
76. Greig, p. xi.
77. Sierz, p. 110.
78. 'Phaedra's Love', [*Blasted* and] *Phaedra's Love* (London: Methuen, 1996), p. 97.
79. Kane, in Stephenson and Langridge, pp. 134–35.
80. E. Aston and J. Reinelt, eds. *Modern British Women Playwrights* (Cambridge University Press, 2000), pp. 214–15.
81. Kane, in Stephenson and Langridge, p. 133.

4 Daughters as Mothers: The Teenager as Potential Parent

1. B. Moore-Gilbert, 'Introduction', *The Arts in the 1970s: Cultural Closure* (London: Routledge, 1994), p. 9.
2. E. Aston, 'Introduction', *Feminist Theatre Voices* (Loughborough: Loughborough Theatre Texts, 1997a), p. 13.
3. M. Wandor, 'Introduction', in *Strike while the Iron Is Hot: Sexual Politics in the Theatre*, ed. Wandor (London: The Journeyman Press, 1980), pp. 11–12.
4. The play's first performance was at the Oval House Theatre Club, London. It was devised, written, performed and directed by WTG, consisting at the time of Frankie Armstrong, Lyn Ashley, Clair Chapman, Sue Eatwell, Anne Engel, Jane Meadows and Mica Nava.
5. 'My Mother Says I Never Should', in *Strike while the Iron Is Hot*, p. 126.
6. Ibid., pp. 127, 124.
7. G. Hanna, [in interview], *Feminism and Theatre: Theatre Papers*, 2nd series, no. 8 (Dartington: Dartington College, 1987), p. 9.
8. 'My Mother Says I Never Should', p. 141.
9. M. Nava, 'Introduction', 'My Mother Says I Never Should', p. 117.

10. A. Scullion, 'Contemporary Scottish Women Playwrights', in *The Cambridge Companion to Modern British Women Playwrights,* eds. E. Aston and J. Reinelt (Cambridge: Cambridge University Press, 2000), p. 109.

11. S. MacDonald, 'When I Was a Girl, I Used to Scream and Shout...', in *Plays: One* (London: Faber, 1995), p. 8.

12. Ibid., p. 7.

13. MacDonald in H. Stephenson and N. Langridge, *Rage and Reason: Women Playwrights on Playwriting* (London: Methuen, 1997), p. 69.

14. Ibid.

15. T.R. Griffiths, 'Waving Not Drowning', in *British and Irish Women Dramatists since 1958,* eds. T.R. Griffiths and M. Llewellyn-Jones (Buckingham, Philadelphia: Open University Press, 1993), p. 50.

16. 'When I Was a Girl, I Used to Scream and Shout...', p. 17.

17. Ibid., p. 31.

18. Ibid., p. 29.

19. Ibid., p. 39.

20. MacDonald, in Stephenson and Langridge, p. 62.

21. Ibid., p. 63.

22. Ibid., p. 69.

23. Besides her own case, Pinnock refers to playwrights such as Jacqueline Rudet, Bernadine Evaristo, Trish Cooke and Michael McMillan. Cf. W. Pinnock, 'Breaking Down the Door', in *Theatre in a Cool Climate,* eds. V. Gottlieb and C. Chambers (Oxford: Amber Lane Press, 1999), p. 31.

24. Ibid., p. 36.

25. S. Croft, 'Black Women Playwrights in Britain', in Griffiths and Llewellyn-Jones, p. 91.

26. M. Wandor, *Carry On, Understudies: Theatre and Sexual Politics* (London: Routledge and Kegan Paul, 1981), p. 183.

27. G. Dayley, 'Endnote to Rose's Story', in *Plays by Women*, vol. 4, ed. M. Wandor (London: Methuen, 1985), p. 80.

28. G. Griffin, *Contemporary Black and Asian Women Playwrights in Britain* (Cambridge: Cambridge University Press, 2003), pp. 34–35.

29. 'Rose's Story', in *Plays by Women*, vol. 4, p. 57.

30. Griffin, p. 211.

31. 'Rose's Story', p. 74.

32. Ibid., p. 65.

33. Pinnock, in Stephenson and Langridge, p. 49.

34. 'Rose's Story', p. 72.

35. Griffin, p. 213.

36. Pinnock, in Stephenson and Langridge, p. 46.

37. T. Cooke, http://peopleplayuk.org/timelines/black_performance.php?year=6 &syear=1&, accessed 15 February 2006.

38. Griffin, p. 25. Griffin references Paul Gilroy's seminal intervention on race relations in Britain, *There Ain't No Black in the Union Jack: The Cultural Politics of Race and Nation* (London: Unwin Hyman, 1987).

39. T. Brown, '*Back Street Mammy*' , Review, *Guardian* (9 October 1989).

40. Cooke, interviewed by J. Komporaly (17 October 2000).

41. Cf. Pam Gems's or Timberlake Wertenbaker's focus on outstanding characters derived from history or myth, such as Queen Christina, Edith Piaf, Marlene Dietrich or Isabelle Eberhardt, Pope Joan, Philomel etc.

42. Cooke, 'Back Street Mammy', in *First Run,* vol. 2, ed. K. Harwood (London: Nick Hern Books, 1990), p. 50.
43. Cooke, in Komporaly.
44. 'Back Street Mammy', pp. 79–80.
45. Croft, p. 92.
46. Cooke, in Komporaly.
47. 'Back Street Mammy', p. 44.
48. K. Harwood, Introduction to 'Back Street Mammy', p. xiv; Cooke, in Komporaly.
49. 'Back Street Mammy', p. 88.
50. Cooke, in Komporaly.
51. 'Back Street Mammy', p. 95.

5 Maternal Desire Against the Odds

1. Mr Brown: 'I didn't know we were to be the first test-tube parents – I wish we weren't!', in G. Corea, The Mother Machine: Reproductive Technologies from Artificial Insemination to Artificial Wombs (London: The Women's Press, 1988), p. 167.
2. M. Warnock, *A Question of Life: The Warnock Report on Human Fertilisation and Embryology* (Oxford: Basil Blackwell, 1985).
3. Nevertheless, innumerable cases of lesbian motherhood have been documented in the late seventies and early eighties.
4. This date was established because embryos start developing a nervous system afterwards.
5. Another related issue is the remuneration of egg and sperm donors. Currently the payment varies considerably from case to case.
6. M. Stanworth, ed. *Reproductive Technologies: Gender, Motherhood and Medicine* (Cambridge: Polity Press, 1987).
7. R. Duelli Klein, quoted in J. Zipper and S. Sevenhuijsen 'Surrogacy: Feminist Notions of Motherhood Reconsidered', in M. Stanworth, p. 136. R. Arditti, R. Duelli Klein and S. Minden, eds. *Test-Tube Women: What Future for Motherhood?* (London: Pandora Press, 1984).
8. G. Corea, *Man-Made Women: How New Reproductive Technologies Affect Women* (Bloomington, IN: Indiana University Press, 1987), p. 39.
9. Dally, *Inventing Motherhood: The Consequences of an Ideal* (London: Burnett Books Ltd, 1982).
10. S. Ruddick, 'Maternal Thought', in J. Trebilcot, ed., *Mothering: Essays in Feminist Theory* (Totowa, NJ: Rowman and Littlefield, 1983), p. 227.
11. T. Gordon, *Feminist Mothers* (London: Macmillan, 1990), p. 2.
12. Trebilcot, p. 1.
13. N. Walter, 'What Feminism Offers Men', *The Independent* (28 June 1999).
14. hooks, *Feminist Theory from Margin to Centre* (Boston, MA: South End Press, 1985), p. 135.
15. Gilligan, *In a Different Voice: Psychological Theory and Women's Development* (Cambridge, MA: Harvard University Press, 1982).
16. Being childless, however, for radical feminists also signified a threat to patriarchal order, as it involved a transgression of the role traditionally defined for women.
17. L. Segal, 'Women's Retreat into Motherhood: Back to the Nursery', *New Statesman,* vol. 113, No. 2910 (2 January 1987), p. 2.

18. S. Kitzinger, *Women as Mothers: How They See Themselves in Different Cultures* (Oxford: Martin Robertson with Fontana Books, 1978), p. 145. Another important British author on the topic was Ann Oakley, see *Becoming a Mother* (Oxford: Martin Robertson, 1979) and *Women Confined: Towards a Sociology of Childbirth* (Oxford: Martin Robertson, 1980). Oakley's work challenged the over-medicalization of childbirth on the grounds of women's basic human right to dignity and privacy.

19. Jong, 'I Am Having It All – So Why Do I Feel Terminally Exhausted?' *Cosmopolitan*, 1985, quoted in S. Faludi, *Backlash: The Undeclared War against Women* (London: Chatto and Windus, 1991), p. 2.

20. C. Hakim, *Key Issues in Women's Work* (London: Athlone Press, 1996), p. 207.

21. M. Benn, *Madonna and Child: Towards a New Politics of Motherhood* (London: Jonathan Cape, 1998).

22. Oakley, 'A Brief History of Gender', in *Who's Afraid of Feminism? Seeing Through the Backlash*, eds. Oakley and J. Mitchell (London: Penguin Books, 1997), pp. 33–34.

23. Brooks, *Postfeminisms: Feminism, Cultural Theory, and Cultural Forms* (London: Routledge, 1997), p. 1.

24. Yeatman, *Postmodern Revisionings of the Political* (London: Routledge, 1994), p. 49. S. Phoca marks the origins of post-feminism in 1968, when the French *po et psyche* group rejected the liberal feminist struggle for equality with men. Drawing on psychoanalytic theory, theorists like Kristeva and Cixous have focused instead on the nature of female subjectivity, and while they situated it in fundamental opposition to the male world they also emphasized its constant fluctuation and multiplicity. Cf. S. Gamble, ed. *The Routledge Companion to Feminism and Postfeminism* (London: Routledge, 2001), p. 298.

25. Benn, p. 234.

26. M. Wandor, *Carry On, Understudies: Theatre and Sexual Politics*, (London: Routledge & Kegan Paul, 1986), p. 138.

27. Wandor, *Time Out* (21–27 November 1977).

28. J. Reinelt, 'Michelene Wandor: Artist and Ideologue', in *Making a Spectacle: Feminist Essays on Contemporary Women's Theatre*, ed. L. Hart (Ann Arbor, MI: The University of Michigan Press, 1989), p. 239.

29. Wandor, *Look Back in Gender: Sexuality and the Family in Post-War British Drama* (London: Methuen, 1987), p. 90. Despite her involvement with feminism, Wandor has recently voiced her reservations to the terms 'feminist theatre' and 'women's theatre' (Wandor, interviewed by Komporaly, 1999). She suggested focusing on the relationship between 'feminism', 'gender' and 'theatre', and in 2000 she presented her views as follows: 'While it may be interesting to know whether a woman playwright considers herself a feminist, in the end her work will consist of a mix of conscious and unconscious impulses.' Wandor, 'Women Playwrights and Feminism in the 1970s', in *The Cambridge Companion to Modern British Women Playwrights*, ed. E. Aston and J. Reinelt (Cambridge: Cambridge University Press, 2000), p. 64.

30. Cf. Wandor quoted in L. Goodman, *Contemporary Feminist Theatre: To Each Her Own* (London: Routledge, 1993), p. 96.

31. K. Crutchley and N. Diuguid, 'Preface to Care and Control', in *Strike while the Iron Is Hot: Sexual Politics in the Theatre*, ed. Wandor (London: Journeyman, 1980), p. 63.

32. Goodman, 1993, p. 77.
33. Gay Sweatshop, 'Care and Control', in *Strike while the Iron Is Hot*, p. 102.
34. Ibid., pp. 89–90.
35. Ibid., p. 113.
36. Ibid., p. 95.
37. Ibid., p. 108.
38. Goodman, 1993, p. 126.
39. J. Davis's list of lesbian plays was compiled for a conference paper (Nene College, Northampton, 19 November 1988), reprinted in Goodman, 1993, p. 140.
40. Wandor quoted in R. Collis, 'Sister George is Dead', in *British and Irish Women Dramatists since 1958: A Critical Handbook*, eds. T.R. Griffiths and M. Llewellyn-Jones (Buckingham: Open University Press, 1993), p. 79.
41. Wandor, in Komporaly.
42. This aspect of Wandor's play references Churchill's 1979 *Cloud Nine*. Both playwrights' focus on communal arrangements is a reflection of their feminist preoccupations in the late seventies.
43. Wandor, 'AID Thy Neighbour', in *Plays* (London: Journeyman Playbooks, 1984), p. 136.
44. Ibid.
45. Ibid., p. 134.
46. Kristeva made these points in her essay 'Stabat Mater', where she claimed that the image of the Virgin Mary did not provide a satisfactory model of maternity, since, with the Virgin Mary, the maternal body was reduced to silence. In 'Motherhood According to Giovanni Bellini', she contended that neither of the two currently available discourses on maternity – Christianity and science – are adequate to explain motherhood. Cf. J. Kristeva, 'Stabat Mater', in *The Kristeva Reader*, ed. T. Moi (Oxford: Basil Blackwell, 1986a); and 'Motherhood According to Giovanni Bellini', in *Desire in Language: A Semiotic Approach to Literature and Art*, ed. L.S. Roudiez (Oxford: Basil Blackwell, 1980), pp. 237–43.
47. S. Daniels, 'Introduction', in *Plays: One* (London: Methuen, 1991), p. ix.
48. Goodman, 1993, p. 35.
49. Daniels, in L. Goodman and J. de Gay, eds., *Feminist Stages: Interviews with Women in Contemporary British Theatre* (Amsterdam: Harwood Academic Publishers, 1996), p. 99; P. Bakker, 'Sarah Daniels', in *Dictionary of Literary Biography*, vol. 245, 'British and Irish Dramatists since World War Two', ed. J. Bull (Detroit, London: The Gale Group: 2001), p. 115.
50. Daniels, in *Rage and Reason,*, eds. H. Stephenson and N. Langridge (London: Methuen, 1997), p. 4.
51 Ibid., pp. 8, 2.
52. Daniels, p. xi.
53. M.F. Brewer, *Race, Sex and Gender in Contemporary Women's Theatre: The Construction of "Woman"* (Brighton, Portland: Sussex Academic Press, 1999), p. 17.
54. Daniels, 'Neaptide', in *Plays: One* (London: Methuen, 1991), pp. 268–69, 287.
55. Brewer, p. 24.
56. Ibid., p. 324.
57. Daniels, in Stephenson and Langridge, p. 5.
58. 'Neaptide', p. 235.

59. Daniels, p. xii.
60. J. Hanmer, 'Foreword to Byrthrite', in *Plays: One* (London: Methuen, 1991), p. 332.
61. Daniels, interviewed by Goodman in 1988 and 1989; quoted in Goodman, 1993, p. 128.
62. Daniels, 'Byrthrite', in *Plays: One*, p. 402.
63. Ibid., p. 404.
64. Ibid., p. 419.
65. Ibid., p. 408.
66. Komporaly, interview with J. Kay, Lancaster University (28 February 2004).
67. J. Dowson and A. Entwistle, *Twentieth-Century British Women's Poetry* (Cambridge: Cambridge University Press, 2005), pp. 183, 198.
68. Her Nigerian father had already four other children, and was not prepared for the meeting. Kay's memoir, *Tracing*, revisits this phase of her life.
69. J. Kay, *The Adoption Papers* (Newcastle upon Tyne: Bloodaxe Books, 1991), pp. 10, 13.
70. Ibid., p. 10.
71. Ibid., p. 21.
72. Ibid., p. 29.
73. Ibid., p. 23.
74. Ibid., p. 24.
75. Kay interviewed by Laura Severin, http://english.chass.ncsu.edu/freeverse/Archives/Spring_2002/Interviews/interviews.htm, accessed 11 September 2005.
76. Kay, in Goodman and de Gay, p. 254.
77. Ibid., p. 255.
78. Kay, in Komporaly.
79. Kay, in Goodman and de Gay, p. 257.
80. Luckham, in A. Pearson, 'Woman on the Verge of a Nervous Breakthrough', *Independent on Sunday* (18 November 1990).
81. Cf., for instance, Gillian Plowman's *Me and My Friend*, Tom Griffin's *The Boys Next Door*, Peter Nichols's *A Day in the Death of Joe Egg*, Mark Medoff's *Children of a Lesser God*.
82. Luckham, in S. Hemming, 'Relative Values: Claire Luckham's New Play is about Down Syndrome', *The Independent* (11 March 1992).
83. Ibid. In this respect she is reminiscent of Charlotte Keatley, who stressed that not having given birth herself at the time had not hindered her from dramatizing generations of mothers.
84. Luckham, afterword to 'The Choice', in *Plays by Women*, vol. 10, ed. A. Castledine (London: Methuen, 1994), p. 114.
85. Luckham, note to 'The Choice', pp. 113–14.
86. 'The Choice', p. 69.
87. Ibid., pp. 74, 97.
88. Ibid., p. 74.
89. Martin, *The Woman in the Body: A Cultural Analysis of Reproduction* (Milton Keynes: Open University Press, 1987). Martin's US-based study focuses on the female body in relation to science and medical intervention. She confronts the way women in different socio-economic positions perceive themselves and their particular society via the medium of events exclusive to women (menstruation, childbirth, menopause).

90. Ibid., p. 13.
91. Ibid., p. 194.
92. J. Murphy-Lawless, *Reading Birth and Death: A History of Obstetric Thinking* (Bloomington, IN: Indiana University Press, 1998), p. 200; A. Oakley and H. Graham, 'Competing Ideologies of Reproduction: Medical and Maternal Perspectives on Pregnancy', in *Women, Health and Reproduction,* ed. H. Roberts (London: Routledge & Kegan Paul, 1981), p. 53.
93. 'The Choice', pp. 88–89.
94. S. Kitzinger, 'Why Women Need Midwives', in *The Midwife Challenge* (London: Pandora Press, 1988), p. 15.
95. L. McMahon, *Home Birth Newsletter* (1991–92), quoted in Murphy-Lawless, p. 236.
96. R. Petchesky, 'Foetal Images: The Power of Visual Culture in the Politics of Reproduction', in Stanworth.
97. R. Betterton, *An Intimate Distance: Women, Artists and the Body* (London: Routledge, 1996), pp. 113–19.
98. 'The Choice', p. 96.
99. Ibid.
100. T. Wertenbaker, interviewed by Komporaly (21 June 1999).
101. Wertenbaker, in D. Edgar, *State of Play: Playwrights on Playwriting* (London: Faber, 1999), p. 75; Wertenbaker, in Stephenson and Langridge, p. 137.
102. Wertenbaker, in Komporaly.
103. Wertenbaker, in Stephenson and Langridge, p. 144.
104. P. Taylor, 'Review of *The Break of Day*', *The Independent* (30 November 1995), p. 13.
105. E. Aston, 'Geographies of Oppression – The Cross-Border Politics of (M)othering: *The Break of Day* and *A Yearning*', *Theatre Research International*, vol. 24, No. 3. (Autumn 1999a), p. 247; Aston, *Feminist Views on the English Stage: Women Playwrights, 1990–2000* (Cambridge: Cambridge University Press, 2003), pp. 157–58.
106. Cousin, 'Revisiting the Prozorovs', *Modern Drama*, no. 40. (1997).
107. Wertenbaker, in Komporaly.
108. Bayley, 'Wanting it All – and More, Review of *The Break of Day*', *New Statesman and Society* (1 December 1995), p. 33.
109. Wertenbaker, in Komporaly
110. Wertenbaker, *The Break of Day* (London: Faber, 1995), p. 35.
111. Wertenbaker, in Komporaly.
112. Ibid.
113. *The Break of Day*, p. 32.
114. Wertenbaker, in Komporaly.
115. *The Break of Day*, p. 73.
116. Ibid.
117. Cf. A. Rich, *Of Woman Born: Motherhood as Experience and Institution* (London: Virago, 1991), p. 55.
118. Canning, 'Feminists Perform Their Past: Constructing History in *The Heidi Chronicles* and *The Break of Day*', in *Women, Theatre and Performance*, eds. M.B. Gale and V. Gardner (Manchester: Manchester University Press, 2000), p. 175.
119. Spivak in interview, 'Subaltern Talk', in *The Spivak Reader*, eds. D. Landry and G. MacLean (London: Routledge, 1996), p. 292. Spivak's article, 'Can

the Subaltern Speak?' was first published in 1988 and reprinted on several occasions; however, she has since withdrawn her support from the original version. Spivak draws upon Gramsci's notion of the subaltern and Ranajit Guha's definition of space as isolated from mobility in a colonized country, and argues that the 'subaltern' woman as a colonized subject is already spoken for, and is positioned as silent, absent or erased. Spivak's theory has been critiqued by several theorists, among others on the account that it homogenizes various subaltern experiences.

120. *The Break of Day*, p. 82.
121. A comparable outsider's perspective on Eastern Europe is Churchill's *Mad Forest*, written as a result of a brief visit to Romania in early 1990. Like Wertenbaker, Churchill also focused on parallel lives and captured the dire economic conditions as well as the inter-ethnic tensions of the period. However, instead of her usual challenge to stereotypes she ended up replicating received perceptions, such as in the case of the Hungarian minority that she presented as the subversive 'other'. She ultimately located Romania itself as 'other' too: as an exotic terrain in opposition to Western values. By inserting brief passages in Romanian (replicating the Brechtian captions that introduce each scene) into her English play she set up an opposition between the two languages that underpins and reinforces the cultural differences mapped out by the characters and events. Cf. Churchill, *Mad Forest: A Play from Romania* (London: Nick Hern Books, 1990).
122. Wertenbaker, in Komporaly.
123. *The Break of Day*, p. 91.
124. S. Carlson, 'Language and Identity in Wertenbaker's Plays', in Aston and Reinelt, p. 146.
125. J.L. DiGaetani, *A Search for a Postmodern Theater: Interviews with Contemporary Playwrights* (New York: Greenwood, 1991), p. 270.
126. Kay, in Goodman and de Gay, p. 255.

6 Alternative Dramaturgies: Rewriting the Maternal Body

1. Komporaly, unpublished interview with J. Sealey (10 July 2005).
2. Komporaly, '"Cripping up is the Twenty-First Century's Answer to Blacking Up": Conversation with Kaite O'Reilly on theatre, feminism and disability', *Gender Forum*, vol. 12. (2005), http://www.genderforum.uni-koeln.de/illuminating/interview_OReilly.html, accessed 14 March 2006.
3. Ibid.
4. Ibid.
5. F. O'Toole, 'Review of Kaite O'Reilly's *Peeling*', *Irish Times* (24 October 2003).
6. R. Bailey, 'Review of Kaite O'Reilly's *Peeling*', *Disability Now* (May 2002).
7. O'Reilly, *Peeling* (London: Faber, 2002), p. 57. *Peeling* was also anthologized in *Graeae Plays: Plays Redefining Disability*, selected and introduced by J. Sealey (London: Aurora Metro Press, 2002).
8. Ibid., p. 54.
9. Ibid., p. 53.
10. Ibid., p. 63.
11. Ibid., p. 50.
12. Ibid., p. 47.

13. Ibid., p. 70.
14. C. Allfree, 'Review of Kaite O'Reilly's *Peeling*', *Metro* (8 April 2002).
15. O'Reilly, in Komporaly.
16. *Peeling*, pp. 46, 39–40.
17. Sealey, in Komporaly.
18. O'Reilly, in Komporaly.
19. *Peeling*, adapted for BBC Radio 3 by Kaite O'Reilly, directed by David Hunter (5 October 2003).
20. *Peeling*, p. 48.
21. L. Mulvey, 'Visual Pleasure and Narrative Cinema', in Mulvey, *Visual and Other Pleasures* (Basingstoke: Macmillan, 1989), p. 19.
22. Cf. feminist work on female spectatorship, L. Gamman and M. Marshment, eds. *The Female Gaze: Women as Viewers of Popular Culture* (London: The Women's Press, 1988).
23. J. McMillan, 'Review of Kaite O'Reilly's *Peeling*', The Scotsman (22 August, 2003).
24. In the 2003 production John was animated and voiced by Steve Tiplady, credited as puppetry consultant in 2005.
25. Komporaly, correspondence interview with S. Woods (13 August 2005).
26. Ibid.
27. Ibid.
28. V. Worsley, in *Feminist Stages*, eds. L. Goodman and J. de Gay (Amsterdam: Harwood Academic Publishers, 1996), p. 221.
29. Ibid., p. 222.
30. Woods, in Komporaly.
31. S. Woods, 'An Introduction from the Writer', *Cake*, Programme (2005), p. 2.
32. Bernard, 'A Note from the Director', *Cake*, Programme, p. 3.
33. Woods, *Cake*, Programme, p. 2.
34. D. Edgar, 'Introduction' to S. Woods, *Grace/Cake* (London: Oberon Books, 2003), p. 8.
35. *Cake*, p. 96.
36. Ibid., p. 100.
37. Ibid., pp. 100–01.
38. Edgar, p. 8.
39. *Cake*, p. 104.
40. A. Furse, *The Infertility Companion* (London: Thorsons, 1997), revised as *Your Essential Infertility Companion* (London: Thorsons, 2001). Furse wrote this book following her infertility treatment and her participation in the 1996 *Making Babies* series for the BBC, both led by Professor Robert Winston. Despite her joy at being having been able to conceive, she found participating in the show a frustrating experience, as it failed to address the economic aspects or the exploitative potential of medically assisted reproduction, and as a result of the heightened media attention and lack of privacy available to patients and new mothers (Komporaly, unpublished interview with Furse, 8 March 2005). *The Peach Child*, a theatre piece for children four–seven years old, was commissioned by The Little Angel Theatre for the Japan Festival 2001/National Children's Theatre Festival funded by the Arts Council of England. This multimedia production, incorporating puppetry, live performance and film, was an adaptation of an ancient Japanese tale about an

elderly childless couple. *Glass Body* (10–24 March 2006) was a 'siteable' (Furse's term for site-specific) installation/performance first created in the atrium of the Chelsea and Westminster Hospital, on a platform visible from walkways and elevators as well as windows of wards.

41. Furse, 'Home Is Where the Art Is, On Longing, Living and Caramel', unpublished presentation, 'Artists Talking the Domestic', Lancaster University (4 March 2005).
42. F. Garcia Lorca, 'Yerma', trans. P. Luke, in Lorca, *Plays: One* (London: Methuen, 1987), pp. 157–206.
43. Furse, 'Director's Note', *Yerma's Eggs*, Programme (2003), p. 2.
44. *Yerma's Eggs*, performance video filmed by Furse and Ajaykumar at the Riverside Studios (28 May 2003). Cf. quotes verbatim from Lorca, pp. 163–64.
45. Komporaly, unpublished conversation with Furse (13 April 2005).
46. *Yerma's Eggs*, performance video.
47. Ibid. Cf. Lorca, p. 168.
48. Ibid. Cf. Lorca, p. 185.
49. Ibid. Cf. Lorca, p. 174.
50. *Yerma's Eggs*, performance video.
51. Ibid.
52. Furse, 'ART of A.R.T', *Gender Forum*, 6 (2003), http://www.genderforum.uni-koeln.de/anybody/furse.html, accessed 27 November 2005.
53. *Yerma's Eggs*, performance video.
54. E.A. Kaplan, *Motherhood and Representation: The Mother in Popular Culture and Melodrama* (London: Routledge, 1992), p. 209.
55. D. Haraway, *Simians, Cyborgs and Women: The Reinvention of Nature* (London: Free Association, 1991), p. 169.
56. E. Martin, *The Woman in the Body*, p. 20.
57. Haraway, p. 150.
58. Furse, 'ART of A.R.T'.
59. S. Plant, *Zeros and Ones: Digital Women and the New Technologies* (London: Fourth Estate, 1997).
60. Martin, p. 46.
61. *Yerma's Eggs*, performance video; cf. Lorca, p. 186.
62. Furse, 'ART of A.R.T'.
63. *Yerma's Eggs*, performance video.
64. J. Edwardes, 'Review of Yerma's Eggs', *Time Out* (4 June 2003) reprinted *Theatre Record*, Issue 11–12 (21 May–17 June 2003), p. 722.
65. 'What is natural? Spring water? Cars? Tinned food? Marijuana? Organ donation? Plastic? Carbon Monoxide? Milk? Bras? Contraception? Hair dye? Paper? Ecstasy? Mice? Electricity? Concrete? Bodybuilding? Wood? Macdonalds? Computers? Blood transfusion? Soap? Tomato Ketchup? Sweat? Earwax? Vitamin pills? Coffee? Organ donation? Alcohol? Airtravel? Fishfingers? Ready to eat salad in a bag? Sunscreen? Coral? Oxygen? Mascara? Condoms? Aspirin? Ice-cream? Boats? Olive oil? IVF? Lemons in winter? The news? Polystyrene cups? Pubic Hair? Saffron? Melodrama? Families? Talcum powder? Sausages? Sofas? Nappies? Sex? Abridged version, *Yerma's Eggs*, performance video.

66. Furse, in Komporaly.
67. Nina Klaff, in *Yerma's Eggs*, performance video.
68. Furse, 'ART of A.R.T'.
69. Furse, 'Home Is Where the Art Is'.
70. Worsley, in Goodman and de Gay, p. 221.

Conclusion

1. Keatley and Wertenbaker interviewed by Komporaly.
2. The Children Act sustains the presumption that father–child contacts are in the child's interest, even in cases of proven domestic violence. For those having children and considering divorce a mandatory period of 'reflection and consideration', lasting up to two years, has been introduced.
3. Cf. the case of Diane Blood, who won the right to use her dead husband's sperm, or the debate raging in 2006 over the right of former cancer patient Natallie Evans to utilize her frozen embryo without the permission of her ex-partner. According to current UK legislation, the consent of both partners are needed; however, this feud has highlighted the clash between ethical and legal matters, as well as the need to examine the distinct perspectives of men and women as potential parents, the issue of denying the last chance to parenthood to someone or the role of genetics in the development of personhood.
4. Other issues, for instance, working mothers' longing to spend quality time with their children or, conversely, the emergence of the 'supermum' who successfully combines work with parenthood, are generally excluded from analysis, due to a lack of dramatic conflict that would make these situations suitable for the stage.
5. Wald, '"No One Claps at the End of a Novel" – A Conversation with Laura Wade', *Gender Forum*, vol. 13 (2006), http://www.genderforum.uni-koeln.de/imagendering2/interview_Wade_Wald.html, accessed 20 March 2006.
6. Wertenbaker, *The Break of Day*, p. 27.

Bibliography

Primary Sources

Arden, J. *Vagina Rex and the Gas Oven* (London: Calder and Boyars, 1971).

Bagnold, E. *The Chalk Garden* (London: Samuel French, 1956).

Carter, R. *A Yearning* (London: Nick Hern Books, 1999).

Churchill, C. 'Owners' and 'Cloud Nine', in Churchill, *Plays: One* (London: Methuen, 1985).

———. *Mad Forest: A Play from Romania* (London: Nick Hern Books, 1990).

———. *Top Girls* (London: Methuen, 1991; originally published 1982)

———. *The Skriker* (London: Methuen, 1994).

———. *A Number* (London: Methuen, 2002).

Cooke, T. 'Back Street Mammy', in *First Run*, vol. 2, ed. K. Harwood (London: Nick Hern Books, 1990).

Daniels, S. 'Neaptide' and 'Byrthrite', in Daniels, *Plays: One* (London: Methuen, 1986).

Dayley, G. 'Rose's Story', in *Plays by Women*, vol. 4, ed. M. Wandor (London: Methuen, 1985).

Delaney, S. *A Taste of Honey* (London: Methuen, 1988; originally published 1956).

Duffy, M. 'Rites', in *Plays by Women*, vol. 2, ed. by M. Wandor (London: Methuen, 1983).

Feinstein, E. and the Women's Theatre Group. 'Lear's Daughters', in *Herstory*, vol. 1, eds G. Griffin and E. Aston (Sheffield: Sheffield Academic Press, 1991).

Furse, A. *Yerma's Eggs*, unreleased performance video filmed by Furse and Ajaykumar (London: Riverside Studios ,28 May 2003).

Gay Sweatshop. 'Care and Control, in *Strike while the Iron Is Hot: Sexual Politics in the Theatre*, ed. M. Wandor (London: The Journeyman Press, 1980).

Gems, P. 'Queen Christina', in *Plays by Women*, vol. 5, ed. M. Remnant (London: Methuen, 1986).

Jellicoe, A. 'The Rising Generation', in *Playbill Two*, ed. A. Durband (London: Hutchinson, 1969).

———. [*The Knack* and] *The Sport of My Mad Mother* (London: Faber, 1985; orig nally published 1958).

Kane, S. [*Blasted* and] *Phaedra's Love* (London: Methuen, 1996).

Kay, J. *The Adoption Papers* (BBC Radio 3, 1990).

———. *The Adoption Papers* (Newcastle upon Tyne: Bloodaxe Books, 1991).

Keatley, C. *My Mother Said I Never Should* (London: Methuen, 1997; originally published 1988).

Lessing, D. *Play With a Tiger* (London: Davis-Poynter Ltd, 1972; originally published Michael Joseph, 1962).

Lochhead, L. *Perfect Days* (London: Nick Hern Books, 1998).

Lorca, F. G. 'Yerma', trans. P. Luke, in Lorca, *Plays: One* (London: Methuen, 1987).

Luckham, C. 'The Choice', in *Plays by Women*, vol. 10, ed. A. Castledine (London: Methuen, 1994).

MacDonald, S. 'When I Was a Girl, I Used to Scream and Shout...', in MacDonald, *Plays: One* (London: Faber, 1995)

Munro, R. *Iron* (London: Nick Hern Books, 2002).

Nagy, P. 'Butterfly Kiss', in Nagy, *Plays: One* (London: Methuen, 1998).

O'Reilly, K. *Peeling* (London: Faber, 2002).

———. *Peeling*, directed by D. Hunter (BBC Radio 3, 5 October 2003)

Page, L. 'Real Estate' and 'Salonika', in Page, *Plays: One* (London: Methuen, 1990).

Pinnock, W. 'Leave Taking', in *First Run: New Plays by New Writers*, ed. K. Harwood (London: Nick Hern Books, 1989).

Raif, A. 'Caving In', in *Plays by Women*, vol. 8, ed. M. Remnant (London: Methuen, 1990).

Samuels, D. *Kindertransport* (London: Nick Hern Books, 1996).

Stephenson, S. *The Memory of Water* (London: Methuen, 1997).

———. *An Experiment with an Air Pump* (London: Methuen, 1998).

Wade, L. *Colder Than Here* (London: Oberon Books, 2005).

Wandor, M. 'AID Thy Neighbour', in *Plays* (London: Journeyman Playbooks, 1984).

———. *Wanted* (London: Playbooks, 1988).

Wertenbaker, T. *The Break of Day* (London: Faber, 1995).

Women's Theatre Group, 'My Mother Says I Never Should', in *Strike while the Iron is Hot: Three Plays on Sexual Politics*, ed. M. Wandor (London: The Journeyman Press, 1980).

Woods, S. *Grace/Cake* (London: Oberon Books, 2003).

Wyvill, K. *Going Potty* (Edinburgh Festival, 2004).

Secondary Sources

Allfree, C. 'Review of Kaite O'Reilly's *Peeling*', *Metro* (8 April 2002).

Andemahr, A., Lovell, T., and Wolkowitz, C., eds., *Feminist Theory: A Glossary* (London: Arnold, 2000).

Arditti, R., Duelli Klein, R., and S. Minden, eds., *Test-Tube Women: What Future for Motherhood?* (London: Pandora Press, 1984).

Artaud, A. *The Theatre and Its Double*, trans. V. Corti (London: Calder Publications, 1993).

Aston, E., ed., *Feminist Theatre Voices* (Loughborough: Loughborough Theatre Texts, 1997a).

———. *Caryl Churchill* (Plymouth: Northcote House, 1997b).

———. 'Geographies of Oppression – The Cross-Border Politics of (M)othering: *The Break of Day* and *A Yearning*', *Theatre Research International*, vol. 24, no. 3 (1999a).

———. *Feminist Theatre Practice: A Handbook* (London: Routledge, 1999b).

———. 'Pam Gems: Body Politics and Biography', in *The Cambridge Companion to Modern British Women Playwrights*, eds. Elaine Aston and Janelle Reinelt (Cambridge: Cambridge University Press, 2000).

———. *Feminist Views on the English Stage: Women Playwrights, 1990–2000* (Cambridge: Cambridge University Press, 2003).

Aston, E. and Reinelt, J., eds., *The Cambridge Companion to Modern British Women Playwrights* (Cambridge: Cambridge University Press, 2000).

Austin, G. *Feminist Theory for Dramatic Criticism* (Ann Arbor: University of Michigan Press, 1990).

Bailey, R. 'Review of Kaite O'Reilly's *Peeling*', *Disability Now* (May 2002).
Bakker, P. 'Sarah Daniels', in *Dictionary of Literary Biography*, vol. 245, ed. J. Bull (Detroit: The Gale Group, 2001).
Bassnett-McGuire, S. 'Towards a Theory of Women's Theatre', in *Semiotics of Drama and Theatre: New Perspectives in the Theory of Drama*, vol. 10, eds. H. Schmid and A. van Kesteren (Amsterdam and Philadelphia: John Benjamins, 1984).
Bayley, C. 'Wanting it All – and More: Review of *The Break of Day*', *New Statesman and Society* (1 December 1995).
Benn, M. *Madonna and Child: Towards a New Politics of Motherhood* (London: Jonathan Cape, 1998).
Bennett, S. 'New Plays and Women's Voices in the 1950s, in *The Cambridge Companion to Modern British Women Playwrights*, eds. E. Aston and J. Reinelt (Cambridge: Cambridge University Press, 2000).
Betterton, R. *An Intimate Distance: Women, Artists and the Body* (London: Routledge, 1996).
Birk, A. and Wald, T., '"Let the Witches and the Magic Back in": Interview with Diane Samuels', *Gender Forum* 6 (2003),
http://www.genderforum.uni-koeln.de/anybody/interview_Samuels.html.
Brewer, M. F. *Race, Sex and Gender in Contemporary Women's Theatre: The Construction of "Woman"* (Brighton, Portland: Sussex Academic Press, 1999).
Brooks, A. *Postfeminisms: Feminism, Cultural Theory and Cultural Forms* (London: Routledge, 1997).
Brown, G. 'Something Out of the Ordinary', *The Independent* (31 January 1996).
Brown, J. 'Caryl Churchill's Top Girls Catches the Next Wave', in *Caryl Churchill: A Casebook*, ed. Phyllis Randall (New York, London: Garland Publications, 1988).
Brown, T. 'Back Street Mammy – Review', *Guardian* (9 October 1989).
Burkman, K. H. 'The Plays of Pam Gems: Personal/Political/Personal', in *British and Irish Drama since 1960*, ed. J. Acheson (London: St. Martin's Press, 1993).
Campbell, B. *The Iron Ladies: Why Do Women Vote Tory?* (London: Virago, 1987).
Canning, C. 'Feminists Perform Their Past: Constructing History in *The Heidi Chronicles* and *The Break of Day*', in *Women, Theatre and Performance*, eds. M. B. Gale and V. Gardner (Manchester: Manchester University Press, 2000).
Carlson, S. 'Language and Identity in Wertenbaker's Plays, in *The Cambridge Companion to Modern British Women Playwrights*, eds. E. Aston and J. Reinelt (Cambridge: Cambridge University Press, 2000).
Case, S.-E. 'The Power of Sex: English Plays by Women, 1958–1988', *New Theatre Quarterly*, vol. VII/27 (August 1991).
Castle, B. *Fighting All the Way* (London: Pan Books, 1994).
Chawaf, C. 'Linguistic Flesh', in *New French Feminisms: An Anthology*, eds. E. Marks and I. de Courtivron (Hemel Hempstead: Harvester Wheatsheaf, 1981).
Chodorow, N. *The Reproduction of Mothering: Psychoanalysis and the Sociology of Gender* (Berkeley: University of California Press, 1978).
Cixous, H. 'The Laugh of the Medusa' in *New French Feminisms: An Anthology*, eds. E. Marks and I. de Courtivron (Hemel Hempstead: Harvester Wheatsheaf, 1981).
Clément, C. and Cixous, H., *The Newly Born Woman*, trans. B. Wing (Minneapolis: University of Minnesota Press, 1991).

Collis, R. 'Sister George is Dead', in *British and Irish Women Dramatists since 1958: A Critical Handbook*, eds. T. R. Griffiths and M. Llewellyn-Jones (Buckingham: Open University Press, 1993).

Corea, G., *Man-made Women: How New Reproductive Technologies Affect Women* (Bloomington: Indiana University Press, 1987).

———. *The Mother Machine: Reproductive Technologies from Artificial Insemination to Artificial Wombs* (London: The Women's Press, 1988).

Cousin, G. *Women in Dramatic Place and Time* (London: Routledge, 1996).

———. 'Revisiting the Prozorovs', *Modern Drama*, no. 40. (1997).

Croft, S. 'Black Women Playwrights in Britain', in *British and Irish Women Dramatists since 1958: A Critical Handbook*, eds. T. R. Griffiths and M. Llewellyn-Jones (Buckingham: Open University Press, 1993).

Dally, A. *Inventing Motherhood: The Consequences of an Ideal* (London: Burnett Books, 1982).

Daly, M. *Gyn/Ecology: The Metaethics of Radical Feminism* (London: The Women's Press, 1978).

DiGaetani, J. L. *A Search for a Postmodern Theater: Interviews with Contemporary Playwrights* (New York: Greenwood, 1991).

Dinnerstein, D. *The Mermaid and the Minotaur: Sexual Arrangements and Human Malaise* (New York: Harper, 1976).

Dowson, J. and Entwistle, A., *Twentieth-Century British Women's Poetry* (Cambridge: Cambridge University Press, 2005).

Edgar, D. *The Second Time as Farce* (London: Lawrence and Wishart, 1988).

———. *State of Play: Playwrights on Playwriting* (London: Faber, 1999).

Edwardes, J. 'Review of *Yerma's Eggs*', *Time Out* (4 June 2003).

Faludi, S. *Backlash: The Undeclared War against Women* (London: Chatto and Windus, 1991).

Firestone, S. *The Dialectic of Sex: The Case for Feminist Revolution* (London: The Women's Press, 1979).

Freeman, J. *The Politics of Women's Liberation: A Case Study of an Emerging Social Move* (New York: McKay, 1975).

Friedan, B. *The Feminine Mystique* (London: Gollancz, 1963).

Furse, A. 'ART of A.R.T', *Gender Forum*, 6 (2003), http://www.genderforum.uni-koeln.de/anybody/furse.html

———. 'Home Is Where the Art Is, On Longing, Living and Caramel', unpublished presentation, Lancaster University (4 March 2005).

Gamble, S., ed., *The Routledge Companion to Feminism and Postfeminism* (London: Routledge, 2001).

Gamman, L. and Marshment, M., eds., *The Female Gaze: Women as Viewers of Popular Culture* (London: The Women's Press, 1988).

Gavron, H. *The Captive Wife: Conflicts of Housebound Mothers* (Harmondsworth: Penguin Books, 1966).

Gilligan, C. *In a Different Voice: Psychological Theory and Women's Development* (Cambridge: Harvard University Press, 1982).

Gilmour, I. *Dancing with Dogma: Britain under Thatcherism* (London: Simon and Schuster, 1992).

Goodman, L. 'Art Form or Platform? On Women and Playwriting' – Interview with C. Keatley, *New Theatre Quarterly*, vol. VI/22 (May 1990).

————. *Contemporary Feminist Theatre: To Each Her Own* (London: Routledge, 1993).

————. 'Overlapping Dialogue in Overlapping Media: Behind the Scenes of *Top Girls*', in *Essays on Caryl Churchill: Contemporary Representations*, ed. S. Rabillard (Winnipeg, Buffalo: Blizzard Publishing, 1998).

Goodman, L., and de Gay, J., eds., *Feminist Stages: Interviews with Women in Contemporary British Theatre* (Amsterdam: Harwood Academic Publishers, 1996).

Gordon, T. *Feminist Mothers* (Basingstoke: Macmillan, 1990).

Greer, G. *The Female Eunuch* (London: MacGibbon & Kee, 1970).

————. *The Whole Woman* (London: Doubleday, 1999).

Grice, A. 'Ten Years after the Fall of Thatcher, Blair Says It's Time Politics Moved On', *The Independent* (23 November 2000).

Griffin, G. *Contemporary Black and Asian Women Playwrights in Britain* (Cambridge University Press, 2003).

Griffiths, T. R. and Llewellyn-Jones, M., eds., *British and Irish Women Dramatists since 1958: A Critical Handbook* (Buckingham: Open University Press, 1993).

Griffiths, T. R. 'Waving not Drowning', in *British and Irish Women Dramatists since 1958: A Critical Handbook*, ed. T. R. Griffiths and M. Llewellyn-Jones (Buckingham: Open University Press, 1993).

Hakim, C. *Key Issues in Women's Work* (London: Athlone Press, 1996).

Hall, S. and Jacques, M., eds., *The Politics of Thatcherism* (London: Lawrence & Wishart, 1983).

Hall, S. *The Hard Road to Renewal: Thatcherism and the Crisis of the Left* (London: Verso, 1988).

Hanna, G. [in interview], *Feminism and Theatre: Theatre Papers*, 2nd series, no. 8 (Dartington: Dartington College, 1978).

Haraway, D. 'A Manifesto for Cyborgs', in Haraway, *Symians, Cyborgs and Women: The Reinvention of Nature* (London: Free Association, 1991).

Hemming, S. 'Relative Values: Claire Luckham's New Play is about Down Syndrome', *The Independent* (11 March 1992).

hooks, b. *Feminist Theory from Margin to Centre* (Boston: South End Press, 1985).

Howe-Kritzer, A. 'Labour and Capital', in *The Plays of Caryl Churchill: Theatre of Empowerment*, ed. A. Howe-Kritzer (Basingstoke: Macmillan, 1991).

Innes, C. *Modern British Drama 1890–1990* (Cambridge: Cambridge University Press, 1992).

Irigaray, I. *Sexes and Genealogies*, trans. G. C. Gill (New York: Columbia University Press, 1993).

Itzin, C. *Stages in the Revolution: Political Theatre in Britain since 1968* (London: Eyre Methuen, 1980).

Jellicoe, A. The Judith Wilson Lecture, *Some Unconscious Influences in the Theatre*, 10 March 1967 (Cambridge: Cambridge University Press, 1967).

————. 'Covering the Ground', in *Women and Theatre: Calling the Shots*, ed. S. Todd (London: Faber, 1984).

Kaplan, E. A. *Motherhood and Representation: The Mother in Popular Culture and Melodrama* (London: Routledge, 1992).

Karpf, A. *The War After. Living with the Holocaust* (London: Heinemann 1996).

Keyssar, H. *Feminist Theatre* (Basingstoke: Macmillan, 1984).

Kitzinger, S. *Women as Mothers: How They See Themselves in Different Cultures* (Oxford: Martin Robertson with Fontana Books, 1978).

———. 'Why Women Need Midwives', in *The Midwife Challenge*, ed. S. Kitzinger (London: Pandora Press, 1988).

Komporaly, J. Unpublished interview with Timberlake Wertenbaker (21 June 1999).

———. Unpublished interview with Michelene Wandor (9 July 1999).

———. Unpublished interview with Charlotte Keatley (17 November 1999).

———. Unpublished interview with Trish Cooke (17 October 2000).

———. 'The Troubles and the Family: Women's Theatre as Political Intervention', in *Representing the Troubles*, ed. E. Walshe and B. Cliff (Dublin: Four Courts Press, 2004).

———. Unpublished interviews with Anna Furse (8 March and 13 April 2005).

———. Unpublished interview with Jenny Sealey (10 July 2005).

———. Unpublished interview with Sarah Woods (13 August 2005).

———. '"Cripping up is the twenty-first century's answer to blacking up": Conversation with Kaite O'Reilly on theatre, feminism and disability', *Gender Forum* 12 (2005), http://www.genderforum.uni-koeln.de/illuminating/interview_OReilly.html.

Kristeva, J. 'Motherhood According to Giovanni Bellini', in *Desire in Language: A Semiotic Approach to Literature and Art*, ed. L. S. Roudiez, trans. T. Gora, A. Jardine, and L. S. Roudiez (Oxford: Basil Blackwell, 1980).

———. 'Stabat Mater', in *The Kristeva Reader*, ed.T. Moi (Oxford: Basil Blackwell, 1986a).

———. 'Women's Time', in *The Kristeva Reader*, ed. T. Moi (Oxford: Basil Blackwell, 1986b).

Kuhn, A. *The Power of Image: Essays on Representation and Sexuality* (London: Routledge and Kegan Paul, 1985).

Lacey, S. *British Realist Theatre: The New Wave in Its Context, 1956–1965* (London: Routledge, 1995).

Littlewood, J. 'Plays for the People', in *The New British Drama*, ed. H. Popkin (New York: Grove Press, 1964).

Llwellyn-Jones, M. 'Claiming a Space', in *British and Irish Dramatists since 1958: A Critical Handbook*, ed. T. R. Griffiths and M. Llewellyn-Jones (Buckingham: Open University Press, 1993).

Martin, E. *The Woman in the Body: A Cultural Analysis of Reproduction* (Milton Keynes: Open University Press, 1987).

McFerran, A. 'Interview with Pam Gems', *Time Out* (7 October 1977a).

———. 'Interview with Caryl Churchill', *Time Out* (21-27 October 1977b).

McMillan, J. 'Review of Kaite O'Reilly's *Peeling*', *The Scotsman* (22 August 2003).

Moore-Gilbert, B. *The Arts in the 1970s: Cultural Closure* (London: Routledge, 1994).

Mulvey, L. 'Visual Pleasure and Narrative Cinema', in Mulvey, *Visual and Other Pleasures* (Basingstoke: Macmillan, 1989).

Murphy-Lawless, J. *Reading Birth and Death: A History of Obstetric Thinking* (Bloomington: Indiana University Press, 1998).

Myrdal, A. and Klein, V. *Women's Two Roles: Home and Work* (London: Routledge and Kegan Paul, 1956).

Neumeier, B. 'Kindertransport: Childhood Trauma and Diaspora Experience', in *Jewish Women's Writing of the 1990s and beyond in Great Britain and the United States*, eds. U. Behlau and B. Reitz (Wissenschaftlicher Verlag, Trier, 2004).

Neustatter, A. *Hyenas in Petticoats: A Look at Twenty Years of Feminism* (London: Harrap, 1989).

Oakley, A. and H. Graham, 'Competing Ideologies of Reproduction: Medical and Maternal Perspectives on Pregnancy', in *Women, Health and Reproduction,* ed. H. Roberts (London: Routledge and Kegan Paul, 1981).

Oakley, A. 'A Brief History of Gender', in *Who's Afraid of Feminism? Seeing through the Backlash,* ed. A. Oakley and J. Mitchell (London: Penguin Books, 1997).

O'Brien, M. *Reproducing the World: Essays on Feminist Theory* (Boulder, London: Westview Press, 1989).

O'Toole, F. 'Review of Kaite O'Reilly's *Peeling*', *Irish Times* (24 October 2003).

Pearson, A. 'Woman on the Verge of a Nervous Breakthrough: From Female Wrestlers to Victorian Actresses; Clare Luckham's Plays Empower the "Weaker Sex"', *The Independent on Sunday* (18 November 1990).

Petchesky, R. 'Foetal Images: The Power of Visual Culture in the Politics of Reproduction', in *Reproductive Technologies: Gender, Motherhood and Medicine,* ed. M. Stanworth (Cambridge: Polity Press, 1987).

Pinnock, W. 'Breaking Down the Door', in *Theatre in a Cool Climate,* ed. V. Gottlieb and C. Chambers (Oxford: Amber Lane Press, 1999).

Plant, S. *Zeros and Ones: Digital Women and the New Technologies* (London: Fourth Estate, 1997).

Pugh, M. *Women and the Women's Movement in Britain, 1914–1959* (Basingstoke: Macmillan, 1992).

Reinelt, J. 'Michelene Wandor: Artist and Ideologue', in *Making a Spectacle: Essays on Contemporary Women's Theatre,* ed. L. Hart (Ann Arbor: University of Michigan Press, 1989).

Rich, A. *Of Woman Born: Motherhood as Experience and Institution* (London: Virago, 1991).

Rickford, F. 'No More Sleeping Beauties and Frozen Boys', in *The Left and the Erotic,* ed. E. Phillips (London: Lawrence and Wishart, 1983).

Riley, D. *War in the Nursery: Theories of the Child and Mother* (London: Virago, 1983).

Rowbotham, S. *A Century of Women: The History of Women in Britain and the United States* (London: Viking, 1997).

Ruddick, S. 'Maternal Thought', in *Mothering: Esays in Feminist Theory* , ed. J. Trebilcot (Totowa, N.J.: Rowman and Littlefield, 1983).

———. *Maternal Thinking: Towards a Politics of Peace* (London: The Women's Press, 1990).

Saunders, G. *'Love Me or Kill Me': Sarah Kane and the Theatre of Extremes* (Manchester: Manchester University Press, 2002).

Scullion, A. 'Contemporary Scottish Women Playwrights', in *The Cambridge Companion to Modern British Women Playwrights,* ed.E. Aston and J. Reinelt (Cambridge: Cambridge University Press, 2000).

Sebba, A. *Enid Bagnold: The Authorized Biography* (London: Weidenfeld and Nicolson, 1986).

Segal, L. 'The Heat in the Kitchen', in *The Politics of Thatcherism,* ed. S. Hall and M. Jacques (London: Lawrence & Wishart, 1983).

———. 'Women's Retreat into Motherhood: Back to the Nursery', *New Statesman* (2 January 1987).

Severin, L. 'Interview with J. Kay', http://english.chass.ncsu.edu/freeverse/ Archives/Spring_2002/Interviews/interviews.htm.

Shellard, D. *British Theatre Since The War* (New Haven: Yale University Press, 1999).

Sierz, A. *In-Yer-Face Theatre* (London: Faber, 2001).

Spencer, C. 'Review of Enid Bagnold's *The Chalk Garden*', *The Daily Telegraph* (4 April 1992).

Spivak, G. [in interview], 'Subaltern Talk', in *The Spivak Reader*, ed. D. Landry and G. MacLean (London: Routledge, 1996).

Stanworth, M., ed., *Reproductive Technologies: Gender, Motherhood and Medicine* (Cambridge: Polity Press, 1987).

Stephenson, H. and N. Langridge, *Rage and Reason: Women Playwrights on Playwriting* (London: Methuen, 1997).

Taylor, J. R. *Anger and After: A Guide to the New British Drama* (London: Methuen, 1962).

Taylor, L. 'Early Stages', in *British and Irish Dramatists since 1958*, ed. T. R. Griffiths and M. Llewellyn-Jones (Buckingham: Open University Press, 1993).

Taylor, P. 'Review of *The Break of Day*', *The Independent* (30 November 1995).

Tynan, K. *Curtains: Selections from the Drama Criticism and Related Writings* (London: Longmans, 1961).

Vidal, J. 'Power and the Woman', *The Guardian* (9 April 1987).

Wald, C. '"No One Claps at the End of a Novel" – A Conversation with Laura Wade', *Gender Forum*, 13 (2006), http://www.genderforum.uni-koeln.de/ima-gendering2/interview_Wade_Wald.html.

Walter, N. *The New Feminism* (London: Little, Brown and Company, 1998).

———. 'What Feminism Offers Men', *The Independent* (28 June 1999).

Wandor, M., ed., *The Body Politic: Writings from the Women's Liberation Movement in Britain 1969–72* (London: Stage 1, 1972).

———. *Carry On, Understudies: Theatre and Sexual Politics* (London: Routledge and Kegan Paul, 1986).

———. *Look Back in Gender: Sexuality and the Family in Post-War British Drama* (London: Methuen, 1987).

———. 'Women Playwrights and Feminism in the 1970s', in *The Cambridge Companion to Modern British Women Playwrights*, ed. E. Aston and J. Reinelt (Cambridge: Cambridge University Press, 2000).

———. *Looking Back in Gender: Post-war British Drama* (London: Routledge, 2001).

Warnock, M. *A Question of Life: The Warnock Report on Human Fertilisation and Embryology* (Oxford: Basil Blackwell, 1985).

White, M. and Norton-Taylor, R. 'Irate Blair Savages Thatcher', *Guardian* (24 November 2000).

Williams, R. 'New English Drama', in *Modern British Dramatists: A Collection of Critical Essays*, ed. J. R. Brown (Englewood Cliffs, New Jersey: Prentice-Hall, 1968).

Wilson, E. *Women and the Welfare State* (London: Tavistock Publications, 1977).

Worsley, T.C. 'The Sweet Smell of Success', *New Statesman* (21 February 1959).

Yeatman, A. *Postmodern Revisionings of the Political* (London: Routledge, 1994).

Young, H. *One of Us: A Biography of Margaret Thatcher* (London: Pan Books, 1993).

Zipper, J. and Sevenhuijsen, S. 'Surrogacy: Feminist Notions of Motherhood Reconsidered', in *Reproductive Technologies: Gender, Motherhood and Medicine*, ed. M. Stanworth (Cambridge: Polity Press, 1987).

———. Platform Performance and discussion of C. Keatley's *My Mother Said I Never Should*, Royal National Theatre, London (8 November 1999),

———. *Yerma's Eggs*, Programme (2003),

———. *Cake*, Programme (2005), http://peopleplayuk.org/timelines/black_performance.

Index